PRAISE FOR

LETTERS TO A YOUNG CATHOLIC

"If I weren't a cradle Catholic, George Weigel's *Letters to a Young Catholic* might make me want to convert."—*Washington Post*

"'Great Expectations,' in fact, could be Weigel's subtitle, for that is what he hopes to inspire in youthful souls with his graceful meditations on truth, beauty, and love."—*Claremont Institute Review*

"But even on the toughest of topics—life and death, and suffering—he manages to quickly hit important notes, quoting scripture and giving the reader something to work with, plus tying these deep issues into the hottest and most crucial public-policy and morality debates of our day. . . . I expect *Letters* will be a long-time Catholic-culture classic."—*National Review*

"This is a luminous work that would appeal to anyone interested in faith, hope, and life itself."—*Booklist*

"Writing in a conversational, epistolary form aimed at young Catholics, Weigel offers a book that simultaneously is, and is not, your grandmother's catechism: he affirms the core doctrines of the Church, but he does so in a way that is refreshingly contemporary and—because of his emphasis on Church sites around the world—catholic as well as Catholic. . . . This book is simply first-rate."—*Publishers Weekly*

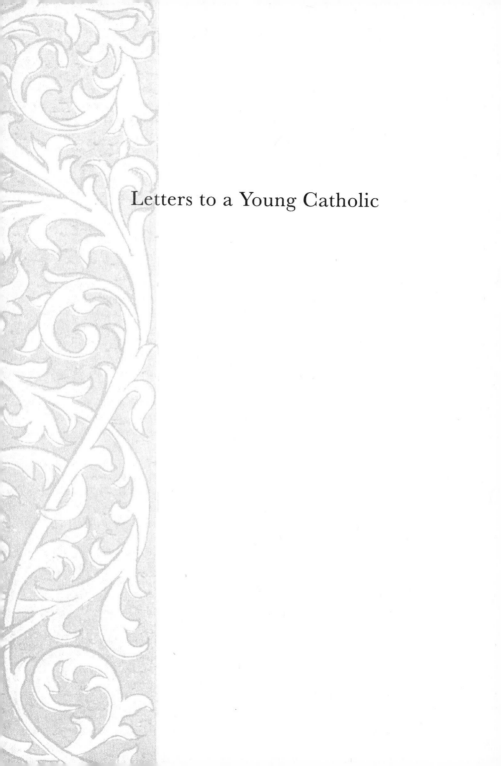

Letters to a Young Catholic

Letters to a
Young Catholic

The Revised and Expanded Edition
of a Modern Spiritual Classic

✦ George Weigel ✦

BASIC BOOKS
A Member of the Perseus Books Group
New York

Published by Basic Books
A Member of the Perseus Books Group

Books published by Basic Books are available at special discounts for
bulk purchases in the United States by corporations, institutions, and other
organizations. For more information, please contact the Special Markets
Department at the Perseus Books Group, 2300 Chestnut Street,
Suite 200, Philadelphia, PA 19103, or call (800) 810-4145, ext. 5000,
or e-mail special.markets@perseusbooks.com.

Designed by Cynthia Young

Library of Congress Cataloging-in-Publication Data
Weigel, George, 1951–
Letters to a young Catholic / George Weigel.—
Revised and Expanded [edition].
pages cm
Includes bibliographical references and index.
ISBN 978-0-465-02832-0 (pbk. : alk. paper) —
ISBN 978-0-465-09750-0 (e-book)
1. Weigel, George, 1951—Travel.
2. Catholic youth—Religious life.
I. Title.
BX2355.W45 2015
282—dc23
2015016113

LSC-H

10 9 8 7 6 5

To

my faculty colleagues and our students

in the

Tertio Millennio Seminar on the Free Society

in Liechtenstein and Kraków,

1992–2014

CONTENTS

A PRELIMINARY POSTCARD

These letters are written to, and for, young Catholics—and not-so-young Catholics, and indeed curious souls of any religious persuasion or none—who wonder what it means to be a Catholic in the twenty-first century and the third millennium. There are lots of ways to explore that question. We could take a walk through the *Catechism of the Catholic Church*, reviewing the key points of Christian doctrine and thinking through the myriad challenges of living a Catholic life today. We could ponder the lives of the saints, ancient and modern, and see what their experiences have to offer by way of example and inspiration. We could think together about the Church's sacraments: What does it mean to be baptized, to celebrate the Mass and receive Christ's body and blood in Holy Communion, to experience the forgiveness of Christ in the sacrament of Penance? We could discuss prayer, and its many forms, styles, and methods.

The more I think about it, though, the more it seems to me that the best way to explore the meaning of Catholicism is to take an epistolary tour of the Catholic world, or at least those parts of the Catholic world that have shaped my own understanding of the Church, its people, its teaching, and its way of life. Catholicism is a very tangible business—it's about seeing and hearing, touching, tasting, and smelling as much as it's about texts and arguments and ideas. Visiting some of the more intriguing parts of the Catholic world will, I hope, be an experience of the mystery of the Church, which is crucial to understanding it. And by the "mystery" of the Church, I don't mean documents filed away in the Vatican Secret Archives. I mean those dimensions of the Catholic experience that are matters of intuition and empathy and insight—experiences which can never be fully captured discursively.

Where to begin our tour? Perhaps a little autobiographical indulgence isn't out of place in a book like this. So let's begin by visiting the Catholic world of my youth. At the very least, it's an interesting slice of Americana. I think it's more than that, though. For when I was a very young Catholic, I absorbed things by a kind of osmosis, things that just may shed light on the fuller and deeper truths of Catholic faith today—even though we're living in a very different time and place and circumstance.

BALTIMORE AND MILLEDGEVILLE

Acquiring the "Habit of Being"

grew up in what now seems to have been the last moment of intact Catholic culture in the United States: the late Fifties and early Sixties, in Baltimore, one of the most Catholic cities in the country. There were lots of places like this—Boston, surely; large parts of New York and Philadelphia; Chicago and Milwaukee and St. Louis. Still, there was something distinctive about Catholic Baltimore in those days. American Catholics past and present are notoriously ignorant of the history of the Church in the United States. In Baltimore, we were very much aware that we were living in the first of American dioceses, with the first bishop and the first cathedral—and, of course, the "Baltimore Catechism," which was used in those days from sea to shining sea.

Catholic Baltimore was different from other parts of America's urban Catholic culture in degree, not in kind. We didn't divide the world into "Baltimore Catholicism" and "Milwaukee Catholicism" (or Philadelphia Catholicism, or New York Catholicism, or Boston Catholicism or whatever). We quite naturally and unselfconsciously divided the world into "Catholics"—people we recognized by a kind of instinct—and "non-Catholics." That instinct wasn't a matter of prejudice. It was the product of a unique experience, and you instinctively recognized people who'd been formed by the same experience.

How were we different? To begin with, we had a singular way of describing ourselves. When someone asked us where we were from, we didn't say "South Baltimore" or "Highlandtown" or "Towson" or "Catonsville." We'd say "I'm from Star of the Sea" (or "St. Elizabeth's" or "Immaculate Conception" or "St. Agnes," or, in my case, "the New Cathedral"). Baltimore was, and is, a city of neighborhoods, but in hindsight it seems instructive that we identified ourselves first by parish, rather than by geographic area. Some might call this "tribal," and there were certainly elements of the tribal (especially ethnic-tribal) in this distinctive way of telling a stranger who you were. It was a different kind of tribalism, though, a *Catholic* tribalism that fostered both fierce rivalries and even fiercer loyalties: rivalries among parishes and schools and teams and youth groups, but beyond and through all those rivalries, an intense sense of belonging to something larger than ourselves, something beyond ourselves that somehow lived inside us, too. All of which was, as I look back on it, a first inkling of "catholicity" (which is another word for "universality") and its relationship to particularity.

We used a different vocabulary, in the Catholic world in which I grew up. With the possible exception of those grinds who were aiming to score 800 on the SAT verbals, the only American kids between the ages of ten and eighteen who regularly used words like vocation, monstrance, missal, crucifer, biretta, chasuble, surplice, ciborium, and paten were Catholics. (That much of this arcane vocabulary was Latin-derived was a source of aggravation to generations of high school and college English composition teachers, eager to get us using short, sharp words of Anglo-Saxon origin rather than those luxurious Latinate nouns and verbs.) We also pronounced words differently: non-Catholics said "Saint AW-gus-teen," but we knew it was "Saint Uh-GUS-tin." Then there was our sense of identification with some local heroes. Other kids could recite the relevant batting and pitching, passing and receiving statistics of their sporting idols, but hadn't a clue (and couldn't have cared less) about their religious affiliation. We were stat-crazy, too, but we also knew exactly who was a Catholic (John Unitas, Art Donovan, Brooks Robinson) and what parish they belonged to. And we sensed a connection to these athletic gods that was . . . different, somehow.

With our Catholic school uniforms, we looked different—and if those uniforms saved our parents a lot of clothes money (which they did), they also reinforced a sense of belonging to something distinctive. So did the fact that we were taught by religious sisters (whom we mistakenly called "nuns," ignorant of the terminological technicality that "nuns" are, by definition, cloistered). Some were magnificent: my first-grade teacher, Sister Mary Moira, SSND, understood "phonics" a generation ahead of time and could teach a stone to read. Others were, to put it gently, less than adequate: my seventy-something fifth-grade teacher, Sister Maurelia, still insisted that the sun orbited the earth. Yet even the bad teachers commanded respect, and through the combined effects of their personal discipline, their austerity, and their devotional lives, even the bad teachers were teaching us something important about life and its purposes, however clumsily or inarticulately. (And yes, there were occasional Ingrid Bergman/*Bells of St. Mary's* moments: the aforementioned Sister Maurelia's devotion to the Ptolemaic universe coexisted with an impressive capacity to clobber a misbehaving boy with a well-aimed chalkboard eraser at twenty paces. Anyone who described such behavior as "abusive" would have been considered insane.)

Our calendar, and the habits it bred into us, also marked us out as distinctive. "Holy Days of Obligation" (like the December 8 feast of Mary's Immaculate Conception) were days off from school then—a source of envy among the "publics," as we sometimes called the kids in the government schools. In that innocent era, before Christian terminology in the government schools had been deemed a danger to the Republic, everybody had "Christmas vacation"; but we had "Easter vacation" while everybody else had "Spring break." Meatless Fridays set us apart from our non-Catholic friends and neighbors: no one else we knew took peanut butter and jelly (or tuna fish, or Swiss cheese on rye) sandwiches to school in their lunch bags (or lunch boxes, among the smaller fry). Our parents couldn't eat meat at breakfast and lunch on the weekdays of Lent, and everyone fasted for three hours before going to church on Sunday morning. First Communion (in the second grade) and Confirmation (in the fourth grade) were major landmarks in our uniquely Catholic lifecycle.

Our Protestant friends knew their Bible a lot better than we did, but we knew our catechism; and, looking back, it strikes me that the memorization of its answers was not only the basic structure of our early religious instruction—it was a first hint that Catholicism is deeply, even passionately, invested in ideas, even ideas boiled down into single-sentence formulas. (Little did we know the titanic struggles that had gone into creating those precise formulations over the centuries.) We had a ritual life that also set us apart. Most of us went to Mass every Sunday (plus those blessed, school-free holy days), and the idea of a churchless Sunday struck us as somehow odd. The Mass was, of course, celebrated in Latin (with the Gospel read in English before the sermon). Catholic boys memorized "the responses" in Latin in order to serve at the altar (the frequent response *Et cum spiritu tuo* giving rise, phonetically, to the old saw about the classic Catholic telephone number: "Et cum speery, two-two-oh"). From constant repetition during Benediction of the Blessed Sacrament and from the weekly Lenten devotion known as the "Stations of the Cross," boys and girls alike learned a few Latin hymns ("Tantum ergo," "O salutaris hostia," "Stabat mater"). And for some reason, perhaps best understood by religious anthropologists, it didn't strike us as the least bit peculiar that we prayed and sang in an ancient language that few of us knew—until, that is, Latin was drummed into us, declension by declension and conjugation by conjugation, when we hit high school.

Some of the things we did raised the eyebrows of our more assertively Protestant neighbors. Our piety had a distinctly Marian flavor, unintelligible and perhaps vaguely blasphemous to non-Catholics. Catholic families were encouraged to say the rosary together, and the annual "May procession" was a great event on the school and parish calendar; its high point came when an especially favored girl from the parish school "crowned" a statue of Mary with a garland of flowers. What truly marked us off as different, though (and, in the eyes of some, not merely different but perversely different), was what everyone in those days called "going to confession." Making one's first confession was an absolute and unchallenged prerequisite to First Communion. So, at age seven or eight we learned an etiquette of self-examination and self-accusation that our Protestant friends (when they got up the nerve to ask) found incomprehensible. Mythologies notwithstanding, "going to confession" wasn't a terrifying or morbid experience: at least once a month we were taken to church from the parochial school and lined up outside the confessional to do our penitential duty, about which, insofar as I can recall, no one complained. All of this (examining conscience, making a "firm purpose of amendment," describing our peccadillos, receiving and saying a brief penance) was simply what we did because of who we were. If other people didn't do such things, they were the odd ducks, not us. They were the ones missing something.

Then there were our international connections, which seemed more richly textured than our neighbors'. American Christians have always been mission-conscious. Still, I don't recall hearing my Protestant friends talk about "ransoming pagan babies," which was something we did during Lent throughout my early years in elementary school. In those days, when a quarter was a lot of money, the idea was to put your pennies and nickels in a small cardboard collection box you kept at home and to accumulate over the forty days of Lent a total of $5.00—which required another self-discipline, to wit, not raiding the collection box too often. This $5.00 would be given to a mission, usually in Africa, and in return, the donor was allowed to give the "pagan baby" its Christian name at its baptism (if memory serves, we got a certificate noting that "James" or "Mary" or whoever had been baptized because of our generosity). I never quite figured out how this worked at the other end, unless all our "pagan babies" were orphans without parents to name them. The point, however, was not the logistics, but the sense that was quickly ingrained in us of being part of a worldwide body. Mission talks were a regular feature of Catholic schools, and the Catholic periodical literature of the day (even for children) was chock-full of stories from the missions, some of them of a blood-curdling sort. The Jesuits and the Religious of the Sacred Heart may have been the up-market religious orders when I was growing up, but the Catholic Foreign Mission Society of America—"Maryknoll"—was where the adventure was.

We were also at least vaguely aware of belonging to a worldwide Church that was being persecuted in various places. The idea of a "Christian-Marxist dialogue" was buried in the womb of the future. What we knew about communism was that communists had killed Yugoslavia's Cardinal Alojzije Stepinac, tortured Hungary's Cardinal József Mindszenty, and locked up the gentle Bishop James

Edward Walsh of Maryknoll (a fellow Marylander and veteran missionary to China). Some of this storytelling had an effect on me that I couldn't possibly have imagined at the time.

A lot of my writing over the past three and a half decades has had to do with Poland, and I can't help but think that the seeds of my Polish passion were planted early—in the third grade, to be precise. In early 1959, the principal of the old Cathedral School in downtown Baltimore, Sister Euphemia, announced that each class in the school would be assigned a communist dictator for whose conversion we were to pray during Lent that year. Everybody wanted Soviet premier Nikita Khrushchev, of course, because he was the only communist dictator most of us had ever heard of. So there was great disappointment in the third grade when, by the luck of the draw, we got the boss Polish communist, Władysław Gomułka. More than thirty years later I would write a book that, among other things, chronicled Gomułka's complex role in Polish Church-state relations; you can't tell me there isn't a connection, somehow, to that third-grade experience.

The other great international linkage that made us different was, of course, the link to what an earlier generation of anti-Catholic bigots (actually, in our grandparents' time) had been pleased to call a "foreign potentate"—the pope. The sense of connection to "Rome" and to the pope himself was strong. Pius XII, the pope of my boyhood, was an ethereal figure; yet every Catholic I knew seemed to feel a personal attachment to him, and I well remember the tears shed when he died in October 1958. I was then in the second grade, and, along with all eight grades of the old Cathedral

School, I was marched across Mulberry Street into the Cathedral of the Assumption, where one of the young priests on the cathedral staff led us in five decades of the rosary. Our elders, for the next few days, said that "there would never be another pope like Pius XII" (a good call, if not for the reasons they imagined at the time). Then, when a portly, seventy-seven-year-old Italian named Roncalli was elected and took what sounded like a bizarre name, "John XXIII," those same elders sagely noted that things just weren't the same (they got that right, too, if again for an entirely different set of reasons). This emotional and spiritual connection to the Bishop of Rome never seemed to us odd, much less un-American, and the anti-Catholic agitations of the 1960 presidential campaign struck us as weird rather than threatening: we knew we were Catholics *and* Americans, and if someone else had a problem with that, well, that was *their* problem, as we used to say. It certainly wasn't ours.

So we were . . . different, and we knew ourselves to be different, yet without experiencing ourselves as strangers in a strange land. Garry Wills and I have never agreed on much, but Wills had it exactly right when, in an elegiac essay written in the early 1970s, he said that our generation of Catholics in America had grown up in a ghetto—just as he was right when he also wrote that it wasn't a bad ghetto in which to grow up. Indeed, the most ghettoized people of all, I've come to learn, are the people who don't know they grew up in a particular time and place and culture, and who think they can get to universal truths outside of particular realities and commitments. There are ghettos and then there are ghettos. The real question is not whether you grow up in a ghetto, but whether the ideas and customs and rhythms of your particular ghetto prepare you to engage other ideas and customs and life experiences without losing touch with your roots. Long before Alex Haley successfully marketed the idea, we had gotten the idea that "roots" were important, because without roots there's no growth, only dryness and decay.

S till, whether we knew it or not (and most of us didn't know it until later in life), this "Catholic difference" wasn't only a matter of how we described ourselves, how we talked, what we wore and ate, where we went to school, and who taught us. The real "Catholic difference"—which was mediated to us by all these other differences—was, at bottom, a way of seeing the world. And, by a roundabout route, this brings us to the first proposition I'd like you to consider: while Catholicism is a body of beliefs and a way of life, *Catholicism is also an optic, a way of seeing things, a distinctive perception of reality.*

What is it? You can describe it in many ways. You can call it the "Catholic *both/and*": nature *and* grace, faith *and* works, Jerusalem *and* Athens, faith *and* reason, charismatic *and* institutional, visible *and* invisible. You can call it the "sacramental imagination" (about which, much more later). You can call it a taste for the analogical, as distinguished from some Protestants' taste for the dialectical. You can, in the broadest terms, call it "Catholic culture." However it's described, though, it's not something you simply argue yourself into. Rather, it's something you experience aesthetically as well as intellectually, with the emotions as well as the mind, through friendships and worship and experiences-beyond-words as well as through arguments and syllogisms. And that, to go back to the beginning, is why, in thinking through the question of what it means to be a Catholic today, it's a good idea to go on a tour of the Catholic world—because there are particular places where this uniquely Catholic way of seeing things comes into clearer focus, as do the particular challenges that twenty-first-century Catholicism faces.

Which brings us to another, perhaps unlikely, place at the beginning of our journey: Milledgeville, Georgia, deep in the heart of Dixie, the least Catholic part of the United States—demographically speaking, at least.

Andalusia Farm, outside Milledgeville, was the home of Flannery O'Connor, one of the most gifted American writers of the past half-century. F. Scott Fitzgerald, another great mid-twentieth-century writer, couldn't escape his boyhood Catholicism, no matter how hard he tried (and he tried *very* hard). Flannery O'Connor wrote the way she did precisely *because* she was a dead-serious Catholic with a deep intuition about the Catholic optic on life.

Born in Savannah in 1925, Mary Flannery O'Connor and her family moved to Andalusia Farm when Flannery was twelve. In 1945 she graduated from the Georgia State College for Women, and then she studied at the famous Writers' Workshop at the University of Iowa. In 1949, the onset of systemic lupus erythematosus, the chronic inflammatory disease that had taken her father's life before Flannery was sixteen, brought her home to Milledgeville, where she spent the rest of her life (save for the occasional out-of-town lecture), and where she died in 1964, at thirty-nine.

Her writing habits were as austere as her prose: her desk faced a whitewashed wall, and she wrote her fiction looking at that blank space. What she wanted to convey in her stories and novels came out of her head and her reading and her reflection and her prayer. And what she wrote was often misunderstood as dark parody and violent satire, when in fact she was holding up a mirror to a modern world that had come to think of its distortions as natural (as she once put it). Fifteen years after her death, her friend Sally Fitzgerald edited and published a collection of her letters under the title *The Habit of Being*. And the world discovered a new Flannery O'Connor—a gifted Catholic apologist and razor-sharp analyst of the "Catholic difference" in its sometimes challenging, sometimes enthusiastic, and always bracing encounter with modern culture.

Flannery O'Connor's novels and short stories struck her first critics, and often strike readers today, as being dominated by grotesques. (Asked why she wrote so frequently about grotesques, Miss O'Connor, who had a very dry wit, used to reply that, in the South, they liked to think they could still recognize them.) In fact, Flannery O'Connor's fiction is pervaded by a deeply Catholic intuition about the temper of our times and what the peculiarly modern determination to identify freedom with radical personal autonomy—"*my* way"—has done to us. As she once put it in one of those posthumously published letters (referring to a "moronic" review of one of her stories in *The New Yorker*), "the moral sense has been bred out of certain sections of the population, like the wings that have been bred off certain chickens to produce more white meat on them." By "moral sense," I think Miss O'Connor meant the "habit of being," that spiritual sensibility which allows us to experience the world not as one damn thing after another, but as the

dramatic arena of creation, sin, redemption, and sanctification. "This is a generation of wingless chickens," O'Connor
continued, "which is I suppose what Nietzsche meant when
he said God is dead." The proclamation of the death of God
had resulted in the death of the truly human: what was left
behind were wingless chickens.

And here's the second proposition to ponder: for all the
sentimentality that occasionally clings to Catholic piety, *there
is nothing sentimental about Catholicism.* "There is nothing
harder or less sentimental than Christian realism," Flannery
O'Connor wrote, because Christianity stands or falls with
the Incarnation—God's entry into history through Jesus of
Nazareth, who is both the Son of God, the Second Person of
the Trinity, and the son of Mary, a young Jewish girl living
on the outer fringes of the Roman Empire. History and humanity are the vehicles by which God reveals himself to the
world he created. History is the arena, and humanity the vessel, through which God redeems the world. History and humanity *count*, and count, ultimately, not because of our pride,
but because of God's merciful love, the unsentimental but
cleansing love of the father who welcomes the prodigal son
home, knowing full well that the prodigal has made a thor-
oughgoing mess of his life by his selfishness, his "autonomy,"
his conviction that nothing, including himself, really counts.

"If you live today, you breathe in nihilism . . . it's the gas
you breathe," wrote Flannery O'Connor; "if I hadn't had the
Church to fight it with or to tell me the necessity of fighting it, I would be the stinkingest logical positivist you ever
saw right now." So, I expect, would I. So, perhaps, would
you. So here's one more way to think about Catholicism and
its distinctive optic on the world and on us: *Catholicism is*

an antidote to nihilism. And by "nihilism" I mean not the sour, dark, often violent nihilism of Nietzsche and Sartre, but what my friend the late Father Ernest Fortin (who borrowed the term from his friend, Alan Bloom) used to call "debonair nihilism": the nihilism that enjoys itself on the way to oblivion, convinced that all of this—the world, us, relationships, sex, beauty, history—is really just a cosmic joke. Against the nihilist claim that nothing is really of consequence, Catholicism insists that *everything* is of consequence, because everything has been redeemed by Christ.

And if you believe that, it changes the way you see things. It changes the way *everything* looks. Here is Flannery O'Connor again, reflecting on the Catholic difference in her own artistic and spiritual life and in the life and work of fellow-author Caroline Gordon Tate:

> I feel that if I were not a Catholic, I would have no reason to write, no reason to see, no reason ever to feel horrified or even to enjoy anything. I am a born Catholic, went to Catholic schools in my early years, and have never left or wanted to leave the Church. I have never had the sense that being a Catholic is a limit to the freedom of the writer, but just the reverse. Mrs. Tate told me that after she became a Catholic, she felt she could use her eyes and accept what she saw for the first time, she didn't have to make a new universe for each book but could take the one she found.

To be sure, Catholicism wants to change the world—primarily by converting it. At the same time, Catholicism takes the world as it is—Catholicism tries to convert *this* world, not some other world or some other humanity of our imagining—because God took the world as it is. God didn't create a different world to redeem; God, in the person of his Son, redeemed the world he had created, which is a world of freedom in which our decisions have real consequences, for good and for evil. Flannery O'Connor used to complain, wryly, that the critics who described her fiction as "horror stories" always had "hold of the wrong horror." The horror isn't wickedness. The horror of the modern world is that, if nothing is really of ultimate consequence, then the wickedness isn't really wicked, the good isn't good, and we're back, once again, to all those pathetic "wingless chickens."

Flannery O'Connor's wry wit may be giving you the impression that being Catholic and being feisty are not mutually exclusive. Good. Let's ratchet that up just one more notch. In the late 1940s, Miss O'Connor, then an aspiring young writer, was taken to a literary dinner in New York at the home of Mary McCarthy, who had made a considerable commercial success out of the story of her break from the Church. Invitations to dinner with Mary McCarthy, a certified heavyweight on the New York literary scene, were gold and frankincense to struggling writers; Flannery O'Connor played the evening rather differently than your typical fledgling author-on-the-make. Here's her description of the self-consciously sophisticated repartee of that dinner party, and her sole contribution to it:

> I was once . . . taken by some friends to have dinner with
> Mary McCarthy and her husband, Mr. Broadwater. (She just
> wrote that book, *A Charmed Life*.) She departed the Church
> at the age of 15 and is a Big Intellectual. We went at eight and

at one, I hadn't opened my mouth once, there being nothing for me in such company to say. The people who took me were Robert Lowell and his now wife, Elizabeth Hardwick. Having me there was like having a dog present who had been trained to say a few words but overcome with inadequacy had forgotten them. Well, toward morning the conversation turned on the Eucharist, which I, being the Catholic, was obviously supposed to defend. Mrs. Broadwater said when she was a child and received the Host, she thought of it as the Holy Ghost, He being the "most portable" person of the Trinity; now she thought of it as a symbol and implied that it was a pretty good one. I then said, in a very shaky voice, "Well, if it's a symbol, to hell with it." That was all the defense I was capable of but I realize now that this is all I will ever be able to say about it, outside a story, except that it is the center of existence for me; all the rest of life is expendable.

Now: there's a lot to be learned from modern philosophy and theology about the difference between a "sign" (which simply conveys a message, like "Stop" or "This is Crest toothpaste") and a "symbol," a more complex reality that makes present, or embodies, the truth it communicates (a wedding ring, for instance). And yes, there's a certain theological sense in which the sacraments are "symbols" through which Christ is really and truly present to his people, the Church. But prior to such distinctions, important as they are, is the gut *Catholic* instinct that Flannery O'Connor defended so rashly in Mary McCarthy's living room. If Mary McCarthy was right, and the Eucharist only represented Christ in some magical way, then Flannery O'Connor was being utterly, thoroughly, radically orthodox when she muttered, "Well, if it's a symbol, to hell with it."

The Catholic imagination, this *habit of being* we've been exploring, is serious business. An evangelical Protestant of my acquaintance once said to a Catholic friend, "If I really believed, like you say you do, that Christ himself is in that tabernacle, I'd be crawling up the aisle on my hands and knees." That's about half-right: for the Catholic habit of being teaches us both the fear of the Lord (in the sense of being awestruck by the majesty and mercy of God) and an intimacy, even familiarity, with God the Holy Trinity, through the personal relationship with Jesus Christ that is the heart of Catholic faith. Inside that distinctively Catholic "both/and" of the intimate and the awesome lies the conviction that *all of this is for real.* Stuff counts. I count. You count. It all counts. Because all of it—you, me, our friends, our critics, the man I jostled on the subway this morning and the bag lady sleeping on the heating grate outside the Farragut North metro stop, the whole mad, sad, noble, degraded, endlessly fascinating human story—is really History, Christ's story, supercharged with that fullness of truth and love that can only come from Truth and Love itself: that can only come from God.

That's what I learned, at least in terms of instincts, in those last years of the intact urban Catholic culture of America. I learned what Flannery O'Connor later named for me as the "habit of being." For all its gaudiness, the world of debonair nihilism in which you've grown up sees the world in black and white, and in two dimensions only. In the world of debonair nihilism, there is only me, and there are only transient pleasures to be grasped and indulged and then quickly forgotten, on the way to the next ephemeral high produced by my willfulness. By contrast, the Catholic imagination, this habit of being, teaches us to see the world in Technicolor and to live in it in three dimensions (or, truth to tell, four, because time counts, too, for Catholicism as well as for Einstein).

That's the habit I hope this correspondence and our tour of the Catholic world helps you acquire: the habit of being, the habit of seeing things in depth, as they are and for what they are. Everything that is, is for a reason. Everything that happens, happens for a purpose. That's what it means to understand history as His-story. Seeing things in their true dimensions is one very large part of what it means to be a Catholic. For learning to see things aright *here* is how we become the kind of people who can see, and love, God forever.

THE PAPAL BASILICA
OF ST. PETER'S, ROME

The Scavi *and the Grittiness of Catholicism*

ope Pius XI died on February 10, 1939. Prior to his election as Bishop of Rome in 1922, he had briefly been the Archbishop of Milan, and the people of the city of St. Ambrose wanted to honor his memory by building a fitting resting place for him in St. Peter's Basilica. So funds were raised, artists commissioned, and a magnificent marble sarcophagus, which was to be the centerpiece of a richly decorated mosaic vault, was prepared and sent to Rome.

According to one story I've heard, when it came time to fit the new tomb into the Grottoes underneath the papal high altar in St. Peter's, it was simply too large. Perhaps that's a case of historical embellishment, which isn't rare in Italy; or perhaps it's just a Roman attempt to tweak the usually efficient Milanese. In any event, there had long been plans for renovating the entire Grotto area, to make it a more appropriate place for pilgrims to pray. So Pope Pius XII, successor to Pius XI, ordered the floor of the undercroft to be lowered to make room for the tomb of his predecessor, and as a first step in the planned renovation.

It was a decision with unforeseen consequences.

What we know today as "St. Peter's" used to be called "New St. Peter's," to distinguish it from "Old St. Peter's," the basilica built by the Emperor Constantine in the fourth century over what he and everyone else understood to be the grave of Peter, Prince of the Apostles. Despite his absorption in planning the new imperial capital at Constantinople, Constantine himself helped a bit with the construction of his magnificent St. Peter's, by carrying twelve baskets of earth to the site, one for each of the twelve apostles. For more than a millennium, "Old St. Peter's" was one of the focal points of the Christian world, a pole toward which Christians' internal compasses naturally pointed.

By the second half of the fifteenth century, however, Old St. Peter's had fallen to rack and ruin; the decision was made to pull it down, stone by stone, to make way for a new basilica. The building of "New St. Peter's," which would eventually include the world's largest dome and the fantastically strong foundations needed to support it, took 120 years and absorbed the attention of 20 popes and 10 architects, including such greats as Bramante, Michelangelo, and Bernini. The building's changing design, the execution of those designs, and the fundraising necessary to support such a vast project caused a lot of controversy and contributed indirectly to the fracturing of Western

Christianity in the Reformation. Amidst all the confusion and construction, little was done to explore the tomb of St. Peter. It was simply assumed to be where tradition and Constantine had sited it. "New St. Peter's" was thus built without any systematic excavation of what was underneath Old St. Peter's.

When the workmen began lowering the floor of the undercroft to accommodate the tomb of Pope Pius XI and renovate the Grotto space, they discovered a series of tombs that, on further examination, seemed to be part of a kind of necropolis, complete with walls, streets, benches, funerary monuments, and so forth. Much of this had been disturbed or destroyed when the ancient Vatican Hill was leveled by Constantine's fourth-century builders, but a fair amount of it was still intact. While World War II raged across Europe, Pius XII quietly authorized a full-scale archaeological excavation of the area, which continued throughout the 1940s.

Digging under the papal high altar of the basilica was something like peeling an onion, or opening one of those nested Russian *matrushka* dolls. Eventually, the excavators found a shrine, the Tropaion (the Greek word for trophy or victory monument): a classic structure, with columns supporting what may have been an altar, surmounted by a pediment. The floor of the Tropaion, in which there's an opening that delineates the boundaries of the grave over which the monument had been built, defined the level of the floor of Constantine's basilica. At the back of the Tropaion was a red wall; exposed to the elements, it began to crack, necessitating the construction of a buttressing wall to support the whole structure. When the archaeologists unearthed the buttressing wall, they found it covered with graffiti—and it contained a secret, marble-lined repository. One piece of graffiti, decoded, seemed to say "Peter is [here]."

Thanks to long-delayed renovation plans, the need to accommodate Pius XI's tomb, and the curiosity of Pius XII (who seems to have been intrigued by the discovery of King Tut's tomb in 1923), the archaeologists eventually unearthed a small city of the dead beneath the foundations of "Old St. Peter's," which had been incorporated into "New St. Peter's" as supports for the colossal new structure. There had been, evidently, a vast pagan burial ground on the Vatican Hill. At some point, Christians began to be buried there. The central grave that defines the Tropaion is surrounded by other graves, which radiate out from it. Thus it seems that the remains of St. Peter, which would have been among the most jealously guarded relics of the ancient Roman Christian community, had been buried, perhaps immediately after his death, perhaps a brief time later, in the Vatican Hill necropolis: secretly, but with sufficient clues to indicate to pious Christian pilgrims the location of Peter's tomb. Perhaps the remains were, during persecutions, moved to a less risky place and then reinterred. Perhaps the Tropaion was part of a Christian complex that, in calmer times, was used for baptisms, ordinations, and funerals. Perhaps, before the Tropaion was built, the grave itself was used as a site for small Christian gatherings in the dead of night.

No one knows for sure. Archaeology isn't algebra; it yields probabilities rather than certainties. But reputable scientific opinion today holds that the excavations under St. Peter's in the 1940s—excavations originally undertaken for an entirely different purpose—did yield the mortal remains of Peter.

Oddly enough, amidst the fragments of Peter's skull, vertebrae, arms, hands, pelvis, and legs, there is nothing from the ankles on down. But perhaps that isn't so odd after all. If a man has been crucified upside down, as tradition says Peter was, the easiest way to remove what was left of his body (which may well have been turned into a living torch during his execution, in another refinement of Roman cruelty) would have been to chop off the deceased's feet and remove the rest of the corpse from its cross.

The remarkable sites beneath St. Peter's are known today as the *Scavi* (excavations). A walk through them is a walk into some important truths about what it means to be a Catholic.

Not so long ago, you couldn't see St. Peter's from the Tiber River, a few hundred yards away: it was fronted by a Roman slum, the Borgo. To prepare for the Holy Year of 1950, the Italian government knocked the slums down and built a broad avenue that runs from the Tiber up to St. Peter's Square: the Via della Conciliazione (Reconciliation Street), so named for the 1929 modus vivendi between the Italian Republic and the Church that created the independent microstate of Vatican City. No matter how many times you do it, the turn into the Conciliazione and that first, startling view of St. Peter's and its dome is always breathtaking. We're fortunate to be doing this today, because the basilica, whose facade was extensively cleaned for the Great Jubilee of 2000, looks better than it has in centuries, and perhaps ever. What was once a blinding mass of white travertine stone has, on cleaning, revealed itself to be a rich mix of colors, including café au lait and some light pastels. Still, it's not the facade and the dome on which we want to concentrate as we walk into the Square, but the obelisk that stands precisely in the center of the Square, framed by Bernini's great colonnade.

The obelisk, a granite Egyptian monolith standing 84 feet tall and weighing 350 tons, was brought to Rome from North Africa by the mad emperor Caligula, who terrorized Rome from 37 to 41, before he was assassinated by the Praetorian Guard; his wickedness, you may remember, was memorably portrayed by John Hurt in the BBC television series *I, Claudius*. Caligula's nephew, Nero, made the obelisk part of the *spina*, or "spine," of his "circus," an elongated oval in which races were held, mock battles staged, exotic animals exhibited—and the condemned executed, often with unimaginable viciousness, for the amusement of the spectators. As you look to the left of St. Peter's, you can see, past the Swiss Guard standing at the Archway of the Bells, the area of Vatican City known as the Piazza dei Protomartiri Romani (the Square of the First Roman Martyrs), so named because that was the part of Nero's now nonexistent circus in which many faithful Christians paid the ultimate price of fidelity.

Tradition tells us that Peter died during one of Nero's spasms of persecution, and if so, he likely died in Nero's circus. If he did, then it's quite possible that the last thing Peter saw on this earth was the obelisk we're now pondering, which was moved to the Square in 1586 by Pope Sixtus V. Think about that as we walk a bit farther into the Vatican.

As we enter through the Archway of the Bells, we come to the Scavi office, the entrance to the excavations beneath the basilica. Scavi tours are not large affairs, and as we go down the stairways and enter the excavations themselves, you can see why. The passageways are narrow and slightly musty, even dampish. As we make our way through the dark corridors that were once streets and alleys in the Vatican Hill necropolis, our guide points out the elaborate pagan funerary monuments as well as Christian tombs. There, after about a twenty-minute walk, is what can be made out of the Tropaion. And after that, reinterred in the graffiti-marked wall I mentioned before, are what the guide tells us are the mortal remains of Peter the Apostle. Leaving through the gilded baroque splendor of the Clementine Chapel, you can't help but think that what we've just seen and touched and smelled is about as close to the apostolic roots of the Catholic Church as it's possible to get.

The Scavi are more than excavations; if we take them seriously, they demand that we think through the meaning of an extraordinary story involving some utterly ordinary people. Here it is. Sometime in the third decade of the first century of the first millennium of our era, a man named Simon, whose father was named John, made his exceedingly modest living as a fisherman in Galilee—which, even by regional standards, was a pretty rough patch of what was itself a fringe of the "civilized world." This man, Simon, became a personal friend of Jesus of Nazareth. Through that encounter, he became not Simon, but Peter, the Rock. But not for a while yet.

His friend Jesus called him "Peter," a wordplay on "rock," but the newly minted Peter hardly seems granite-like in the pre-Easter sections of the gospels. He is impetuous; he often doesn't understand what Jesus is saying. No sooner does he get his new name than he starts telling Jesus that he, Jesus, is flat wrong when he says that the promised Messiah of God must suffer; Jesus calls him a "Satan" and tells him to "get behind me" [Matthew 16.13–23]. When Jesus is arrested, Peter insinuates himself into the courtyard near where his master is being interrogated. But when challenged to acknowledge that he, too, was with Jesus the Galilean, Peter starts cursing and denies that he ever knew the man. None of the gospels suggests that Peter was present at Jesus's crucifixion; they do tell us that, after his denial, Peter "went out and wept bitterly" [Matthew 26.69–75].

In the Catholic view of things, Easter changes everything; it certainly changed Peter. After having encountered the Risen Christ on Easter Sunday morning and along the lakeshore of the Sea of Galilee, Peter truly *is* the Rock. Filled with the Holy Spirit on Pentecost, fifty days after Easter, he becomes the Church's first great evangelist; the tale is told in Acts 2.14–41, where the holiday crowd initially assumes that this suddenly eloquent Galilean fisherman must be drunk—and then many convert to The Way after each hears in his own language Peter's proclamation of the Resurrection. Peter welcomes the centurion Cornelius, a Gentile, into the Christian fellowship, enabling his fellow Jews to see that God intends the saving message of Christ for the whole world [Acts 10.1–11.18]. As the early Church struggles with what it means to be a Christian, Peter is recognized as the center of the Church's unity, the man before whom issues of Christian identity and practice are thrashed out [Acts 15.6–11]. Later, according to the most ancient traditions, Peter goes to Rome, where he eventually meets his death—thus fulfilling what the Risen Christ had said to him at breakfast along the Sea of Galilee after the miraculous catch of fish: that "when you are old, you will stretch out your hands and another will gird you and carry you where you do not wish to go" [John 21.18].

The Scavi and the obelisk—Peter's remains and the last thing Peter may have seen in this life—confront us with the historical tangibility, the sheer grittiness, of Catholicism. For all that critical scholarship has taught us about the complex story of the early Christian movement, certain unavoidable facts remain. Here, in the Scavi, you can touch them. A Galilean fisherman—a man whose personal characteristics, warts and all, were carefully recorded by his followers—ends up buried on Vatican Hill. Why? For more than 1,900 years, pilgrims from all over the world have come to venerate this man's remains. Why?

Catholicism does not rest upon a pious myth, a story that floats away from us the more we try to touch it. Here, in the Scavi, we're in touch with the apostolic foundations of the Catholic Church. And those foundations are not in our minds. They exist, quite literally, in reality. Real things happened to real people, who had to make real, life-and-death decisions—and who staked their lives not on stories or fables, but on what they had come to *know* as the truth about the Risen Lord Jesus Christ. Beneath the layers of encrusted tradition and pious storytelling, there is something real, something you can touch, at the bottom of the bottom line of Catholic faith.

And that forces us to confront some decisions.

Y ou've asked me to help you explore some of the truths of Catholic faith and practice. One of the most important truths that you might ponder is this: *the truth of faith is something that seizes us*, not something of our own discovery (still less, our invention). The Peter who was led from Galilee to Rome did not make the journey because of something he had discovered and wanted to explore to satisfy his curiosity. Peter went from the security of his modest Galilean fishing business to the dangerous (and ultimately lethal) center of the Roman Empire because he had been seized by the truth, the truth he had met in the person of Jesus.

Being seized by the truth is not cost-free. "You have received without pay, give without pay," Jesus tells his new disciples, including Peter [Matthew 10.8]. In Peter's case, the call to give away the truth that had seized and transformed his life eventually cost him his life. And that, too, is a truth to be pondered: *faith in Jesus Christ costs, not just something, but everything*. It demands all of us, not just a part of us.

One of the most touching scenes in the gospels is St. John's story of Peter's encounter with the Risen Christ along the Sea of Galilee, to which I've referred earlier. In that story, the Risen One asks Peter, who's surrounded by the other apostles, "Simon, son of John, do you love me more than these?" Peter, perhaps abashed, answers, "Yes, Lord, you know that I love you." The question then comes again, "Do you love me?" And Peter replies, again, "Yes, Lord, you know that I love you." Still evidently unsatisfied, the Risen Lord poses the question a third time: "Simon, son of John, do you love me?" Peter, the gospel tells us, was "grieved" because the questions kept coming, and finally answers, "Lord, you know everything, you know that I love you" [John 21.15–17]. Generations of preachers have presented this as a matter of the Risen Christ rather teasing Peter, matching Peter's three denials before the crucifixion with three questions about Peter's love. I think there's something far deeper, something at that border between the intimate and the awesome, going on here.

Peter, who has been given his new name because he is to be the Rock on which the Church rests, is being told, gently but firmly, that his love for Christ is not going to be an easy thing. His love is not going to be a matter of "fulfilling" himself. His love must be a pouring out of himself, and in that self-emptying he will find his fulfillment—if not in terms that the world usually understands as "fulfillment." In abandoning any sense of his autonomy, in binding himself to feed the lambs and sheep of the Lord's flock, Peter will find his true freedom. In giving himself away, he will find himself. Freely you have received, freely you must give—if the gift is to continue to live in you. That is what the Risen Christ tells Peter on the lakeshore.

As we've seen, in the gospels Peter is constantly make a hash of things—which should predispose us to think that those stories really happened; the leader's mistakes and failures and betrayals are not something his followers would likely have invented. In a world deeply skeptical of the miraculous, perhaps the hardest of these stories to accept is the story of Peter's walking on water. Put aside your skepticism for a moment and think about what the story is teaching us—about Peter and about ourselves.

You know the basic narrative. The disciples are out on the Sea of Galilee, in a boat by themselves, when they see what they imagine to be a ghost walking toward them across the stormy waters. Jesus tells them not to be afraid: "Take heart, it is I." And Peter, whose crusty skepticism has a modern ring to it, responds, "Lord, if it is you, bid me come to you on the water." Jesus raises the ante: "Come." And Peter climbs out of the boat and starts to walk toward Jesus across the water—until, that is, he starts looking around at the waves blown up by the wind, at which point he starts sinking and calls out to Jesus to save him. Jesus takes him by the hand and leads him to safety in the boat, at which point the weather calms [Matthew 14.25–32].

Did it happen just like that? I don't know, although I'm inclined to think that something extraordinary happened on the Sea of Galilee that night. However we work out the meteorology and hydrology, though, the lesson of the story—the truth it's trying to convey—remains, and helps fill in our portrait of Peter and our understanding of faith as radical and life-transforming gift. When Peter keeps his eyes fixed on Jesus, he can do what he imagines impossible: he can "walk on water." When he starts looking around for his security—when he starts looking elsewhere—he sinks. So do we. When we keep our gaze fixed on Christ, we, too, can do what seems impossible. We can accept the gift of faith, with humility and gratitude. We can live our lives as the gift for others that our lives are to us. We can discover the depths of ourselves in the emptying of ourselves.

In the Catholic view of things, "walking on water" is an entirely sensible thing to do. It's staying in the boat, hanging tightly to our own sad little securities, that's rather mad.

There are many other Peter stories we could revisit—including, while we're here in Rome, the famous *Quo Vadis* story of Peter's alleged flight from Nero's persecution. As the legend has it, Peter had decided to flee Rome at the outbreak of persecution, perhaps in fear, perhaps because he thought "the Rock" should be somewhere safe so others could eventually find and cling to it, and to him. In any case, heading out the Via Appia, Peter meets Jesus, who's heading *into* the city and the persecution. *"Quo vadis, Domine,"* Peter asks—"Lord, where are you going?" "I am going to Rome to be crucified," Jesus answers—and disappears. At which point Peter turns back into the city to embrace martyrdom. In Rome, to this day, you can visit the spot on the Via Appia Antica where all of this is said to have happened.

The *Quo Vadis* legend is interesting for its tenacity. It's also interesting for the same reason it's interesting that the Church, in deciding which books to include in the canon of the New Testament, included four gospels that all describe, sometimes in great detail, Peter's failures. Those stories could have been discreetly edited out, airbrushed from history; they weren't. And that tells us something.

What it tells us is that weakness and failure are part of the Catholic reality *from the beginning*. Weakness and failure, too, are part of the grittiness of Catholicism—including weakness and failure, stupidity, and cowardice among the Church's ordained leaders. Flannery O'Connor was speaking a very ancient truth when she wrote in 1955 that "it seems to be a fact that you have to suffer as much from the Church as for it." Almost fifty years later, Catholics in the United States relearned that lesson the hard way, in the scandal of clerical sexual abuse and the crisis that scandal caused when it was so badly handled by some bishops—by the successors of the apostles. I don't detect any massive abandonment of the Catholic Church because of this crisis. But it does force us to come to grips with the fact that the people of the Church, including its ordained leadership, are earthen vessels carrying the treasure of faith in history (as St. Paul put it in 2 Corinthians 4.7).

Only the naive would expect it to be otherwise. Like Peter, all the people of the Church, including the Church's ordained leadership, must constantly be purified. And purified by what? Like Peter, we must be purified by love, by a more complete and radical emptying of self. "Smugness," Flannery O'Connor once wrote, "is the Great Catholic Sin." Looking at Peter, we might almost say, "as it was in the beginning."

But here, too, the Scavi help us get to the deeper truth of Catholic things. For, while the early Church insisted on including weakness and failure in its narrative of its first years and decades, the storyline of the New Testament—of the gospels and the Acts of the Apostles—is not, finally, a story of failure, but of purified love transforming the world. To be sure, that transformation comes with a price: imagine Peter, in the agonized moments before his death, looking at that obelisk we can see today, and you can understand that none of this is easy. Then consider all those pilgrims who, like Peter, were seized by the truth of Christ, and who have come, over the centuries, to place themselves in the presence of Peter's remains. Pious nostalgia? Raw curiosity? I don't think so. Whether articulate or mute, what those millions of pilgrims were and are saying, as they pray in the Scavi or over the Scavi, surrounded by the baroque magnificence of the basilica, is that *failure is not the final word*. Emptiness and oblivion are not our destiny. Love is the final word. And love is the most living thing of all, because love is of God.

To know that, and to stake your life on it, is to have been seized by the truth of God in Christ—amidst and through, not around, the gritty reality of the world.

St. Catherine's Monastery, Mt. Sinai / The Holy Sepulcher, Jerusalem

The Face of Christ

s you saw in Milledgeville, Georgia, the "Catholic world" isn't confined to sites owned or operated by the Catholic Church. In this letter, I'd like to take you to two different kinds of sites within the "Catholic world": one is a Greek Orthodox monastery; the second is a church divided among a gaggle of Christian communities, who can (and do) argue for decades about which of them gets to fix the roof. As I've said before, Catholicism and grittiness go together. Let's go now to two very gritty places located on the border where the divine and the human touch—places where *things happened*, things with ultimate consequences.

No one knows for certain where Mt. Sinai, the mountain where God met Moses in the Hebrew Bible, is. A pilgrimage tradition that dates back to about AD 400 identifies "Mt. Sinai" with Jebel Mûsā, a 7,500-ft. twin-peaked mountain at the southern tip of the Sinai Peninsula. The landscape seems appropriate to the story. Jebel Mûsā is a steep, craggy place, with two neighboring mountains close at hand and a large plain at the base of the mountain cluster; its colors and topography are a little reminiscent of the stark beauty of the American Southwest. Arguments about the precise location of biblical sites have fueled doctoral dissertations beyond numbering; most expert opinion today agrees that the early Christian pilgrims got it right—Jebel Mûsā (The Mountain of Moses) is the site of the encounter at the burning bush, the giving of the Ten Commandments, and the Mosaic covenant between God and the people of Israel.

After twelve centuries of Islamic dominance of the Middle East and North Africa, it's easy to forget that the Egyptian desert was the great cradle of monasticism in early Christian history, beginning with St. Anthony in the mid-third century. These monks led lives of extraordinary, even desperate, rigor, none more so than the "anchorites" or "eremites" who lived by themselves in small hermitages. Once the word got around, through pilgrims, that Jebel Mûsā was where some of the most dramatic events in the Book of Exodus had unfolded, hermitages sprang up on the shadier northern slope of the mountain, the traditional site of the burning bush through which Moses had first encountered the God of Abraham, Isaac, and Jacob. In 527, the Byzantine emperor Justinian built a great monastery on that same northern slope. High, thick walls had to be erected later to protect the monks from robbers; still later, a modus vivendi was achieved with invading Muslims by allowing them to build a small mosque inside the compound. If you talk to the Bedouins who have taken care of security at St. Catherine's for a very long time, they'll tell you that this is where they come to venerate Moses, whom they regard as a prophet.

Justinian dedicated the monastery church to Mary and to the commemoration of Christ's Transfiguration; later, in the eighth century, when the relics of St. Catherine of Alexandria were brought to Jebel Mûsâ for safekeeping, the whole complex was renamed in her honor. Today, the Monastery of St. Catherine is an autonomous Orthodox monastery, and its abbot (or Hegumen, in Orthodox terminology) is consecrated by the Greek Orthodox Patriarch of Jerusalem with the impressive title "Archbishop of Sinai, Pharan, and Raitho." For all its isolation, and notwithstanding the hardness of the surrounding area, St. Catherine's is a living Christian community, its two dozen monks offering pastoral care to some 9,000 local Christians, most of them Red Sea fishermen.

Those same monks also care for some of the greatest treasures of the Christian world: the Codex Sinaiticus, one of the earliest extant copies of the Greek Bible, discovered by the German biblical scholar Constantin Tischendorf in the monastery library in 1844; the Codex Syriacus, a fourth-century rendering of the canonical gospels in Syriac; some 3,000 other manuscripts in Arabic, Georgian, and Slavonic as well as Syriac and Greek; and an incomparable collection of icons. (Read Janet Soskice's book, *The Sisters of Sinai*, for a marvelous tale of discovery centered on the monastery and its artifacts.)

One of the monastery's treasures is why we've come to this place—a place where timelessness is tangible. Because that's the perfect setting in which to ponder the truths embodied by St. Catherine's most famous icon, *Christos Pantokrator*—Christ the All-Sovereign, Christ the Universal King.

A word about icons and the first-millennium controversy over "iconoclasm" is in order. First, icons.

An icon is not intended to be a work of representational art, in the usual way that we think of paintings by, say, Rembrandt. Rather, an icon is "written" (not "painted") by an iconographer, for whom his work is both a vocation (not merely a job) and a form of prayer: an iconographer "writes" icons because he believes himself called by God to do so, and he writes specific icons as the result of meditation and prayer on some mystery of the faith. The product, the icon, is intended to be another border-crossing between the divine and the human, a window into the mystery that it pictorially conveys.

To use some Western theological terminology we've used before, and with apologies to the learned for the anachronism, an icon is a *symbol* that *makes present* what it conveys. A conventional Western painting—Holbein's portrait of Sir Thomas More—simply says, "This is what this man looked like." Holbein didn't intend to make Sir Thomas *present*, in the sense that those viewing the painting would "meet" the former Lord Chancellor and "man for all seasons." The anonymous iconographic genius who wrote *Christos Pantokrator* intended precisely that: that, in the *Christos Pantokrator*, we would meet the Lord Jesus Christ.

But how could this be? To go back to Moses and the Ten Commandments: What happened to the Bible's condemnation of idolatry, its absolute prohibition against pictorial or other artistic representations of God? How is an icon not an idol?

When the Christian movement largely displaced the gods of Greek and Roman antiquity, everyone, whether Christian or not, might well have imagined that this meant the death of religious art. Mainstream Christianity accepted the Hebrew Bible as divine revelation, and as God himself had put it, that meant (in the wonderful translation done by King James's committee) "Thou shalt not make unto thee any graven image" [Exodus 20.4]. When Christianity met the neo-Platonic thought then dominant in the Mediterranean world, some Christian philosophers began to teach that the "image of God" in us, and preeminently in Christ, is located in the "rational soul"—and you can't paint or sculpt or make a mosaic representation of the rational soul. So for these thinkers, attempts to portray the "image of God" in us was both idolatrous and philosophically absurd. Had they won the day, religious art would have been doomed.

Yet the triumph of Christianity in the Roman world actually produced an extraordinary and unprecedented outpouring of artistic creativity, which continues to this day. What happened? What happened is that the grittiest, most earthy of Christian claims—that the Son of God became flesh in Jesus of Nazareth—eventually became the rationale for both Christian iconography and Christian representational art. Rather than negating art, the Incarnation became the ultimate warrant for religious art. This is worth thinking about for a moment.

The theological battle between the iconoclasts, who literally destroyed icons, and the defenders of icons lasted for almost two hundred years. A lot of blood was spilled as the Byzantine emperors got into the fray, and what must have been some of the greatest religious art in history was destroyed in the process. Although the politics of the controversy dragged on until 843, the issue was resolved theologically in 787 at the Second Council of Nicaea. And, as I said a moment ago, the argument that prevailed was an argument from grittiness: it turned on the tangibility, so to speak, of Christ, the Incarnate Son of God.

At Nicaea II the icon-defenders told their iconoclastic adversaries, yes, of course we agree that the Son is the Image of God the Father; that's what the Council of Chalcedon had declared in 451 and we all accept that. But you iconoclasts are missing the further point: the Image of the Father has been made human in the Incarnation. When Mary said "yes" to the angel Gabriel's startling message, *the Image of God became a man.* Jesus Christ was not a crypto-human, God in a fleshy disguise; to take that seriously means taking the physical and the material seriously. And that brings us to icons.

As historian Jaroslav Pelikan once put it in summarizing the winning argument in this debate, an icon is "not an idol but an image of the Image." Indeed, Pelikan reports, the defenders of icons pushed their argument all the way back, proposing that the "making of images" begins within God himself: for the Son is the Image of the Father, and through this Image—this Second Person of the Trinity, this *Logos,* this Word—God creates the world. Everything in the world is part of what Pelikan calls a "great chain of images," whose origins are within the interior life of God the Holy Trinity.

What about idolatry?

Idolatry, the defenders of icons taught, was the arrogant human attempt to "get at" and control the divine through images, to cross the infinite gulf between the human and the divine by our own efforts. What happened in the Incarnation, they continued, is that *that gulf was crossed for us.* Jesus Christ, truly divine and truly human, is the living, enfleshed Image that completes the great chain of images—the incarnate Son of God who brings the divine into the human world and lifts the human up into the interior life of God himself. The God who had once forbidden the people of Israel to make images of himself had given us the true Image, and in the flesh. When God enters history, the events of salvation history, "written" iconographically for us, can become true images of the Image.

Whew.

I'd apologize for this brief and admittedly high-altitude theological detour, except that it's very important in nailing down a theme we've already touched upon: that *Catholicism is realism.* Why was the iconoclastic controversy so important? The defenders of icons were right, and the Church was right to vindicate them, because what was at stake here was nothing less than the Christian claim that *we can touch the truth of our salvation.* Christianity, even in its most abstract neo-Platonic dress, is not simply a matter of ideas, even true ideas. Christianity is a matter of truths enfleshed: God become man, and man deified.

That is Who we meet in the *Christos Pantokrator.*

Because it lies so far from the beaten track, St. Catherine's and its icons escaped the ravages of the iconoclasts. Discovered under layers of paint, the *Christos Pantokrator* is an image of Christ in a typical iconographic pose, full-face toward us, the Lord's head surrounded by a golden corona or halo, his left arm clutching a jeweled Bible to himself (the Word of God, the Second Person of the Trinity, holding the Word of God, the Holy Scripture), his right hand raised in a gesture that is both greeting and blessing, the thumb and ring finger touching (in acknowledgment of the two natures united in the one person of Christ), the index and middle fingers crossed (in acknowledgment of the instrument of salvation). The colors are impressively rich: gold and ivory, lavender and vermillion. But it is the Holy Face—majestic, calm, strikingly masculine—that draws us into the icon and into an encounter with the Lord himself.

It is one face, for Christ is one. Yet the iconographer, by painting a face with two subtly different expressions, has drawn us into the mystery of God Incarnate, the Son of God come in the flesh. For all its humanity, we see— perhaps better, we *sense*—that, while this is a truly human face, it's unlike any face we've seen before. He is in time, in one dimension of his face, but beyond time, in another. He is like every other human person, i.e., a person of time and space and history; but he is also transcendent, eternal. We meet him in his humanity; he draws us into his divinity. As Jaroslav Pelikan wrote, he is the embodiment of three transcendentals: the "one who was the embodiment not only of the True in his teaching and of the Good in his life, but of the Beautiful in his form as 'the fairest of the sons of men' [Psalm 45.2]." In the truth, goodness, and beauty of his majesty, we glimpse the glory of our own human destiny, if we believe in him and his power to transform our lives into a participation in his own divine life. The true, the good, and the beautiful meet in Christ, the Image of the Father from all eternity, the son of Mary of Nazareth according to the flesh.

The *Christos Pantokrator*, which was probably written in Constantinople in the sixth century, iconographically embodies a theme that was key to the teaching of the Second Vatican Council in the twentieth century: that, in Jesus Christ, we meet both the truth of the merciful Father and the truth about our humanity. As the Council fathers wrote, "Christ, the final Adam, by the revelation of the mystery of the Father and His love, fully reveals man to man himself and makes his supreme calling clear" [*Gaudium et Spes*, 22].

"Spirituality," as it's defined in those hundreds of books you find listed under that topic, is our search for the "religious." Catholicism is emphatically *not* "spirituality" in that sense of the term. Catholicism (according to the great twentieth-century Swiss theologian Hans Urs von Balthasar) is about God's search for us—and our learning, over the course of a lifetime, to take the same path through history that God is taking. Human reason, the Catholic Church insists, can "get" us to God, in the sense that human reason can "find" the fact of God's existence through rational argument. But we cannot meet the God of Abraham, Isaac, and Jacob, the God who is the Father of Jesus Christ, by reason alone; nor can we discover

God's attributes. That required a demonstration—and the demonstration of the truth about God, the merciful Father, comes through the Incarnation of the Son of God, who shows us the Father and his mercy.

You've heard since you were a child about the parable of the "prodigal son" [Luke 15.11–32]—which is more accurately called the Parable of the Merciful Father. Yes, the profligate son sets the dramatic stage by his dissipation and his (rather calculating) decision to return home as a hired hand. But it's the father, who watches from afar and who runs out to greet his wayward son before he has even arrived home, who is the center of the dramatic action. It's the father who casts all pragmatism, all rational calculation, aside—who cannot imagine taking his son back as a hireling, but lavishly embraces him and welcomes him home as a son. The merciful Father revealed by Jesus Christ does not wait for us to figure out our dependency; nor will he respond to our acknowledgment of our failures by bringing us "home" in a lesser station. He comes in search of us: he rushes out to embrace us, to restore to us what is ours by heritage—that which we have lost by our own squalid selfishness. In his incarnate Son, the merciful Father wishes to make us sons and daughters again. In language that the writer of the *Christos Pantokrator* might have used, what he offers us, profligately and freely, is *theosis*, "divinization," the restoration of what he intended for us in the beginning, but which we lost by our willfulness.

This is the "good news" of the Gospel—but there is more. For as we learn by being drawn into the *Christos Pantokrator*, and as the Second Vatican Council insisted, *Jesus*

Christ reveals who we are, as well as *who God is*. And who we think we are has a lot to do with the unfolding of modern history. Let me show you how.

In June 1959, the commission preparing the agenda for the Second Vatican Council wrote all the bishops of the world, asking them what the Council should discuss. The answers, from all over the world, fill the first several volumes of the *Acta*, the "Acts," or official record, of Vatican II. Some of the proposals are striking anticipations of the key themes that would dominate the Council's debates: the shape of Catholic worship, the relationship of Scripture and Tradition in God's revelation, the role of the local bishop and the "college" of bishops, religious freedom as a human right. But what's even more striking, in thumbing through the first volumes of the *Acta*, is how mundane so many of the submissions are. Clearly, many, many bishops did not expect the Council to undertake a root-and-branch examination of Catholic self-understanding and practice. Anticipating a brief, clear-cut Council in which their role would be to ratify documents pre-prepared in Rome, many bishops were far more concerned that the mundane matters they worried about on a daily basis were addressed: some wanted various modest changes in canon law; others wanted to be able to give permissions or grant exemptions from this or that without referring the matter to Rome. If you read the *Acta*'s opening volumes, you get the distinct impression that many bishops imagined that Vatican II would be an exercise in ecclesiastical housekeeping. (My favorite submission came from the Archbishop of Washington, DC, Patrick J. O'Boyle.

After listing a half-dozen or so housekeeping items, Archbishop O'Boyle proposed that the Council pronounce, "in light of the doctrines of creation and redemption," on "the possibility of intelligent life on other planets." When I read that in a Roman archive, I laughed out loud—it's even funnier in Latin—and the archivist asked me what was so funny. To which I could only reply, "Well after fifteen years of working there, I should have thought that the first thing the Archbishop of Washington would have wanted to determine was the possibility of intelligent life in his own diocese.")

Amidst all that paper in the *Acta* you can find the submission from the forty-year-old auxiliary bishop of Kraków, a philosophically inclined Pole named Karol Wojtyła, whom very few people in Rome had ever heard of. Wojtyła didn't send a laundry list of ecclesiastical housekeeping chores. He sent a kind of philosophical essay, built around a single, sharp question—What in the world *happened*? How did a twentieth century that had begun with such high expectations for the human future produce, within five decades, two worlds wars, three totalitarian systems, Auschwitz, the Gulag, mountains of corpses, oceans of blood, the greatest persecutions in Christian history, and a Cold War that threatened the future of the planet? *What happened?*

What happened, Karol Wojtyła suggested, was that the great project of Western humanism had gone off the rails. Desperately defective ideas of the human person, married to modern technology, had turned the twentieth century into a slaughterhouse. Ideas have consequences, and bad ideas can have lethal consequences. Perhaps as many as 100 million human beings had paid with their lives, in the first half of the twentieth century, for the consequences of some desperately defective ideas of *who we are*.

What was to be done? Wojtyła proposed that the Catholic Church should undertake a gigantic intellectual, cultural, and spiritual rescue mission. The Church should help rescue humanism—rescue the whole project of modernity—by proposing once again, with full clarity and conviction, that we see the true meaning of our humanity in the face of Christ. In Christ, we meet the truth that man without God has lost touch with the deepest yearnings of his humanity. In Christ, we meet the truth that willfulness is not freedom but a form of slavery. In Christ, we meet the truth that men and women who live their lives against a horizon of transcendent possibility are the true servants of human betterment here-and-now. In Christ, we meet the merciful Father, whose mercy redeems our humanity and fulfills its true destiny, which is an eternal destiny. Humanism without God is unhuman, and ultimately, inhuman. As St. Augustine wrote in his *Confessions*, "Thou has made us for Thyself, O Lord, and our hearts are restless until they rest in Thee." The restless yearnings of the modern heart will be satisfied in Christ; a Christ-centered humanism is a true and ennobling humanism.

As I said a moment ago, the truth about God and about us that the Catholic Church carries in history required a demonstration. That demonstration was the life of Jesus Christ, culminating in the events of Christ's passion, death, and resurrection. So let's go now to the site where tradition tells us the drama of salvation reached its final act.

Entering the Old City of Jerusalem through the Jaffa Gate, we walk about a hundred yards until we turn left into David Street, full of Arab *suqs*. The shallow steps of David Street take us another sixty yards or so until we reach Christian Quarter Road, into which we make another left turn; the vast stone blocks in the pavement date from the time of Herod the Great. A sign directs us into a covered street on the right; by following it to its end, we turn left into the courtyard in front of the Church of the Holy Sepulcher.

You'll find it disorienting, for it hardly seems, on walking in, like a single "church" at all, but rather a jumble of shrines. Stepping inside the front door, we're immediately confronted with a stone embedded in the floor. Tradition calls it the "Stone of Unction," where the body of Christ was anointed after it was taken down from the cross; it is jointly "owned" by the Armenian Apostolic Church, the Greek Orthodox Church, and the Catholic Church. To our right, up a winding set of nineteen steep stone stairs, is a kind of loft containing two major shrines, one cared for by the Catholic Church and one in the control of the Orthodox Church: this is the traditional site of Calvary and the eleventh and twelfth "stations" of the cross—Jesus being nailed to the cross and Jesus crucified. Between the two chapels in the loft is the thirteenth "station," the *Stabat Mater*, where a Catholic altar commemorates Mary receiving the dead body of her son in the famous pose known the world over from Michelangelo's *Pietà*.

If we turn left at the Stone of Unction, we wind our way around to an enormous circular stone structure supported by ugly steel girders, erected to counter the damage caused by an earthquake in 1927. This is the Aedicule. The area surrounding it, the *Anastasis* (Resurrection), is surmounted by a rotunda, recently restored and decorated in a slightly delirious, modern-Italian style; it took decades for the squabbling Orthodox, Armenians, and Catholics to agree on its restoration, despite the ever-present possibility of its collapse. Inside the Aedicule are two chapels, the first called the Chapel of the Angel, referring to the angel who met the surprised women on Easter morning [Matthew 28.2–7; Mark 16.5–7]. A low doorway gives access to the second chapel; marble-lined and full of candles, it is so small that only three people can kneel inside at once. Here, according to tradition, lay the body of Christ from late Good Friday afternoon until Easter. An officious Orthodox monk hustles pilgrims and tourists in and out, his hand held out for an "offering"; on the back side of the Aedicule, a Coptic monk conducts prayers and services in a loud voice, some of which strike the untrained ear as barely disguised protests at the Copts' exclusion from responsibility for the Aedicule. But the Copts have less to complain of than the Ethiopian Orthodox, who are confined to a ramshackle "monastery" on the roof, the monks' cells being corrugated steel sheds that remind you of the sweatbox from which Alec Guinness conducted his battle of wits with Colonel Saito in *The Bridge on the River Kwai*. If you come to the 6:30 a.m. Sunday Mass conducted by the Franciscans at the Aedicule, you will notice that, at the precise stroke of 7:30 a.m., the "Catholic rug" is rolled up from the front of the Aedicule and the "Orthodox rug" put back down.

At first blush, it's hard not to think of all this as a shambles—and a disgraceful shambles at that. The noise, the smells, the poor lighting, the rather garish rotunda dome, the barely repressed competition of the various Christian communities (whose relations are governed, to this day, by a status quo imposed by the Ottoman Turks, as the quarreling factions can agree together on nothing else)—all of this seems, not simply strange, but scandalous. Christians conducting a form of civil war over what they all agree are the most important places in human history?

And yet, and yet . . . you notice, it being a Sunday morning, that the Mass being celebrated by the Franciscans is not the usual Mass for that Sunday, but the Mass of Easter—and you join in the simple Latin antiphon, *Haec dies quam fecit Dominus, exultemus et laetemur in ea* (This is the day the Lord has made, let us rejoice and be glad in it), and you are reminded, as you've never been before, that *every* Sunday is Easter, the day of the Lord's resurrection. After Mass, you notice the pilgrim, lost in silent prayer at the back of the twelfth station, the tears running through the hands covering his face. Then you kiss the rock of Calvary, and the Stone of Unction, and the Holy Sepulcher itself—and none of the rest makes any difference at all. The squawking Copts and the emaciated Ethiopians and the surly Greek Orthodox and the torpid Franciscans all seem, somehow, transformed. If God came searching for us in history, if the Son of God redeemed us in the flesh, then why be repelled by the grittiness of it all? God wasn't, and neither was God's Son.

And you understand that the Greek Orthodox are right to have named a spot on the marble floor of their cathedral, opposite the Aedicule, the *omphalos* (navel). This *is* the center of the world, the center of history.

One writer who got all that and turned it into art was the great English novelist and Catholic convert Evelyn Waugh. Critics have never had much use for what they consider one of Waugh's decidedly minor efforts, *Helena*, but it's well worth reading. Waugh himself thought it his "most ambitious work," and beneath its veneer of technical experimentation—as a young woman, the Empress Helena, mother of Constantine (who built the first Basilica of the Holy Sepulcher in 325), talks like a British teenager of the Flapper Era—the novelist was constructing a fictional account of the confrontation between myth and history. *Something had happened*, Helena was convinced, and she was determined to find what Waugh described in a letter as "the essential physical historical fact of the redemption"—the True Cross of Christ.

In this deceptively simple novel, Waugh took on the false humanisms of which young Bishop Karol Wojtyła wrote in his letter to the commission preparing the agenda of Vatican II. To Waugh, what admirable but muddle-headed naturalistic humanists like Aldous Huxley (*Brave New World*) and George Orwell (*1984*) didn't understand was that modern agnostic or atheistic humanism was a variant on Christianity's ancient foe, gnosticism: the heresy that denies the importance, even the reality, of the material world—which is, at bottom, a denial of the essential facts of life, including the facts of suffering and death. The True Cross, for which Helena searches in her old age, is the emblem of both our createdness and our redeemedness—this "remorseless lump of wood, to which Christ was nailed in agony," as one Waugh biographer puts it. That is what we confront in the Church of the Holy Sepulcher. Without that grittiness, Christianity is just another of the mystery cults of the ancient Mediterranean world. With this "remorseless lump of wood," a tangible witness to the mystery of the Incarnation, the window to the supernatural is open, and the "real world" in both its agonies and its joys is put into proper perspective—the perspective of the Kingdom of God, which breaks into the world and history through the life, death, and resurrection of Jesus Christ.

Evelyn Waugh had all this in mind when he wrote to Orwell thanking him for a gift copy of *1984*, Orwell's great dystopian novel of the terrors of a totalitarian future. Waugh complimented Orwell on his novelistic ingenuity. But then he wrote that "the book failed to make my flesh creep as presumably you intended." Why? Because "men who have loved a crucified God need never think of torture as all-powerful."

Indeed, as Catholicism thinks of these things, men and women who have loved a crucified God are the true humanists, because they have been given the grace of knowing, in their flesh, the true measure of our humanity, redeemed at such a cost and destined for glory. That is why, on March 26, 2000, something happened in the Church of the Holy Sepulcher, away from the eyes of the world, that speaks volumes about this place and its meaning. It was Pope John Paul II's last afternoon in Jerusalem, after a weeklong pilgrimage to the Holy Land that had riveted international attention. During one of the last formal events of the day, a lunch at the residence of the papal representative, the Pope quietly asked if he might be permitted to go back to the Church of the Holy Sepulcher, where he had celebrated a televised Mass that morning—privately, as an ordinary pilgrim. The authorities agreed, and John Paul, almost eighty years old, a man who walked with difficulty and pain, climbed those nineteen stone steps to the twelfth station of the cross, in order to pray. This old Polish priest, who had displayed unshakable courage in the face of the worst of modern tyrannies, was determined to pray at Calvary, the place where all the world's fears had been offered by the Son to the Father in order to set humanity free from fear. And he did, meeting a deep longing of his own Christian soul and vindicating the proposal he had urged on the Second Vatican Council forty years before—that the Church should bear witness to the Christ who reveals to us *who we are* and thereby enables us to be truly, fully, radically human.

"And the Word became flesh and dwelt among us, full of grace and truth; we have beheld his glory, glory as of the only Son from the Father" [John 1.14]. *He* is the true measure of *who we are*. In his Holy Face, we meet the truth about ourselves, in the flesh.

The Dormition Abbey, Jerusalem

Mary and Discipleship

ust south of the Old City of Jerusalem is Mt. Zion, the site of King David's original fortress (the "City of David" in 2 Samuel 5.7). Mt. Zion has been the site of battles for millennia. Somewhere in the vicinity of 1000 BC, David captured an ancient Jebusite acropolis, called "Zion," and refortified it as his own city (hence the "City of David"); this was the starting point from which David made adjacent Jerusalem (which hadn't previously been the territory of any of the tribes of Israel or Judah) the capital of his unified monarchy. The Crusaders built a church dedicated to Mary here in 1100; it was destroyed by the Sultan of Damascus in 1219. About 3,000 years after David conquered the Jebusite stronghold, Mt. Zion was again a battleground, during Israel's 1948 War of Independence and the 1967 Six-Day War. As we come through Zion Gate, you'll

notice the bullet holes in the white Jerusalem stone of the Old City walls.

Mt. Zion is thick with history and memory. The cenotaph of David is here, as is the traditional site of the Cenacle, the room in which Jesus celebrated his last supper with his disciples, and the room in which the disciples were later to receive the Holy Spirit on Pentecost. From Mt. Zion, we can look south to the pool of Siloam, site of one of Jesus's miraculous cures [John 9.7]; east over the Kidron Valley to the Monument of Absalom, David's rebellious son; and slightly northeast to the Mount of Olives, where we see the gnarled olive trees of the Garden of Gethsemane and one of Jerusalem's most touching pieces of architecture—the tear-shaped Church of the Dominus Flevit, which reminds us that "the Lord wept" (*Dominus flevit*) over his beloved Jerusalem before his death [Luke 19.41–44].

We've come to Mt. Zion to visit the Dormition Abbey, which is about a hundred yards or so south of the Old City walls. This striking octagonal stone structure, with its distinctive conical roof and a handsome bell tower, is one of the city's most visible landmarks. It was built by Kaiser Wilhelm II, who had been given a parcel of land on Mt. Zion by Sultan Abdul Hamid II during the German emperor's visit to Jerusalem in 1898; the kaiser's architect took as his model the cathedral in Aachen, where Charlemagne is buried (itself modeled on San Vitale, the great octagonal basilica in Ravenna). That bit of imperial place-marking notwithstanding, the *Dormitio* (as the locals call it) is a magnificent building. Just beyond the sometimes jarring bustle of the Old City, it's an oasis of calm and quiet. Its circular interior, surmounted by that conical roof, breathes the spacious openness of transcendence. A splendid golden mosaic of the Virgin and Child focuses our attention in the apse; beneath are mosaic portraits of the prophets who foretold the Messiah's coming: Isaiah and Jeremiah, Ezekiel and Daniel; Haggai, Malachi, Micah, and Zechariah.

The floor beneath the dome is another gem of the mosaicist's art. A series of concentric circles represents the spread of God's saving Word throughout the world, which begins from within the Holy Trinity itself; thus the inner ring contains three interlocking circles, each with the word *hagios* (holy), reminding us of the one God Who is three Divine Persons. The adjoining circle depicts the *traditio* (tradition, or "handing on") of the Word announced to the world with the names of the four major prophets (Isaiah, Jeremiah, Ezekiel, Daniel), while the third circle commemorates the twelve minor prophets (Hosea, Joel, Amos, Obadiah, Jonah, Micah, Nahum, Habakkuk, Zephaniah, Haggai, Zechariah, and Malachi). The fourth circle is the circle of the Christian evangelists, depicted by their traditional symbols: a man (Matthew), a lion (Mark), a calf (Luke), and an eagle (John). Then comes the circle of the twelve apostles (in which, interestingly enough, Paul, not Matthias, takes the place of Judas Iscariot). The apostolic circle touches a circle depicting the months of the year and the signs of the Zodiac, which Christian artists sometimes use to represent the totality of the universe. The mosaic is completed by a final circle, a Latin rendering of Proverbs 8.23 and its paean to divine Wisdom: "He formed me from of old, from eternity, before the earth. The abyss did not exist when I was born, the springs of the sea had not gushed forth, the mountains were not set in their place, nor the hills when I was born."

As magnificent as the Dormitio is, though, we've not come here to admire the architecture and art, or even to spend time in the main body of the church. Rather, we want to go downstairs, to the crypt, to think about Mary, the mother of Jesus and the mother of the Church. And, through Mary, we can think about the mystery of vocation—of "being called"—which is at the center of the Catholic life.

No one knows where Mary lived out her life after the Resurrection, or where Mary died. (Indeed, one of the more intriguing arguments for the bodily "assumption" of Mary into heaven, which was defined as an article of Catholic faith in 1950, is the quite remarkable fact that there is no site in the Christian world at which the pious have ever seriously claimed to hold the relics of Mary—which would surely have been a place of pilgrimage.) One venerable tradition has Mary dying in Ephesus, where it is assumed that her guardian, the apostle John, was living. Another tradition has Mary living out her life on Mt. Zion, and "falling asleep" here. Thus the formal name of this great church is the Dormitio Sanctae Mariae, the "Church of the Falling Asleep of St. Mary."

The tradition of Mary's "dormition" on Mt. Zion is embodied in a small shrine at the center of the crypt. There, atop a sarcophagus, is a life-size statue of the Virgin "asleep," carved from ivory and cherry wood. Keeping watch from the interior of a small cupola above are some of the prominent women of the Old Testament, depicted in mosaics: Eve, mother of humanity; Miriam, sister of Moses and songstress of Israel's liberation; Jael, the Kenite who defended Israel from the Canaanite warrior Sisera; Judith, the beautiful widow who saved Jerusalem from the army of Nebuchadnezzar; Ruth, the faithful Moabite who became the great-grandmother of King David; and Esther, who saved her exiled Jewish kinsmen from the murderous plot of Haman.

Here, in the quiet of the Dormitio's crypt, is as good a place as I know to ponder the meaning of Mary for Catholics.

Mary is both an invitation to Catholicism and, for many Protestants, an obstacle to Catholicism. Curiously enough, Mary was also a bit of an obstacle at one point in the spiritual journey of a very Catholic young Pole named Karol Wojtyła, who grew up in a land thick with Marian piety and who later became Pope John Paul II. John Paul was the first pope to publish a memoir of his struggle to discern his Christian vocation, and in that small book, *Gift and Mystery*, he told us that, when he left his hometown of Wadowice to enter the Jagiellonian University in Kraków in 1938, he felt the traditional Marian piety of his birthplace as burdensome: "I began to question my devotion to Mary, believing that, if it became too great, it might end up compromising the supremacy of the worship owed to Christ."

During the brutal Nazi occupation of Kraków in World War II, Karol Wojtyła started reading the French theologian, St. Louis Grignion de Montfort (1673–1716). Montfort's master work, *True Devotion to Mary*, taught Wojtyła that all true Marian piety was Christocentric, or

Christ-centered—all "true devotion to Mary" *necessarily* pointed us to Christ, and through Christ (who is both Son of God and son of Mary) into the mystery of God himself, God the Holy Trinity. Montfort's language is a bit ornate for contemporary tastes (John Paul gently referred to the Frenchman's "rather florid and baroque style"), but he got the essential point right: rather than being an obstacle to an encounter with the living Christ, Mary was and is a privileged vehicle for meeting Christ the Lord.

The New Testament itself supports Montfort's proposal. The last words of Mary recorded in the gospels—"Do whatever he tells you" [John 2.5], her instruction to the waiters at the wedding feast of Cana—sum up Mary's singular role in the history of salvation: Mary is the unique witness who, from the moment of the Incarnation, always points beyond herself ("Do whatever *he* tells you") to her son. And because her son in the flesh is the incarnate Son of God, by pointing us to her son Mary also points us into the heart of the Trinity. All "true devotion to Mary," in Montfort's phrase, is Christocentric and Trinitarian: all true Marian piety is an invitation to a deeper encounter with the mystery of the Incarnation and the mystery of the Trinity. All true Marian piety is thus an invitation to a deeper reflection on *who we are* and *who God is*. It must be, to be true to itself.

Contemporary Catholic theology has developed this insight in intriguing ways that give a rich texture to the Church's Marian piety. We've already met the Swiss theologian Hans Urs von Balthasar, a kind of pyrotechnic genius of the modern Catholic world. Thinking through the complex reality of the Church in one of his books, *The Office of Peter and the Structure of the Church*, Balthasar suggested that the Church in every age is formed in the image of the great figures of the New Testament. The Church of proclamation and evangelization, for example, is formed in the image of St. Paul, the great apostle of the Gentiles. The Church of contemplation and mystical insight is constantly being formed in the image of the apostle John, the beloved disciple who rested his head on the Lord's breast at the Last Supper. The Church of authority is formed in the image of Peter, to whom Christ gave the power of the keys, the power to bind and loose, and the parallel injunction to "strengthen your brethren" [Luke 22.32]. And the Church of discipleship—which is the basis of everything else—is formed in the image of a woman, Mary, who is the first of disciples and thus the Mother of the Church.

How? Because it is in Mary's *fiat*—"Be it done unto me according to *your* word" [Luke 1.38]—that we discover the pattern or form of all Christian discipleship. Mary's *fiat* makes possible the Incarnation of the Son of God, whose redeeming and sanctifying work in history continues in the Church through its proclamation, its contemplation, and its authority. Mary is the first disciple of the son she bore and nursed and raised; because all Christians are grafted onto Christ in the sacrament of Baptism, Mary is the Mother of the Church, the mystical body of Christ extended in history. Through Mary's *fiat*, we glimpse one of the primary lessons of discipleship, a lesson it takes a lifetime to learn. And the lesson is that *we are not in charge of our lives—God is in charge of our lives*. To know that is to be liberated in the truest sense of human freedom. To know that is to be set free from the restlessness that besets every human heart in every age.

Mary's articulated *fiat* at the Annunciation—"Be it done unto me according to your word"—is completed by Mary's silent *fiat*, the reception of the dead body of her son at the foot of the cross, which some ancient spiritual writers referred to as Mary's "martyrdom" (a theme we'll return to later). In both instances, Mary teaches us to *trust*: to trust in God's wisdom, which so often contradicts "the evidence"— the "evidence" about ourselves, and the "evidence" about the world and its fate. To enter into the mystery of the Blessed Virgin Mary is to take our first steps in the spiritual discipline of trust.

That trust extends beyond time to eternity. For Mary, in Catholic teaching, is the first of disciples in every way: that is the meaning of the doctrine of the Assumption, which teaches that Mary was "assumed," body and soul, into heaven at her death—her "dormition," her "falling asleep." As she is the first of disciples at the beginning, so she is the first of disciples in the anticipation of what God intends for all of us: a bodily resurrection to eternal life forever, within the light and love of the Trinity. The more we think about it, here in the crypt of the Dormition Abbey, the more striking it is that there has never been a serious claim in Christian history, "Here is Mary" (as there is, for example, in the Scavi: "Peter is here"). In the development of Catholic understanding, it took almost 2,000 years to bring this intuition—that Mary must be the pattern of Christian discipleship *all the way*—to a formulation of doctrine; as I mentioned a moment ago, that only happened in 1950. But the trajectory was there from the beginning.

God's demonstration of his purposes for all of us is completed, in a sense, by the Assumption: here is *our* destiny, because we, too, have been configured to Christ, the son of Mary and the Son of God. The Church teaches that the saints enjoy the fullness of God's life in heaven; but the saints, too, await the completion of God's saving purposes in the resurrection and transformation of their mortal bodies. *God saves all of us*, not just the "spiritual" within us. That is what the Catholic Church affirms in teaching the Assumption of Mary, the first of disciples in all things—the first to experience the fullness of that which awaits all the saved.

We might want to pray the rosary together here. The rosary has been the most popular form of Marian piety in the Catholic world for centuries. Praying the rosary fell out of favor in some Catholic circles in the years immediately after Vatican II, but the revival of the rosary in recent years tells us something important: that this is a privileged form of prayer precisely because it points us, through Mary, to the truth about her son and the truths about us that he reveals and confirms.

For a very long time, the rosary was composed of fifteen "decades" (ten recitations of the *Ave Maria*, the prayer known as the "Hail Mary"), each decade preceded by the Lord's Prayer and completed by a prayer to the Trinity. The fifteen decades, in turn, were clustered into three groups of five "mysteries": the "Joyful Mysteries" (involving events in the pre-public life of Christ), the "Sorrowful Mysteries" (the events of Christ's passion and death), and the "Glorious Mysteries" (the resurrection and its effects in the life of the early Church). In 2002, Pope John Paul II surprised the Catholic world by suggesting that the Church add five new mysteries to the recitation of the rosary: the "Luminous Mysteries," or "Mysteries of Light," recalling events in the public ministry of Christ—his baptism; the wedding at Cana and Christ's first public miracle; the preaching of the Kingdom; the Transfiguration; and the Last Supper and the institution of the Eucharist.

When I first heard that the Pope was "adding" mysteries to the rosary, I couldn't quite understand what he was up to. It seemed a bit odd: rather like adding two or three innings to the normal baseball game. Shortly afterward, though, I found myself lecturing at a prestigious—and thoroughly, even aggressively, secular—college in New England. After my lecture, a group of Catholic students invited me to the chapel they had set up. There, we prayed together the "Luminous Mysteries." And I was sold. John Paul, it came clear to me, had filled a "gap" in the rosary. The traditional fifteen-decade rosary leaps from the late childhood of Christ (the last Joyful Mystery is the finding of the boy Jesus in the Temple) to the Passion (the first Sorrowful Mystery being the Agony in the Garden). Something was missing—an opportunity to meet Christ, in the rosary, in his public life. The new "Luminous Mysteries" suggested by John Paul II are another opportunity to drink in the meaning of Mary's *fiat*—"Do whatever *he* tells you"—by reflecting through this rhythmic form of prayer on just what Jesus did and said in five key moments of his ministry.

As my young friends at that college intuitively understood, the rosary is a prayer that lends itself well to reflection on *vocation*, on what it means to be called by God to a unique

Christian mission. The first of the rosary's "mysteries"—the Annunciation—takes us back to Mary's *fiat*, reminding us that Mary as the first of disciples is also the pattern of Christian vocation. The Gospel of Luke tells us that Mary found the angel's greeting "troubling." And why not? But Mary's response, amidst her fears and doubts—Mary's *fiat*—vindicates the angel's greeting, that she is "full of grace." Mary doesn't negotiate. She doesn't ask for a pre-maternal contract, like today's "prenuptial agreements." Mary doesn't have an exit strategy. Mary doesn't "keep her options open." In fear and trembling, but with confidence in God's saving purposes, she gives the answer: *fiat*. Let it be. I am the Lord's servant, and the Lord will provide.

"Keeping your options open" is not the path to happiness, wholeness—or holiness. That's an important Marian insight from the New Testament for every generation, but perhaps especially for yours. We've all heard, time and again, that young people in the twenty-first century are "not ready to commit." Is that because yours is a generation short on trust? If so, it's not hard to understand why. You've seen the wreckage caused by the sexual revolution and its dissolution of trust between men and women, within marriage and outside of marriage. You've seen public officials betray their oaths of office, and priests and bishops betray the vows they swore to Christ and the Church at their ordinations. You've seen teachers and professors betray the truth because of expediency, cowardice, or an addiction to political correctness. If this is a generation that finds it hard to trust, and thus hard to "commit," that's understandable.

But not persuasive.

Perhaps this "trust deficit" is one of the reasons why so many young people found Pope John Paul II such a compelling figure. Here was commitment embodied in an irresistible way—particularly as the Pope's physical difficulties became an instrument for preaching the Gospel of life, the Gospel of God's powerful and transforming love. Unlike popular culture, John Paul II didn't pander to you—he challenged you: never settle for less than the greatness of soul that God has made it possible for you to live because of Christ. At the same time, he demonstrated with his life that he asked of you nothing that he hasn't asked of himself; he asked no commitment that he has not made, no struggle that he had not struggled through.

How could he do this? I think he gave the answer at Częstochowa, the great Polish shrine of the Black Madonna, Poland's most famous Marian icon, in 1979. There, John Paul said, quite simply, "I am a man of great trust; I learned to be one here." I learned to trust here, in prayer before this image of Mary that draws us into the mystery of Mary's special role in salvation history—which is the world's history, read in its true depth. I learned to trust, not in "options" or "exit strategies," but in the mother who always points us toward her son, toward the Christ who never fails in his promises.

That's why the inclusion of the wedding feast at Cana in the new Luminous Mysteries of the Rosary is another invitation to think and pray about your vocation. Every Catholic, every Christian, has a vocation—a unique *something* that only *you* can do in the providence of God. That, too, can be a disturbing thought—until we recognize that that same providence will, mercifully, repair and make straight whatever false steps we take in living out our vocational commitments. "Do whatever *he* tells you": that is Mary's message to us, as well as to the waiters at the wedding feast in Cana. "Do whatever *he* tells you" is Mary's gentle invitation to make her *fiat* your own. Don't look for an exit strategy. Live in trust, not in calculation. Stake everything on Christ.

In his embrace, to which Mary points us, you'll find the path to happiness, wholeness, and holiness that can never be found by keeping your options open.

LETTER FIVE

The Oratory, Birmingham, England

Newman and "Liberal" Religion

n February 2003, I visited the famous Birmingham Oratory, founded by John Henry Newman in 1848. It's sometimes said, and not without reason, that Newman was the most important Catholic thinker of the past two centuries. The remarkable subtlety of Newman's theology (especially his thinking about the act of faith) is one facet of his enduring impact on contemporary Catholicism; his often exquisite prose is another. But even those who have a tough time working through the intellectual thickets of Newman's *Grammar of Assent* find the drama of his life and his conversions irresistible: the evangelical who made a brief detour into theological liberalism before becoming one of the leading lights of the "Tractarian" reform of High Church Anglicanism, a movement that eventually led him to Rome and, after no little trouble, a cardinal's red hat. On September 19, 2010,

Pope Benedict XVI celebrated Mass for the beatification of John Henry Newman in Cofton Park outside Birmingham— an acknowledgment of Newman's sanctity that gratified Catholics throughout the world who revered him as a man of exceptional virtue as well as one of the intellectual fathers of the Second Vatican Council. (The confirming miracle that made Newman's beatification possible involved the cure of an American deacon, Jack Sullivan.)

I was in Birmingham to deliver the *laudatio*, a kind of keynote address, at the Oratorians' annual celebration of Newman's birthday, which falls on February 21. The Congregation of the Oratory was founded by St. Philip Neri in Rome in 1564; today, there are more than seventy Oratorian communities around the world—the Birmingham Oratory being the first of several in England. The congregation is one of those quirky curiosities that crop up throughout the Catholic world. Oratorians live in community, but there's no specific line of work assigned to them by the congregation's founding documents. The Oratories are very loosely organized, with each Oratory being a virtually independent clerical kingdom; they typically combine genteel poverty with refined taste, a high-powered intellectual life, a fondness for good wine, and a minimum of creature comforts. As one of the Birmingham Oratorians led me to the guest room through somewhat musty corridors and showed me how to open the antique oak washstand near my bed (I couldn't tell whether the chamber pot had been hidden or retired), he said, quite cheerfully, "Walking through these halls gives you a real feeling for what it must have been like in the old cardinal's day." To which I could only murmur in reply, "It certainly does."

The "Musical Oratory" in honor of Newman's 202nd birthday was a splendid affair in the beautiful Birmingham Oratory church (itself a sign of contradiction and hope in a neighborhood that's seen better days). My address was preceded and followed by wonderful music from the church's lay *a capella* choir (singing pieces by Victoria, Stanford, and Mozart); a visiting string trio did a very nice job with Telemann's A-minor sonata for violin and basso continuo. Having begun with a hearty rendering of Newman's hymn "Firmly I Believe and Truly," we finished with an all-stops-pulled rendition of his "Praise to the Holiest in the Height" before repairing en masse to the Upper Hall of the Oratory's Cloister Buildings, where a copious amount of Côtes du Rhône was drunk in honor of Newman and of our fellowship in honoring him.

The next morning, after a bracingly chilly night and a wrestling match with the oaken washstand, I came down to breakfast, where the other side, so to speak, of English Oratorian life was on display. One of the fathers munched happily on a bit of carbonized stale bread (smeared with just a touch of marmalade) while reading his mail (in several languages) and, perhaps, contemplating his work as one of the Church's best translators of Latin into English: the Birmingham Oratory, you see, holds the civilized view that no man should be burdened with conversation that early in the morning. So talk is forbidden at breakfast, according to one of the Birmingham Oratory's delightfully odd rules.

All in all, as I told my wife, it was rather like stepping into a cartoon from *Punch* sometime in the last quarter of the nineteenth century. What *Punch* would have satirized, though, seemed more like interesting, even holy, eccentricity to me.

Which is an entirely appropriate ambiance in which to ponder Newman, a great hero of Catholic "progressives" who spent much of his intellectual life combating what he called "liberal religion," and what he might mean for you.

Newman's rooms and library are preserved at the Birmingham Oratory just as he left them when he died, at age eighty-nine, on August 11, 1890. And when I say "just as he left them," I mean that quite literally. With one of the Oratorians as my guide, I could sit at Newman's small desk, finger his rosary beads, and examine the Latin breviaries he and his friend Hurrell Froude had used as Anglicans (causing great scandal). On the wall to my left was a faded clip from one of the London newspapers: a map of Egypt and Sudan tracing General Kitchener's path en route to Khartoum, from which he was supposed to rescue General Gordon; perhaps someone had gotten word to Newman that Gordon, besieged in Khartoum by the wild-eyed forces of the Mahdi, was preparing for death by reading Newman's lengthy poem "The Dream of Gerontius." Behind me was the small fireplace at which the aged cardinal tried to take the chill from his bones before retiring for the night, aided by a glass or two of brandy (and the glasses are still there, too).

Getting up from the desk and walking around a bookcase that separates the sitting room from a small chapel, I could open the door of an antique wardrobe to find Newman's red hat, the cardinal's *gallero*, complete with tassels, propped up against the back wall. The altar is still set as if for Mass; the walls behind and on both sides of it are covered with notes and cards, pinned in place by Newman to remind him of the people for whom he had promised to pray.

In another part of the Oratory, a small band of devoted archivists were systematically organizing, editing, annotating, and publishing Newman's vast correspondence and his diaries, one thick volume at a time. The most recent editor of the series, Gerard Tracey, had died just a month before my visit. With long, flowing gray locks that hung past his shoulders, this meticulous scholar looked like nothing so much as one of the elves in *The Lord of the Rings*; the Oratorians, with a fine sense of the appropriate, buried a layman who had devoted his entire working life to Newman near the cardinal's grave in their cemetery at Rednal. In this workspace, you can actually touch Newman's work thanks to the labors of men like Tracey: pulling the box marked "Apologia" from the shelf, you can read through the originals of Newman's correspondence with his publisher about his extraordinary memoir of his spiritual and ecclesial journey, perhaps the only autobiography in Christian history worthy to be mentioned in the same breath as Augustine's *Confessions*.

It's all as if it were . . . today. And that feeling is intensified when you open another wardrobe in the archivists' workshop and find Newman's cardinalatial robes, which he may have worn only once in his life, when he sat for the famous portrait by Sir John Millais that's now in the National Portrait Gallery in London. Or, if you like, pick up and try on one of the two or three cardinal's birettas that rest in the same wardrobe.

It's in Newman's library, though, that Newman "lives" most powerfully—or so it seemed to me. The library is a large, high-ceilinged horseshoe with an iron catwalk that allows you access to the books shelved on the second tier. Go to the left, on the first tier, and take out the large white folio volume of the collected works of St. Gregory the Great: there, on the flyleaf, you'll find a dedication of this gift to Newman from his friend and fellow-Tractarian Edward Pusey, in Pusey's own hand. Turning around, you see a stand-up desk; here, in the white heat of controversy, Newman wrote the *Apologia pro Vita Sua*, his spiritual autobiography, in a mere two months, tears falling onto the pages as he wrote. (Charles Kingsley, an Anglican divine and writer, had accused Newman, and the Catholic clergy in general, of dishonesty—of being willing to dissemble, even lie, without any qualms of conscience, if that served the interests of the Church. Newman's devastatingly effective response in the *Apologia* demolished Kingsley's reputation, a fact that Kingsley never quite seemed to grasp.)

Newman could be precious, bordering on vain, and he was adept at satirical polemic; the subtleties of his thought could be taken by less intelligent readers (like Charles Kingsley) as dissembling or evasion; the originality of his mind could strike the guardians of a brittle form of Catholic orthodoxy as dangerously innovative, perhaps even heretical. So it was no wonder that Newman's entire adult life was spent in controversy—often bitter controversy. In addition to suffering Kingsley's calumnies, Newman was long held suspect by Catholics who, in the old saw, imagined themselves to be more-Catholic-than-the-pope.

Newman believed that the pope could, under certain well-defined circumstances, infallibly define matters of faith and morals. Given the intellectual, political, and ecumenical circumstances of the second half of the nineteenth century, however, he wondered whether it was prudent to assert this truth through the action of an ecumenical council. This put Newman into conflict with a former friend and fellow convert from Anglicanism, Henry Edward Manning, Archbishop of Westminster and one of the chief lobbyists for defining papal infallibility at Vatican I (1869–1870). The Council eventually affirmed the doctrine, and despite the moderation of its formulation, the Council's decision prompted a sharp public attack on Catholicism by William Gladstone, the former British prime minister and one of the great political figures of the day. Newman's defense of the doctrine against Gladstone, in his *Letter to the Duke of Norfolk*, was much more effective, among both Anglicans and Catholics, than Manning's—but for his pains Newman fell again under a Roman shadow when a bad translation of the *Letter* prompted yet another round of questions about Newman's orthodoxy. In 1879, however, the new pope, Leo XIII, created him a cardinal and permitted him to remain at the Birmingham Oratory (in those days, cardinals who were not residential bishops were required to live in Rome). Newman's vindication was at hand. He made the most of the occasion, thereby leaving all of us with something to think about.

Despite his age (he was seventy-eight at the time), Newman traveled to Rome to receive the red hat—the one that's still in the wardrobe in his rooms—from the hands of Pope Leo XIII himself. There, on May 12, 1879, the newest cardinal delivered an address in which he said that "for thirty, forty, fifty years I have resisted to the best of my powers the spirit of liberalism in religion." What did Newman mean by "liberalism"? The *Apologia* contains a long "Note" in which Newman spelled out eighteen "liberal" propositions that he "earnestly denounced and abjured." They're worth your reading—indeed, the entire *Apologia* is worth your reading—but, for the moment, let's stick with Newman's Roman address of 1879, when he gave a more concise account of what it was that he had been fighting against for decades:

> Liberalism in religion is the doctrine that there is no positive truth in religion, but that one creed is as good as another, and this is the teaching which is gaining force and substance daily. It is inconsistent with any recognition of any religion, as *true*. It teaches that all are to be tolerated, for all are matters of opinion. Revealed religion is not a truth, but a sentiment and a taste; not an objective fact, not miraculous; and it is the right of each individual to make it say just what strikes his fancy. Devotion is not necessarily founded on faith. Men may go to Protestant Churches and to Catholic, may get good from both and belong to neither. They may fraternize together in spiritual thoughts and feelings, without having any views at all of doctrine in common, or seeing the need of them.

Newman's enemies accused him of emotional instability and intellectual shiftiness, citing his several conversions as evidence. Newman thought of his life as of a piece. When he was converted to evangelical Anglicanism from a brief adolescent experiment in atheism; when his evangelicalism gave way to a dalliance with liberal Anglicanism; when dissatisfaction with the liberal camp led him to High Church Anglicanism and the Tractarian movement; when his historical research and theological reflection as a Tractarian led him to the conclusion that the Catholic Church was in fact what it claimed to be, the embodiment of the apostolic Church willed by Christ—all of this, in Newman's mind, fit together. He was embarked on a great spiritual journey that had led him from willfulness to obedience; from a skepticism answerable only to his own judgments to a conviction that there were truths God had revealed to which *we* were accountable; from the loneliness (and pridefulness) of doing things and believing things *my* way to the sometimes difficult but ultimately consoling conviction that a God who had revealed himself would have also given the world a vessel in which the truth of that revelation would be preserved and defended—the Catholic Church. Newman was no romantic about the Catholic Church; he knew all about its weaknesses and flaws, and he suffered repeatedly at the hands of Catholic incompetents and Catholic heresy-hunters. But he read his own life, and his journey into Catholicism, in the terms he asked to have inscribed on his tombstone: *Ex umbris et imaginibus in veritatem* (From shadows and appearances into truth).

Catholicism, he insisted, is not a matter of *opinion* but of *truth*. "Liberal" Catholicism, like every other form of "liberal" Christianity, was its own worst enemy, in Newman's view. "Liberal" religion had no internal brake, no way of saying, "Here is where opinion stops and truth begins." It had no mechanism to keep itself from unraveling, from changing itself to the point where there was no self left.

"Liberal" religion couldn't tell the difference between appearances and reality, shadows and the truth of things.

That's as true today as it was in Newman's day. And it's just as hard a saying today as it was then—perhaps harder.

We live in a culture saturated by what Newman called "liberalism"—a culture in which about all that can be conceded is that there may be *your* truth and *my* truth, what's good for you and what's good for me. To assert that there might, in fact, be something properly described as *the* truth is not only considered odd; it's usually considered intolerant, and, in a culture that values "tolerance" (or what it imagines to be tolerance) above all else, to be called "intolerant" is about as bad as it gets. Newman's life and work suggests that that's a risk worth taking. If, that is, you understand that genuine tolerance means engaging differences with respect and civility, not in avoiding differences as if they make no difference. If, that is, you're interested in traveling *ex umbris et imaginibus*—from shadows and appearances—into the light. Newman's life and work remind us that the quest for truth is one of the greatest of human quests—*if* we understand that the purpose of the journey is not the journey itself, but getting to the destination, which is the light.

To stand with Newman against "liberal" religion is emphatically *not* to stand against questioning and probing and developing our understanding, and the Church's understanding, of the truth. Newman's was a modern mind. He knew about skepticism, having lived in it and with it. He had no use for forms of Catholic philosophy and theology that reduced the faith and its truths to a series of coldly logical deductions. He was a thinker from the bottom up, so to speak, rather than from the top down. And because of that, he knew that questions and questioning were essential to mature faith. Catholic faith, he understood, was not a matter of saying "yes" to truth in the same way that we say "yes" to the truth that 2+2 always equals 4 in the base-ten system. The act of faith was richer, more complex than that. In the *Grammar of Assent*, his most technically difficult work and a marvel of finely honed distinctions in its exploration of the religious mind, he coined a phrase, the "illative sense," to describe how a convergence of factors reaches a point where probabilities, added together, drive us to certainties. This can be so powerful a force within us that it functions like a proof, even though it isn't a proof strictly speaking.

Let's try to see what Newman was driving at through another conversion story. In the summer of 1921, Edith Stein, a brilliant young German philosopher who, as a teenager, had abandoned her parents' Judaism, was wrestling with questions of faith. She was spending a few days with some Lutheran friends, fellow-philosophers, who had to go out of an evening. Edith Stein stayed at their home, and looking for something to read, pulled the *Autobiography* of St. Teresa of Avila out of her hosts' library. She got no sleep that night. At dawn, she finished the *Autobiography*, said, simply, "This is the truth," and went out to buy a catechism and a missal. Four months or so later, she was baptized. Twenty-one years later, as a Carmelite nun, she was martyred in the gas chambers of Auschwitz. Edith Stein was canonized in October 11, 1998, under her Carmelite name, St. Teresa Benedicta of the Cross.

One of Edith Stein's biographers sums up her conversion, and its "trigger" in her reading of St. Teresa's *Autobiography*, like this: "So convinced was she of the truth of St. Teresa's experience that she had to acknowledge the source of that experience as Truth itself." Here is Newman's "illative sense" at work. But don't get blocked by that somewhat strange phrase. Think of what Newman was talking about, and what Edith Stein experienced, as a form of *grace*, mediated through powerful human experiences. In this sense, God's grace does for the believer what "genius" does for the artist or the theoretical physicist. It *brings things together* in so powerful a way that the force of the truth demands a response, an affirmation, a "yes." Even if, as for Newman, that conversion leads to broken friendships, loss of career, loneliness and controversy; even if, as for Edith Stein, that conversion leads to martyrdom.

What does all this have to do with Newman's polemic against "liberal" religion? Everything. "Liberal" religion creates what the Jewish scholar David Gelernter calls an "ice-your-own-cupcake world," because "liberal" religion is religion-we-make-up. *Revealed* religion, on the other hand, is religion-into-which-we-are-incorporated. Liberal religion has no confidence in the human capacity to be seized by the truth of things—by a saving word of revelation from the God of Abraham, Isaac, Jacob, and Moses, whom Jesus calls "Father": a God who reveals *himself*, not propositions *about* himself. Mature Catholic faith is a matter of being seized by the truth in such a way that we *know*, in a special way of knowing, that, as Edith Stein said in the guestroom of Hedwig Conrad-Martius's home, "This is the truth." It's not something we invent. It's not something we can buy. It's something we can only receive. It's a gift, a gift that demands a response.

And the name of that response, to be even more countercultural, is *obedience*. Not childish servitude. Mature *obedience*. Courageous obedience. John Henry Newman described the special joy of this obedience to revealed truth in one of his novels: "Certainty, in its highest sense, is the reward of those who, by an act of will, and at the dictate of reason and prudence, embrace the truth, when nature, like a coward, shrinks [from it]. You must make a venture; faith is a venture before a man is a Catholic; it is a gift after it. You approach the Church in the way of reason, you enter it in the light of the Spirit."

As you consider what it means to be a Catholic today, here's one of the things you must wrestle with: liberal Christianity is dying. When the legitimate questioning, probing, and developing that are essential for theology erode into religion-we-make-up, Christian communities decay. For there seems to be an Iron Law built into the Christian encounter with modern life and culture: according to that law, Christian communities that maintain a clear sense of their doctrinal and moral borders flourish, while Christian communities whose borders become so porous that it's hard to tell who's in and who's out wither to the point of stagnation and death. Even a cursory examination of the demographics of world Christianity bears this out.

That Iron Law is as true within Catholicism as it is within the wider Christian world. Just as liberal Protestantism is dying today, a century and three quarters after Newman diagnosed the lethal disease that beset it, so is what often calls itself "liberal" or "progressive" Catholicism. It's not an accident that the Catholic Church is flourishing where the Second Vatican Council is understood to be a bracing affirmation of Christian orthodoxy and where the adventure of dynamic orthodoxy is understood to be the greatest of human adventures. It's not an accident that the religious orders and seminaries that are growing are those that take seriously the distinctive mission, way of life, and dress of religious life and the priesthood, while it's the self-consciously liberal religious orders and seminaries that are dying. It's not an accident that the fastest-growing lay renewal movements are those that take the hardest demands of Catholic life most seriously. And it's no accident that the Church is in deep, deep trouble in those parts of Europe, Canada, and Oceania where the romance of orthodoxy has been displaced by the siren songs of what Newman described as "liberal" religion: of Christianity understood as opinion, or hobby, or lifestyle "choice," not truth. Catholic Lite, as I've called it, has no real future.

For the better part of forty years now, ever since Vatican II, the Catholic story has been presented in the media (and, truth to tell, in a lot of the Church) as a story of "good" liberals vs. "bad" conservatives. To get identified with the latter—even if the term "conservative" makes no sense in terms in describing people who, within the boundaries of orthodoxy, are exploring the frontiers of Catholic faith in a thoroughly modern way—is to find yourself in the crosshairs of the culture and the crosshairs of those Catholic liberals for whom everything is to be tolerated except those dreadful conservatives (much less neoconservatives!). And that can get very uncomfortable.

It's worth it, though. At the same time, when we stand up for the great adventure of orthodoxy, we always have to remember Flannery O'Connor's injunction against Catholic smugness. So always remember that there are many, many Catholics who, according to the regnant categories, think of themselves as good *liberal* Catholics, just as there are bishops who believe that the function of religious leadership is to "walk straight down the middle," as one prominent American prelate put it, "touching both sides as you go." It's not our role to question the commitment of obviously committed Catholics (although it may be our role, on occasion, to challenge both ourselves and our liberal friends to a deeper fidelity and a more radical commitment). And yes, that bishop was on to something when he told his seminarians that he wanted them to be in touch with everybody in the Church, not just the people they agreed with.

But remember, too, that you can't split the difference quite so neatly as that. John Henry Newman staked his life on the judgment that liberal religion and revealed religion aren't two forms of the same thing; they're two different things. Too much of what calls itself "liberal Catholicism" today is very much like what Newman described in his 1879 polemic against liberalism: sentiment and taste rather than revealed religion. That it hasn't got much of a future seems pretty clear from the demographics. But that's not the real problem. The real problem, as Newman understood, is that this kind of liberalism deprives us of the joy that only comes from the obedience of faith.

I have to confess that it took me a while to accept this. Perhaps a brief outline of how that happened will be of some interest to you as you consider your own position.

When I studied theology in college and graduate school, in the heady years just after the Second Vatican Council, it really did seem as if we could, and should, reinvent the Catholic world anew. In that atmosphere (which was, of course, deeply influenced by currents in the wider culture), the "obedience of faith" was not a phrase you regularly encountered. We didn't spend very much time considering Newman's critique of "liberal religion." Modernity was standing in judgment on doctrine; doctrine wasn't the standard by which we were to judge modernity. Everything seemed plastic and malleable, and we were filled with an exhilarating sense of living on the cutting edge of the Catholic future.

I vividly remember a party that seems, in retrospect, to have captured the temper of those times. One of my professors, an official theological adviser (or *peritus*) at Vatican II and a founder of *Concilium*, the international journal of self-consciously "progressive" theology, regaled us with Council stories: machinations over getting draft texts of Council documents secretly printed, various theological and political plots, back-channel negotiations. It was, he memorably said, a "theologians' paradise." At the time, it sounded like a terrific description (and experience) to me, because I had absorbed the conventional storyline and assumed he was referring to the Council as a great contest of ideas, a Catholic Waterloo or Gettysburg at which theologians who had long been squashed by Roman bureaucrats were vindicated in their efforts to bring the Catholic Church into dialogue with the modern world.

To give my old teacher the benefit of the doubt, I think that *is* what he thought he was describing: a contest of ideas, in which people who believed in the vitality of ideas had won. In his own way, I'm sure he understood that struggle to be a struggle for the truth (even if he once summed up his basic theological position in these rather lame terms: "That God is alive means that tomorrow will be different from today"—which is not exactly what Edith Stein found in the *Autobiography* of Teresa of Avila). At the same time, my professor was also talking, if unconsciously, about power: Vatican II had been a "paradise" for many theologians because it was their first, enticing taste of power. To be sure, distinguished theologians helped the bishops craft the many fine documents of the Second Vatican Council. While they were doing that, though, some of these intellectuals also came to think of themselves as a new form of teaching authority in the Church. And what they were promoting through that self-validating authority was, by and large, what John Henry Newman would have called "liberal" religion. Go to many Catholic theology departments in the United States today, and you'll find a lot of it on tap, at least among professors over fifty.

I first started questioning the liberal Catholic project when I left graduate school and started teaching and writing—two activities that force you to think through what you really think. Native contrariness probably played some role in my intellectual journey away from Catholic liberalism; by the same token, I can say in all honesty that I found the two great enthusiasms of those years—liberation theology and feminist theology—intellectually shallow and unsatisfying. In college and graduate school, the influential German theologian Karl Rahner, who dominated "liberal" Catholic theology for decades, had been my lodestar. Yet well do I remember the night when, after reading the tedious prologue to Rahner's *Foundations of Christian Faith*, which described the modern crisis of belief, something suddenly dawned on me—"I don't know anyone he's talking about." And I began to think that a theology whose primary reference point was the contemporary academy and its profound nervousness about the very idea of "truth" was not going to be of much interest beyond the seminar room. My fondness for history was probably another factor in getting me to embrace Newman's critique of liberalism. Having always been intellectually excited by history, I suppose the liberal tendency to dismiss the past as largely irrelevant to contemporary concerns finally grated on me once too often.

A lot of my discontent with the categories in which I had been intellectually trained came into clearer focus in the late 1970s, when I read an ecumenical broadside called "An Appeal for Theological Affirmation," which was widely known as the "Hartford Appeal." Its signatories included some of the most influential religious thinkers in North America, only a few of whom would—in those days, at least—have welcomed being described as "conservatives." Yet, as I remembered it, the "Hartford Appeal" had been mocked in my graduate school as the "Hartford Heresies," and dismissed as a matter of onetime "good liberals" losing their nerve. On closer examination, and through the prism of my new skepticism about liberal Catholic shibboleths, a much more interesting picture came into focus—in their own way, the signatories of the Hartford Appeal were bringing John Henry Newman's critique of liberal religion up to date. For Newman had, in fact, gotten it exactly right in his *Apologia* and its appended "Note" on liberalism. The real issue was not "liberals vs. conservatives," but rather liberal religion vs. revealed religion.

What case did the Hartford Appeal make?

It began by challenging the view that "modern thought is superior to all past forms of understanding reality," such that "modern thought" stands in judgment on classic Christian doctrine and practice. Rather, Christian thinking should employ an ecumenism of time, employing wisdom and insight from any historical era.

The Hartford signatories argued against the suggestion that "religious language refers to human experience and nothing else." Why? Because if that's the case, then God is "humanity's noblest invention." With Newman, the Hartford Appeal insisted that *We did not invent God; God invented us.*

Again, with Newman, the Hartford Appeal denied that "all religions are equally valid," with its corollary that "the choice among them is not a matter of . . . truth but only of personal preference or lifestyle." Christianity reduced to a lifestyle choice is Christianity emptied of its power.

Salvation, the Hartford signatories affirmed, includes a "promise of human fulfillment." But it is false to suggest that "to realize one's potential and to be true to oneself is the whole meaning of salvation." God's promises are not to be trivialized, and God promises more than the "human fulfillment" that psychobabble imagines. By the same token, the Hartford Appeal insisted that, while worship is personally and communally enriching, it's a fundamental mistake to assume that the purposes of worship are "self-realization and human community." Worship, the Appeal teaches, is a response to God's initiative. We worship God not because it makes us feel good, or feel more connected; "we worship God because God is to be worshiped," and doing so arises out of the fundamental human "desire to know, love, and adore God."

The Hartford signatories flatly denied that "the world sets the agenda for the Church" (a theme then being promoted by the World Council of Churches), and insisted that Christian social action, which is imperative, must be informed by distinctively Christian understandings of the world. Moreover, the Appeal insisted, it is precisely because of their confidence in God's transcendence—"God's reign over all aspects of life"—that Christians can engage in the fray against all forms of human oppression. To identify God's reign with any mundane political or economic program is idolatry, because "God has his own designs which confront ours, surprising us with judgment and redemption."

Why revisit the Hartford Appeal now? Read it as an invitation to Newman and his critique of liberal religion. Hartford's language may be a little more accessible than Newman's, which takes some getting used to; and Hartford's reference points, in the Church and in the world, are all around us, unlike Newman's. Remember, though, that Newman and the Hartford signatories saw the same great truth: that *obedience to Christian truth is liberating*, in the deepest sense of human liberation. That truth comes from God and invites us to a personal encounter with God through Jesus Christ and his Church. It's not something we make up for ourselves. It's something we can only receive as a gift.

Cherish it for the great gift it is.

The Olde Cheshire Cheese, London

Chesterton's Pub and a Sacramental World

he "Catholic world" has a lot more to it than churches. It's also a world of libraries and bedrooms, mountains and the seaside, galleries and sports fields, concert halls and monastic cells—places where we get glimpses and hints of the extraordinary that lies just on the far side of the ordinary (to borrow from Alfred North Whitehead, who wasn't a Catholic but who had a Catholic sensibility in this respect). That's why I want to take you now to a pub, the Olde Cheshire Cheese, on London's Fleet Street. One of the great Catholic troubadours of the world and its sacramentality, Gilbert Keith Chesterton, spent more than a few evenings here. We should pay it a visit, too.

The dark wooden interiors of the Olde Cheshire Cheese have seen a lot of English literary history. Samuel Johnson used to hold forth here, as only he could; his house was a few steps away, and according to some accounts he was in the Cheese daily. So, we may assume, was his biographer, Boswell. Dryden, Thackeray, and Dickens were all regulars in their day. As we go into the pub from a narrow alley, Wine Office Court, you'll cross a metal grate that protects the old stone step at the entrance. Once upon a time, before the grate was in place to protect this second-class relic, you could walk into the Cheshire Cheese in the footsteps, literally, of some of the greats of English literature. Now for the first-floor bar. The portrait over the fireplace is of one William Simpson, a waiter, who served the Cheshire Cheese and its distinguished clientele in the first third of the nineteenth century. Dickens's favorite drinking table is the one to the right of the fireplace.

Had you come to the Cheese in the early twentieth century, you might well have had the luck to find G. K. Chesterton here, often with his brother Cecil and their friend Hilaire Belloc: three men convinced that the truths God wants us to find in this world were to be found not only in churches and lecture halls, but in places like the Olde Cheshire Cheese—places that provided the good food and good drink that enabled good fellowship and good conversation. Imagine Belloc at the table, regaling his friends with stories of his 1906 campaign for Parliament in South Salford, where Belloc's Conservative Party opponents had adopted a bigoted slogan, "Don't vote for a Frenchman and a Catholic" (Belloc's father was French). Never one to duck an argument, Belloc deliberately chose a Catholic school for his first campaign speech. The local priests advised him to avoid the issue of his faith; Belloc was having none of it. The hall was packed, and he pulled no punches: "Gentlemen, I am a

Catholic. As far as possible, I go to Mass every day. This is a rosary. As far as possible, I kneel down and tell these beads every day. If you reject me on account of my religion, I shall thank God that He has spared me the indignity of being your representative." The workers of South Salford gave him a standing ovation and elected him a few weeks later. G. K. Chesterton, who wouldn't become a Catholic for another sixteen years, would have roared his approval and then, perhaps, wiped the tears of laughter off his ample face. Here were men who knew, as Belloc biographer Joseph Pearce once put it, that "love and laughter were linked in a mystical unity," because "beyond the mere love of laughter was to be found the laughter of love."

All of which makes it entirely appropriate that the Olde Cheshire Cheese stands today, as it did in the days of what Londoners used to call the "Chesterbelloc," on the site of a thirteenth-century Carmelite monastery. There are "Catholic places," and then there are "Catholic places"—and some of them are recycled, so to speak, in different livery in different centuries.

But I digress. On to Chesterton.

The British ambassador in Washington once said of his friend, Theodore Roosevelt, "You must always remember that the President is about six." G. K. Chesterton (or "GKC," as he signed his journalism) was always about five. He was born in 1874 and died in 1936 at the age of sixty-two. And yet, through religious struggles, the hard grind of journalism, political controversies, and intellectual combat, GKC retained a five-year-old's wonder at the world around him and at the people he met, loved, and ate, drank, and argued with. The Encyclopedia Britannica, after listing his credits as "English critic and author of verse, essays, novels, and short stories," remarks that Chesterton was "known also for his exuberant personality and rotund figure." At first blush, it can seem a rather odd description for a literary genius who was a respectable amateur theologian and a first-rate Christian apologist. But, with GKC, what you see is what you get: the manner of the man spoke volumes about his conviction that the human comedy is, in the deepest sense, a divine comedy.

We've spoken before about the bedrock Catholic conviction that *stuff counts*. Chesterton fervently believed that, although it took him until age fifty-two to enter into full communion with the Catholic Church. Thus, even in his pre-Catholic years, GKC was an ardent defender of the *sacramental imagination*—the core Catholic conviction that God saves and sanctifies the world through the materials of the world. You've probably heard it said that Catholicism is uneasy in the world, that Catholicism demeans the world and the flesh. Don't believe it for a second.

Catholicism takes the world, and the things of the world, far more seriously than those who like to think of themselves as worldly. Water, salt, and oil are the tangibles by which sanctifying grace is conferred in the *sacrament* of Baptism; bread and wine are the materials through which Christ gives his body and blood to his people in the *sacrament* of the Holy Eucharist; in the *sacrament* of Matrimony, the consummation of marital love completes the vows exchanged at a Catholic couple's wedding; oil brings healing in the *sacrament* of the Anointing of the Sick, as it conveys the gift of the Holy Spirit in the *sacrament* of Confirmation. And all of this happens not by Harry Potter–like wizardry, but *because the world was sacramentally configured by God from the start* [cf. Genesis 1.1]—*and still is today* [cf. everything around you]. What we experience here—in what skeptics call the "real world"—is a window into the *really* real world that makes this world possible, the world of transcendent Truth and Love. The ordinary stuff of the world is the material God uses to bring us into communion with the truly extraordinary—with God himself.

The ancient enemy of this sacramental imagination is what we might call the *gnostic imagination*. Gnosticism, one of the first of Christian heresies, is remarkably resilient, even protean. It crops up time and again, generation after generation, in slightly different guises and disguises: from the Manichees, who once seduced Augustine, through the medieval Albigensians and Cathari, and down to the present. Whenever and however it appears, though, gnosticism teaches the same seductive and devastating message: stuff *doesn't* count; the material world is a distraction (even a wicked distraction); what counts is the *gnosis*, the arcane knowledge, that lifts the elect, the elite, out of the grubbiness of the quotidian. Gnosticism can't handle the Incarnation—the truth that God enters the world in the person of his Son, the second person of the Trinity, to redeem and sanctify us *in* our humanity, not to fetch us out of it. And God does that because, as in the beginning, God understands that what He has created is *good*, even *very good* [Genesis 1.31]. Because gnosticism can't accept the goodness of the world, it can't "get" the Incarnation, and it can't accept the sacraments. Which means that, whether it appears in

ancient guise or modern dress, gnosticism is the polar opposite of Catholic earthiness. It's also, invariably, elitist.

As far as I know, Chesterton never used the terms "sacramental imagination" and "gnostic imagination." But the former is what he passionately defended, and the latter is what
he passionately criticized. Chesterton's genius was in seeing
how the modern gnostic imagination had taken a devilishly
clever turn: it demeans the material through the guise of
materialism. Let me take you on a tour of Chesterton's analysis and argument by way of some of my favorite Chester-
tonisms, drawn from his small book *Orthodoxy*, published
thirteen years before he entered the Catholic Church.

ON THE RIGHT KIND OF WORLDLINESS

*Thoroughly worldly people never understand even the
world; they rely altogether on a few cynical maxims that
are not true.*

Here is GKC's master-indictment: a worldliness closed
in on itself misses the full truth of the world. Worldliness is
no bad thing, if by "worldliness" we mean taking seriously
the stuff of the world, most especially including the lives and
loves, passions and commitments of ordinary, unexceptional
people. But that's not what modern worldliness does. For
self-consciously "worldly" moderns, usually found in elite
circles, *nothing* counts. Everything is ephemera; everything
is plastic, changeable, manipulable. (Think of the more delirious forms of "gender theory," which insist that maleness
and femaleness are only cultural "constructs." Or think
of the Freudian reduction of the human condition to *sola*

psyche.) The wrong kind of worldliness thinks of the world as a closed house, without windows or doors; and nothing in the house's layout or decoration is of very much consequence, expect insofar as it bears on transient pleasures. GKC's world, by contrast, is an open house, with windows, doors, and skylights. The light illuminates the givenness of the things in the house, helping us see that what's given is full of meaning (like maleness and femaleness and their interrelation and complementarity).

On Why We Need Our Imaginations

Imagination does not breed insanity. Exactly what does breed insanity is reason. Poets do not go mad; but chess-players do. Mathematicians go mad, and cashiers; but creative artists very seldom. I am not . . . in any sense attacking logic: I only say that this danger does lie in logic, not in imagination. . . . To accept everything is an exercise, to understand everything is a strain. The poet only desires exaltation and expansion, a world to stretch himself in. The poet only asks to get his head into the heavens. It is the logician who seeks to get the heavens into his head. And it is his head that splits.

Here's another lesson in the sacramental imagination. To reduce what we can "know" to what we can rationally "prove" is dehumanizing—and it's another deprecation of the world and its sacramentality. You can't "prove" the "truth" to be found in friendship or love; in intellectual or political or spiritual passion; in Mozart's Prague Symphony, in Rachmaninoff's *Vespers*—or in hitting the low outside corner with a 90+ mph cut fastball. But these "truths" exist, and they give life not only its tang, but its meaning. To deny the truth of these things is to lock oneself into the prison of a windowless world. It's stifling. And you'll eventually suffocate. Chesterton argued that a lot of the modern world was dying of suffocation. Look at the history of the twentieth century, and see if you don't think he had a pretty strong case.

On Small and Large Infinities

The madman is not the man who has lost his reason. The madman is the man who has lost everything except his reason. . . . [H]is mind moves in a perfect but narrow circle. A small circle is quite as infinite as a large circle; but, though it is quite as infinite, it is not so large. . . . There is such a thing as a narrow universality; there is such a thing as a small and cramped eternity. . . . [The] strongest and most unmistakable mark of madness is this combination between a logical completeness and a spiritual contraction.

What's wrong with the way many skeptical moderns "see" the world? They see the world as a narrow infinity, because they've lost a sense of sacramentality. As GKC put it, the modern materialist skeptic—the modern gnostic—"understands everything, and everything does not seem worth understanding." Catholicism offers a different kind of infinity: a larger infinity, in which reason is enriched by imagination and imagination is disciplined by reason. As I suggested a moment ago, in the Catholic sacramental imagination, we "think" with our brains, our senses, and our emotions. Thinking with our brains only gives us a headache; it also gives us an aching soul. For the deepest longings within us—for communion with others, for wisdom, for joy, for accomplishment, for love—cannot be satisfied by reducing the world to syllogisms. Human beings were made for a wider infinity, for a more ample eternity.

On Our Need for Mystery

Mysticism keeps men sane. As long as you have mystery you have health; when you destroy mystery you create morbidity. The ordinary man has always been sane because the ordinary man has always been a mystic. He has permitted the twilight. He always has one foot in earth and the other in fairyland. He has always left himself free to doubt his gods; but (unlike the agnostic today) free also to believe in them. . . . The whole secret of mysticism is this: that a man can understand everything by the help of what he does not understand. The morbid logician seeks to make everything lucid, and succeeds in making everything mysterious. The mystic allows one thing to be mysterious, and everything else becomes lucid.

When GKC says "mysticism" here, I think what he's getting at is the sacramental imagination—the experience of the extraordinary through the ordinary. That's the mysticism to which every Catholic is called. The "dark night" mysticism of St. John of the Cross is not a universal experience; neither is the burning mystical exaltation Bernini captured in marble in his *Ecstasy of St. Teresa of Avila*. What *can* be every Catholic's "mysticism" is the experience of an open world, a world open to the transcendent. That's why, for Chesterton, the cross is the most apt of Catholic symbols. A circle, he wrote, suggests perfection and infinity, but a perfection "fixed for ever in its size." The cross, by comparison, "has at its heart a collision and a contradiction." But precisely because of that it "can extend its four arms forever without altering its shape. Because it has a paradox in its center it can grow without changing. The circle returns in upon itself and is bound. The cross opens its arms to the four winds; it is a signpost for free travelers."

On Tradition

Tradition may be defined as the extension of the franchise. Tradition means giving votes to the most obscure of all classes, our ancestors. It is the democracy of the dead. Tradition refuses to submit to the small and arrogant oligarchy of those who merely happen to be walking about. All democrats object to men being disqualified by the accident of birth; tradition objects to their being disqualified by the accident of death. Democracy tells us not to neglect a good man's opinion, even if he is our groom; traditions asks us not to neglect a good man's opinion, even if he is our father.

Or our grandfather. Or our great-grandmother's great-grandmother. Because the gnostic imagination can't take the world with the true seriousness it deserves, modern gnostics have little use for the past: everything has to be recreated anew, over and over again. In a sacramentally configured world, by contrast, the past counts—not because of nostalgia, but because of reverence. Because it's part of this sacramentally configured world, what was lived and learned in the past can also be a window into the truth, beauty, and goodness of things here and now. And that's another dimension of authentically Catholic liberation: we don't have to make it up for ourselves. We can stand on the shoulders of spiritual and intellectual giants, and we can see all the more clearly from that vantage point.

On Optimism and Pessimism

When I was a boy there were two curious men running about who were called the optimist and the pessimist. I constantly used the words myself, but I cheerfully confess that I never had any very special idea of what they meant. . . . Upon the whole, I came to the conclusion that the optimist thought everything good except the pessimist, and the pessimist thought everything bad, except himself.

A little later in his ruminations on optimism and pessimism, GKC suggests that the choice between them is a false one, because both assume that "a man criticizes this world as if he were house-hunting, as if he were being shown over a new suite of apartments." But no one, he continues, is in that position: "A man belongs to this world before he begins to ask if it is nice to belong to it. . . . My acceptance of the universe is not optimism, it is more like patriotism. . . . The world is not a lodging-house at Brighton, which we are to leave because it is miserable. It is the fortress of our family, with the flag flying on the turret, and the more miserable it is the less we should leave it. The point is not that this world is too sad to love or too glad not to love; the point is that when you do love a thing, its gladness is a reason for loving it, and its sadness a reason for loving it more." That's a *sacramental* appreciation of the world. Today's gnostics, for whom nothing really counts, can be optimists or pessimists, because optimism and pessimism are mere matters of optics, of how you look at things, and that can change from day to day, or with a new prescription for your glasses—or with a new set of ideological filters. (It's no accident that the post-9/11 political commentaries of a premier modern gnostic, the French critic Jacques Derrida, were notable for their utter incoherence, even meaninglessness.) In the sacramental imagination, which teaches us a profound loyalty to the world and how it's been made, we're neither optimists nor pessimists. As Catholics, we're men and women of *hope*: and hope is a far sturdier thing than optimism, because hope is a virtue, a virtue that rests on another virtue, faith.

On Laughter, or Why Satan Fell

Seriousness is not a virtue. It would be a heresy, but a much more sensible heresy, to say that seriousness is a vice. It is really a natural trend or lapse into taking one's self gravely, because it is the easiest thing to do. It is much easier to write a good Times *leading article than a good joke in* Punch. *For solemnity flows out of men naturally; but laughter is a leap. It is easy to be heavy: hard to be light. Satan fell by force of gravity.*

His own, that is: Satan fell by force of his own gravity. By taking himself too seriously—by taking himself with ultimate seriousness—Satan fell. His weight became too much for him to bear, and so he fell. Crashed. Cratered. Isn't that rather like the modern gnostic mindset? Because nothing in the world counts, only *I* count: only my imperial, autonomous, self-generating *self* counts. Now *that's* heavy; far too heavy. A sacramental outlook on the world teaches us that, yes, we count (and infinitely). But so does everyone else. Moreover, everyone and everything else is caught up in the same cosmic drama in which we find ourselves. That gives us some distance on us—the distance that can lead to laughter, which is another window into the transcendent. Catholics laugh; gnostics frown.

On the Dangers in Narrow Worldliness

There is only one thing that can never go past a certain point in its dalliance with oppression—and that is orthodoxy. I may, it is true, twist orthodoxy so as partly to justify a tyrant. But I can easily make up a German philosophy to justify him entirely.

Gnosticism is not only dangerous for your mental and spiritual health; it's also dangerous for your political health—and everyone else's, too. Take the more assertive scientists on the frontiers of today's biotech revolution. These men and women are highly sophisticated, supremely intelligent gnostics, for whom *nothing* is a given. And they'll tell you quite openly (if usually on the second or third drink, after hours at an academic conference) that they're in the immortality business: making human beings immortal, or as immortal as we want to be, until boredom or some other factor causes us to want to die of our own will. Humankind, in their view, is infinitely plastic; remanufacturable, if you will. And that's what they intend to do—to remanufacture the human condition by manufacturing human beings. Anyone who imagines that that can be done without massive coercion hasn't read their Aldous Huxley. The "brave new world"—the gnostic world writ large—is a world of overwhelming coercion, coercion in the name of the highest ideals. The sacramental imagination is a barrier against the brave new world, because the sacramental imagination teaches us that the *givens* in this world have meaning—including the final givenness, which is death.

On God's Transcendence and Us

By insisting specially on the immanence of God we get introspection, self-isolation, quietism, social indifference— Tibet. By insisting specially on the transcendence of God we get wonder, curiosity, moral and political adventure, righteous indignation—Christendom. Insisting that God is inside man, man is always inside himself. By insisting that God transcends man, man has transcended himself.

The sacramental imagination builds civilizations. It's precisely *because* medieval Frenchmen believed in a world sacramentally configured—a world in which the true, good, and beautiful could be revealed through *stuff*—that they could build the great towers and fashion the miraculously luminous stained glass of Chartres (which we'll be visiting in due course). It's precisely because Frederick Hart had a sacramental imagination that he could sculpt such lifelike figures at the Vietnam Veterans Memorial—and such a magnificent evocation of the creation over the main doors of Washington Cathedral. If who we are and what we do *counts*, then it's worth being good, and it's worth doing as well as we can with what materials and talent we have at hand. If *nothing* counts—if the world is simply an ephemeral stage for working out the "needs" of my *self*—then why sculpt? Why paint? Why write poetry or compose music? Or, perhaps better, why do any of that in any way other than as a protest against the emptiness and meaninglessness of it all?

In a fine, book-length essay on St. Thomas Aquinas, G. K. Chesterton had this to say about his times, which have set the stage for yours: "As the eighteenth century thought itself the Age of Reason, and the nineteenth century thought itself the Age of Common Sense, the twentieth century cannot . . . think itself anything but the Age of Uncommon Nonsense." The uncommon nonsense that has spilled over from the twentieth century into the twenty-first is the gnostic nonsense that takes everything in the human condition as infinitely malleable and infinitely plastic, subject to change by acts of human willfulness. As GKC noted above, this strange attitude involves a deep disloyalty to the world, even as it imagines itself to be taking the world seriously by denying the transcendent.

Confronted by this disloyalty, Catholicism must declare its loyalty to the world—the world as created, redeemed, and sanctified by God, which is *the world as it is, transformed*. Declaring our loyalty to the world, Catholics have to propose to the world a different reading of history. It's certainly possible to read "history," and learn something about the truth of history, according to the conventional chapter headings: Ancient Civilizations; Greece and Rome; the Middle Ages; Renaissance and Reformation; the Age of Revolution; the Age of Science; the Space Age. The sacramental imagination suggests another set of chapter headings: Creation, Fall, Promise, Prophecy, Incarnation, Redemption, Sanctification, the Kingdom.

The trick is to see, with Chesterton, that *the two stories are one story.* "World history" (understood as what shows up on The History Channel) and salvation history aren't running on parallel tracks. Salvation history *is* the human story, read in its true depth and against an appropriately ample horizon. Thus the romance of orthodoxy—getting the story of salvation history straight as *His*-story—is the romance of the world. And the adventure of orthodoxy is the greatest of *human* adventures. It's not an add-on, a kind of spiritual frequent-flyer upgrade. It's the real deal, the thing itself. That's what the sacramental imagination teaches us.

The sacramental imagination gets the world into proper focus. Its critics often say that the Catholic Church is all about denying the world and ourselves; G. K. Chesterton insisted that Catholicism was about thick steaks, cigars, pubs, and laughter. Catholicism is more than that, of course. But it's also that, and to miss that is to miss something crucial in the Catholic world. The Catholic world isn't nervous about its legitimate pleasures. In fact, it's a world in which those pleasures can be fully enjoyed, because they're understood for what they really are—anticipations of the joy that awaits us in the Kingdom of God.

And that, I suggest, is a lot more appealing than granola-and-Corona-Lite gnosticism.

But let's end this on a more literary than gustatory note. Chesterton's was a remarkably clean prose; as you've seen from the brief citations we've been pondering, his genius lay in giving unexpected twists to familiar things. Gerard Manley Hopkins was a different kind of literary man, whose genius involved sprung rhythms, word-inventions, and a deliberate breaking of the conventions. As far as I know, Hopkins never frequented the Olde Cheshire Cheese. But it's entirely appropriate to finish our reflections here with a reading from this ascetic Jesuit.

What unites Chesterton and Hopkins is that they were both saturated with the sacramental imagination. So let me end this letter not with Hopkins's more familiar poem about the sacramentality of *stuff*, "God's Grandeur" ("The world is charged with the grandeur of God / It will flame out, like shining from shook foil . . . "), but with a less familiar hymn to the truth and beauty to be found in a profoundly Catholic loyalty to the world, to the open-ended givenness of things:

> Glory be to God for dappled things—
> > For skies of couple-colour as a brinded cow;
> > > For rose-moles all in stipple upon trout
> > > that swim;
> Fresh-firecoal chestnut-falls; finches' wings;
> > Landscape plotted and pieced—fold, fallow,
> > and plough;
> > > And all trades, their gear and tackle and trim.
> All things counter, original, spare, strange;
> > Whatever is fickle, freckled (who knows how?)
> > > With swift, slow; sweet, sour; adazzle, dim;
> He fathers-forth whose beauty is past change:
> > > Praise him.

CASTLE HOWARD, YORKSHIRE, ENGLAND

Brideshead Revisited *and the Ladder of Love*

astle Howard in Yorkshire has been the home of various descendants of the 4th Duke of Norfolk for more than three hundred years. This masterpiece of architecture, decoration, and landscaping is set in a thousand-acre park, replete with rolling lawns, lakes, a magnificent rose garden, and a great fountain; the fountain's centerpiece is a Portland stone rendition of Atlas holding the earth on his shoulders. The main building, crowned by an ornate dome, borders three sides of a large cobblestoned courtyard. Going inside, you'll find Chippendale and Sheraton furniture, paintings by Gainsborough, Holbein, Joshua Reynolds, and Peter Paul Rubens, and statuary gathered from ancient Greece and Rome. Castle Howard got a lot of attention in the early 1980s when it was used in filming Evelyn Waugh's novel *Brideshead Revisited*. And while it seems

that this remarkable country estate was only one of several models for the fictional "Brideshead," home to the aristocratic Flyte family, that really doesn't matter. What counts is what happened, in a place like this, in Evelyn Waugh's deeply Catholic imagination.

Brideshead Revisited is one of the few novels to be successfully "translated" into a film—in this case, a ten-hour British made-for-television extravaganza with an all-star cast: Jeremy Irons, Anthony Andrews, Diana Quick, Sir Laurence Olivier, Sir John Gielgud, Claire Bloom. I hope you'll read the book and then watch the film. When you do, I think you'll agree that Castle Howard / "Brideshead" is not simply the setting for much of the novel's action and the film's beauty. Through Waugh's artistry and insight, it becomes a kind of Everyplace in which we can watch the unfolding of a Catholic conversion—a privileged place where we can watch a man learning to climb the ladder of love.

Waugh himself found that ladder a steep one. Accosted at a party by a formidable matron who asked him how he, a prominent Catholic convert, could be so rude, Waugh replied, "Madame, were it not for the Faith, I should scarcely be human." Some might regard that as yet another example of Waugh's extraordinary eccentricity—the kind of anarchic humor that once led him to ask a superior officer in the Royal Marines whether it was true that "in the Romanian army no one beneath the rank of Major is permitted to use lipstick." But I don't think so. For here is Waugh, in a more sober and reflective moment, writing essentially the same thing about the steepness of the ladder of love to his friend and fellow-author Edith Sitwell when she was received into the Catholic Church:

Should I as Godfather warn you of probable shocks in the human aspect of Catholicism? Not all priests are as clever and kind as Father D'Arcy and Father Caraman. (The incident in my book of going to confession to a spy is a genuine experience.) But I am sure you know the world well enough to expect Catholic boors and prigs and crooks and cads. I always think to myself: 'I know I am awful. But how much more awful I should be without the Faith.' One of the joys of Catholic life is to recognize the little sparks of good everywhere, as well as the fire of the saints.

One way to think about *Brideshead Revisited* and its insight into Catholicism is to think of it as a story in which those small sparks of goodness are slowly fanned into the flame of genuine conversion—despite some hard resistance from the principal characters.

It will do scant justice to the richness of Waugh's novel, but let me give you a desperately brief summary of the plot. Brideshead's protagonist is Charles Ryder, a lonely and artistically inclined young man who has been sent to Oxford by his determinedly off-hand father, his mother having died while serving as a nurse in the First World War. In postwar Oxford, Charles meets and befriends Sebastian Flyte, youngest son of Lord Marchmain, hereditary master of Brideshead. Sebastian, who carries a Teddy bear named Aloysius, is at the center of an Oxonian circle of aesthetes and cranks. Yet even as he fritters away his Oxford days in four-hour lunches and drunken nocturnal escapades, he introduces Charles to the wonders of natural beauty and the intensity of adolescent male friendship. As that friendship unfolds, Sebastian brings Charles on several occasions to Brideshead itself; there, Charles, overwhelmed by the sensuousness of the place, undergoes what he calls a "conversion to the baroque." The mystery of the Flyte family and its relationship to the Catholic Church intensifies when, during one summer break from university, Sebastian takes Charles to meet his father, who lives in Venice with a wise and discerning mistress, having abandoned his wife and England after leading the local yeomanry in France in World War I.

As Sebastian slowly sinks into alcoholism, Charles's friendship with Sebastian's beautiful sister, Julia, ripens—even as his relationship with the pious Lady Marchmain deteriorates. Stoically bearing her husband's infidelity and hatred, Lady Marchmain has remained at Brideshead, where she spends hours a day in the art-nouveau chapel Lord Marchmain had once built her as a wedding present; her intense but humanly inept piety has an element of the tragic about it, suggests her younger daughter, Cordelia—"When people wanted to hate God they hated Mummy." That turns out to be the case with Lord Marchmain himself, who returns to Brideshead after his wife's death. Charles Ryder, who has become a successful painter, and Julia are now living together at the great house after the failure of their marriages: Julia's to Rex Mottram, a soulless politician, and Charles's to Celia Mulcaster, the society-conscious sister of a boorish Oxford classmate. After his brittle elder son, Bridey, marries a not altogether attractive widow, Lord Marchmain decides to leave Brideshead to Julia, thumbing his nose at the proprieties and effectively disinheriting the son who most closely resembles the wife he abandoned.

As the hand of death tightens around Lord Marchmain's throat, a fierce argument breaks out between Charles and Julia. Bridey is determined to have a local priest called to Brideshead to see his dying father; Charles is just as determined that no such concession be made to what he, and, he assumes, Lord Marchmain, regard as superstition. Julia, struggling with her own conscience and her lover's incomprehension, finally agrees to the visit when Lord Marchmain is on his deathbed, seemingly comatose. At the bedside, Charles finds himself torn:

> Then I knelt, too, and prayed: "O God, if there is a God, forgive him his sins, if there is such a thing as sin . . . " I suddenly felt the longing for a sign, if only of courtesy, if only for the sake of the woman I loved, who knelt in front of me, praying, I knew, for a sign. It seemed so small a thing that was asked, the bare acknowledgment of a present, a nod in the crowd . . .
>
> The priest took the little silver box from his pocket and spoke again in Latin, touching the dying man with an oily wad; he finished what he had to do, put away the box, and gave the final blessing. Suddenly Lord Marchmain moved his hand to his forehead; I thought he had felt the touch of the chrism and was wiping it away. "O God," I prayed, "don't let him do that." But there was no need for fear; the hand moved slowly down his breast, then to his shoulder, and Lord Marchmain made the sign of the cross. Then I knew that the sign I had asked for was not a little thing, not a passing nod of recognition, and a phrase came back to me from my childhood of the veil of the temple being rent from top to bottom.

Later that day, Charles and Julia meet by themselves and admit to each other what their hearts had sensed for some time—that something terrible and wondrous had been confirmed at Lord Marchmain's death; that, as Julia puts it, "I can't shut myself out from [God's] mercy . . . the bad thing I was on the point of doing, that I'm not quite bad enough to do, [is] to set up a rival good to God's. . . . Now we shall both be alone, and I shall have no way of making you understand." To which Charles replies, "I don't want to make it any easier for you. . . . I hope your heart may break; but I do understand." Then they part.

Years later, when Charles, now Captain Ryder, returns to a Brideshead commandeered by the army as a training depot during World War II, it is as a convert to Catholicism, newly struck by the significance, for his own life and those of the Flytes he loved, of the "small red flame" in the chapel he had once disdained aesthetically. And as this often saddened man leaves the chapel, his subaltern remarks, "You're looking unusually cheerful today."

C ritics have often missed the unmistakable thread running through *Brideshead Revisited*. Some, concentrating on the brilliant evocation of Oxford undergraduate life in the aftermath of World War I, imagine it as another exercise in Waugh's social satire. In a Britain starved of luxuries during and after the Second World War, some read *Brideshead* as a nostalgic evocation of a more sumptuous past, even as others take the novel as further evidence for Waugh's snobbery. All of these readings quite miss the main point. *Brideshead Revisited*'s theme is exactly what Waugh said it was, in his preface to the revised edition: "the operation of divine grace on a group of diverse but closely connected characters." This is a novel about conversion, and conversion understood as a climb up the sometimes steep steps of the ladder of love.

Seen another way, Charles Ryder's story is the story of a man growing from lesser affections to harder, yet truer, loves. Evelyn Waugh's Catholic genius really kicks in, though, when we understand that Charles grows into the richest of loves—love for God in Christ—not merely *from* lesser loves, but *through* them.

Starved of love as a boy by his cold and aloof father, he climbs one rung up the ladder of love through his friendship with Sebastian—even if that friendship involved a dalliance with what Charles later describes as a "naughtiness . . . high in the catalogue of grave sins." But the love that Charles and Sebastian share is an immature one, as Charles himself admits; Oxford and the visits to Brideshead and Lord Marchmain's home in Venice with Sebastian were "a brief spell of what I had never known, a happy childhood." Sebastian, fearing the loss of that happy childhood, escapes into alcoholism (and finally finds a home as a sometimes-drunk, sometimes-sober lay doorman at a North African monastery). Sebastian's own fear of adult love, and of the responsibility it entails, doesn't destroy his friendship with Charles; but it limits its scope and depth.

Charles's love for Julia is a higher, nobler love than his love for Sebastian, because it's a love directed to a truer end—even though it's an adulterous love, on both sides. But this love, too, has it limits. For this is also love-as-escape—in this instance, the effort to create a new and solitary

"Arcadia" with Julia at Brideshead, like the "Arcadia" that life at Oxford in the first flush of friendship with Sebastian had been. Yet even as they try to convince themselves that this is the genuine love for which they have been yearning, Julia seems ineffably and inexplicably sad; Bridey's characteristically tactless (if accurate) remark about her "living in sin" with Charles sends her into a rage of anger and tears. Similar outbursts follow, and Julia slowly begins to recognize that, while her anger seems aimed at her lover, its real target is herself.

The deathbed drama of Lord Marchmain crystallizes in both Julia and Charles the realization that their love, however deep, cannot be a new "Arcadia"—there is no escape to any such mythical paradise from the truth about love and its demands. Recognizing that, Charles and Julia together take the next and even harder step up the ladder of love when, by mutual consent, they agree to part. Lesser loves have led to higher loves, and ultimately to a confrontation at Lord Marchmain's deathbed with the Love that is the hardest, most brilliant, of all—the love of God, manifest in Christ, which shows us the truth about ourselves and our loving.

I learned a lot of this from my friend Douglas Lane Patey, who strikes me as Waugh's most insightful literary interpreter. As Doug Patey once noted, Waugh intuitively understood the Catholic critique of modern sentimentality; he knew that love is not merely a feeling or sentiment, but rather a spiritual drive within us, a drive for communion, for "man is a being motivated by an inbuilt hunger for an adequate object of love." Thus Waugh takes Charles Ryder through a series of loves that form the stages of a spiritual ascent "from Sebastian through Julia to God. Each lesser love is real and valuable, but at the same time inadequate: each is a means pointing beyond itself to a more satisfactory end. And because the progression embodies a providential design, each is a seeming detour or retrogression that in fact constitutes an advance."

This deeply Catholic reading of the spiritual life may help explain why some critics regard *Brideshead* as little more than an evocative period piece—and why the back cover of a recent Penguin paperback edition of the book gets it spectacularly, smashingly wrong when it sums up Charles Ryder's journey as one in which he "finally comes to recognize his spiritual and social distance" from this "doomed Catholic family." Once again, Professor Patey is an able guide when he suggests that *Brideshead* is, rather, the story of "a providential plan: a design by which, in the usual manner of providence, good is educed from ill, meaning from the seeming chaos of events." Waugh, no fool, knew he was writing against the grain of the modern sensibility by making divine providence the subtle engine of his story. Perhaps that's why, in a brilliant set piece, he puts the contemporary skeptic's view of Christianity in the mouth of a young, agnostic Charles Ryder, before Charles begins to feel the twitch of a divine pull on the thread of his own life. Thus Charles's description of himself during the early phase of his relationship with the Flyte family:

> I had no religion. . . . The view implicit in my education was that the basic narrative of Christianity had long been exposed as a myth, and that opinion was now divided as to whether its ethical teaching was of present value, a division in which the main weight went against it; religion was a

hobby which some people professed and others did not; at
the best it was slightly ornamental, at the worst it was the
province of "complexes" and "inhibitions"—catchwords of
the decade—and of the intolerance, hypocrisy, and sheer
stupidity attributed to it for centuries. No one had ever
suggested to me that these quaint observances expressed
a coherent philosophical system and intransigent historical claims; nor, had they done, would I have been much
interested.

Nor are some—perhaps many—"interested" today. And
this brings into focus one of the great questions *Brideshead* puts squarely before you: Is life a permanent pleasure
hunt, as so much of contemporary culture suggests (and as
Charles Ryder once imagined)? Or is life a matter of learn-
ing-to-love? As I read it, *Brideshead Revisited* is a powerful
invitation to invest in love. Which is, to be sure, a risky
investment. But taking the risk of a genuine love, a love
that attaches itself to what is truly worthy of the gift of
one's self, is the only way to satisfy that yearning for communion that is at the heart of our humanity. Hard as love
can be, love is the only eternal reality—for God himself is
Love.

It would be misleading to suggest that any of this is easy.
It isn't, and Waugh knew it. That's why *Brideshead Revisited* doesn't smooth over the travail of climbing the ladder of
love. During their idyllic Oxford days, Sebastian keeps telling Charles Ryder that he wishes it weren't true: "I suppose
they try and make you believe an awful lot of nonsense,"

the skeptical Charles asks his friend about Catholicism. "Is it nonsense?" Sebastian replies, somberly. "I wish it were. It sometimes sounds terribly sensible to me."

A similar struggle with that challenging link between truth and love takes place in Charles's relationship with Julia. On the night that Bridey announces his engagement, he also mentions that his intended, a "woman of strict Catholic principle fortified by the prejudices of the middle class," would never agree to being Charles and Julia's guest at Brideshead. "I couldn't possibly bring her here," Bridey continues. "It is a matter of indifference to me whether you choose to live in sin with Rex or Charles or both—I have always avoided inquiry into the details of your *ménage*—but in no case would Beryl consent to be your guest." After Julia storms out of the room in tears, she calms herself, and she and Charles walk out on the lawn to the great Atlas fountain. Trying to distract Julia from Bridey's comment, Charles asks, "You do know at heart that it's all bosh, don't you?" "How I wish it was!" Julia replies; and then Charles remembers—"Sebastian once said almost the same thing to me." But Charles still doesn't understand the ferment in Julia's soul. As they stand by the foundation, he tries another distracting conversational gambit: what they've been through that night, he suggests, is "like the setting of a comedy." Or perhaps it was "Drama. Tragedy. Farce. What you will. This is the reconciliation scene." At which Julia explodes again: "Oh, don't talk in that damned bounderish way. Why must you see everything second-hand?" Although she's not yet ready to accept all its implications, Julia has begun to understand that the love for which she has been yearning can never be "second-hand," can never be a matter of acting a part. The only true comedy, she is beginning to intuit, is the divine comedy.

Charles's friendship with Sebastian, Doug Patey suggests, was "a kind of secular communion." His relationship with Julia takes place on a higher rung of the ladder of love, but it's still a spiritually deformed love, an incomplete communion—indeed, a communion that can never be complete, and thus must be abandoned, at least in its present form. Love, and the truth about a true love's true object, can never be separated. And that is why Charles, on the brink of conversion, can say, and mean without meanness, "I don't want to make it easier for you. I hope your heart may break. But I do understand."

Why is love so hard a thing to grow into? A contemporary of Waugh's, the great British apologist C. S. Lewis, was probably on to the beginning of an answer when he once observed that, for most of us as we now are, the joys of heaven would be an "acquired taste." Dante had the same idea—he had to become accustomed to heaven in his journey through the Paradiso; he had to learn to see things as they really are. That's why life cannot be lived "second-hand," as Julia angrily tells Charles. Christians have to learn to live with reality, with the truth about truth and the truth about love, if we're going to fulfill our human and spiritual destiny and live happily with God forever—the God who is Truth and Love all the way through. That takes getting used to. And that's what the spiritual life is—climbing the ladder of love, with the help and prod of grace, to that summit where we can be happy living with Love itself, forever. For there, at the top of the ladder, we find the Love that is capable of fulfilling love's longing for an absolute fulfillment.

All over the London Underground—on the walls, on tiled floors, and even on London Underground souvenir t-shirts— riders are confronted with an admonition: "Mind the Gap." The designers of London's colossal subway system thought that injunction a sensible warning about the danger of get- ting your foot caught between the edge of the train and the subway platform; in fact, they were giving us a metaphor and a motto for our growth in faith, hope, and love. We all live in "the gap" between the person we are today and the per- son we ought to be. That's the inherent *dramatic* structure of the spiritual life, and of the moral life. Living in and closing that gap—better: living in and letting God's grace, at work in our lives, close the gap—is a matter of becoming the kind of people who can live with God forever, the kind of people for whom heaven is a (super)natural pleasure, not an acquired taste.

Such people have learned, among other things, that sin and forgiveness are the warp and woof of the Christian life. Julia explodes at Bridey's crude comment about her "living in sin" precisely because she knows he's right. For Julia to grow into love, she has to accept that she's been living as she shouldn't, and that the only remedy for that is to stop, confess, and seek forgiveness and reconciliation. It's not enough to say "I take responsibility," the ubiquitous catchall for *not* taking real responsibility in our society. We have to take the consequences that go along with the responsibility, even if that means being pulled, yet again, up another steep rung on the ladder of love. In a society that isn't altogether secure in saying "This is right" and "This is wrong," period, "I take responsibility" is what irresponsible people often say to deflect attention from their irresponsibility—to change the subject, to get on with getting on. That's not the way Christians climb the ladder of love. That's not the way we become the kind of lovers who can live with Love for all eternity. That's not how our sundry human comedies (and tragedies) are integrated into the divine comedy—"the love that moves the sun and the other stars," as Dante ended the greatest poem in history.

Brideshead Revisited, the film, has a marvelous soundtrack composed by Geoffrey Burgon. Its elegiac main theme, whether rendered by flute, French horn, or a single, muted trumpet, reminds us that love, while no easy business, is at the center of our humanity—and the *Brideshead* theme does that without descending into sentimentality. So does one of the great hymns of the Catholic tradition, *Ubi Caritas et Amor*, typically sung at the Mass of the Lord's Supper on Holy Thursday, while the priest washes the feet of a dozen congregants (as Jesus washed his disciples' feet on their last night together), or during the congregation's procession to Holy Communion. The text is a simple one:

> *Ubi caritas et amor, Deus ibi est.*
> *Congregavit nos in unum Christi amor.*
> *Exultemus, et in ipso iucundemur.*
> *Timeamus, et amemus Deum vivum,*
> *et ex corde diligamus nos sincero.*

[Where charity and love are, there God is.
We have been brought together as one in the love of Christ.
Let us exult and rejoice in him.
May we fear and love the living God,
and may we love with a sincere heart.]

Take a moment now and listen to the setting of this ancient text by the modern French composer Maurice Duruflé, who died in 1986; it's the first of his *Four Motets*, opus 10. Faithful to the hymn's foundations in Gregorian chant, Duruflé marries this melodic line to a contemporary four-part harmony in which sopranos and altos, tenors and basses, remind each other, back and forth, that *ubi caritas et amor, Deus ibi est*. The entire motet lasts less than two minutes, yet through the mysterious interplay of text and musical setting, it captures everything we've been exploring here: the human thirst for love; the struggle to find appropriate loves; the ladder of love to which Christ beckons us; the forgiveness of Christ that makes the ascent to truer loves possible; our sometimes difficult growth into the maturity of lovers who can love Love forever. I have often thought that I should like to listen to certain pieces of music on my deathbed (if God is kind enough to grant me a deathbed); Duruflé's *Ubi caritas* would certainly be one of them.

For here we really are at the center of the Catholic and Christian claim—that love is the most living thing there is, for God himself is love. *This* is "the love that moves the sun and the other stars." This is what makes us, and this is what we are made for—we are made for love, so that we may live with Love.

There's another historic site in England where the bracing demands of love come into focus—the Tower of London, in which we find the cell where St. Thomas More lived for the last fifteen months of his life. You know his story from another great film, *A Man for All Seasons*. You may remember the heart-wrenching scene in the final act, when More's family is allowed into that cell to visit him, in order to talk him into truckling to the king's determination to make himself head of the Church in England. More's beloved daughter Margaret, whom he has taken care to educate in the classics, is designated to appeal to both her father's heart and mind:

MORE: You want me to swear to the Act of Succession?

MARGARET: "God more regards the thoughts of the heart than the words of the mouth." Or so you've always told me.

MORE: Yes.

MARGARET: Then say the words of the oath and in your heart think otherwise.

MORE: What is an oath but words we say to God?

MARGARET: That's very neat.

MORE: Do you mean it isn't true?

MARGARET: No, it's true.

MORE: Then it's a poor argument to call it "neat," Meg. When a man takes an oath, Meg, he's holding his whole self in his own hands. Like water. And if he opens his fingers *then*—he needn't hope to find himself again. Some men aren't capable of this, but I'd be loath to think your father one of them.

Margaret tries another tack, arguing that More is making himself into a hero. He parries that thrust easily enough—with the world being what it is, "why then perhaps we *must* stand fast a little, even at the risk of being heroes." Margaret, close to tears, then cries out: "But in reason! Haven't you done as much as God can reasonably want?" To which More replies, haltingly, "Well . . . finally . . . it isn't a matter of reason; finally it's a matter of love."

Love of what? Of truth, I suggest—the truth with which Christ seizes our lives. And what is that truth? It is the truth that we have come from love; that we have been redeemed by an infinite love; and that we are destined for an eternity of love with Love itself. In the final analysis, this isn't something that's settled by rationality, by argument. It's settled, in an often unsettling way, by Someone. It's a matter of being seized by the Truth who is Love—the Love that became incarnate in the world in Jesus of Nazareth, especially in his suffering, death, and resurrection.

To be seized by the truth mirrored in the face of Christ, and to love that truth with everything we have in us, is emphatically not something we do by ourselves. We meet Christ in his Church, which Catholicism often calls the "mystical body of Christ." The Church, as you well know, is a very earthen vessel, full of cracks and fissures. Learning about that can also be a step up the ladder of love. Let me give you an example.

When I was a boy, our parish pastor was a kind of godlike figure to me. A "late vocation," he had been a Princeton classmate of F. Scott Fitzgerald, had made money on Wall Street, and seemed to know everyone worth knowing. He'd been close to my paternal grandparents and was a frequent guest in our home. When, during high school, I discovered that he was an alcoholic, I was devastated. That devastation turned, I must confess, to feelings of contempt: the contempt that comes from learning abruptly about an idol's clay feet, especially during those adolescent years with their painful combination of certainties and uncertainties.

I rarely saw this man in my twenties. But in 1987, I was returning to my old parish to lecture on my first major book, and I somehow got it into my head that I should visit him at the retirement home where he was then living—or, more precisely, dying, of a cancer of the throat. His condition made it difficult to talk, but we managed a fifteen-minute conversation, and I gave him a copy of the book, assuming that he was too ill to come to my lecture. When I was taking my leave, he asked me to come closer. Reaching up from his wheelchair to draw me into a half-embrace, he whispered, in his cancer-hoarsened voice, "You know that I have always loved your family." I couldn't hold back the tears, and told him that, now, I knew that. That night, he staggered on a cane into the back of the parish hall; he had taken a cab from his retirement home, and he could only stay for five minutes, but he was going to give witness, if only for that long, to the fact that he had loved me, and loved my family.

I don't mean to be overly dramatic, but that afternoon and evening were a great lesson for me in the absolute centrality of love within Catholicism. Was my old pastor a weak and sinful man? Yes, and I had to come to grips with that. Was he also a man who, in the final analysis, had given his life to love, and to Love? That's how he taught me to read his life during that last time we were together. The giving, and the loving, had been transformed by Love itself into what St. Paul calls in Philippians 4.18 an "acceptable sac-rifice": a sacrifice in which all that he had done wrong had been consumed by fire.

His ladder of love had been a steep one; indeed, he'd fallen off it more than once. I thank God that he lived long enough, and that providence brought us back together again, so that I could learn how, through the falls, he had completed the climb—and so I could learn one last lesson from him.

What does all this business about love and Love come down to for you? Simply this: never settle for less than the spiritual and moral grandeur, which, by grace, can be yours. They are your baptismal birthright as a Christian.

You will fail. You will stumble on the ladder, and you will fall. That's no reason to lower the bar of expectation. That's a reason to get up, dust yourself off, seek forgiveness and reconciliation, and try again. If you settle for anything less than the greatness for which you were made—the great-ness that became your destiny at baptism—you're cheating yourself. If you settle for anything less than the greatness that has been made possible for you by Christ, you're ignor-ing the twitch of the divine weaver on the thread of your life. Let the grace of God lift you up to where, in your heart of hearts, you want to be.

LETTER EIGHT

The Sistine Chapel, Rome

Body Language, God-Talk, and the Visible Invisible

he Sistine Chapel in Rome may be the most extraordinary room in the world. Millions of people come here every year to admire the beauty of the chapel's decoration: the ceiling frescoes and *Last Judgment* of Michelangelo; the scenes from the life of Christ and the life of Moses that rim the chapel walls, painted by such masters as Botticelli, Ghirlandaio, Perugino, Pinturicchio, and Signorelli. It's usually a very busy place.

Yet even if you come here during the height of the tourist season, you may notice a curiosity—when tourists enter the Sistine Chapel, the buzz that usually surrounds tour groups often fades away, if only briefly. People are stunned into silence, or at least something approaching silence. Is that a reaction to the magnificence of the frescoes' colors, which, since their restoration, are far bolder than any photograph can convey? Are visitors awestruck at the human genius that could produce such painting? I suspect the answer is "yes" to both.

But let me suggest that something else—something *more*—is going on here. A great travel writer, H. V. Morton, once wrote that "a visit to Rome is not a matter of discovery, but of remembrance." That's what the Sistine Chapel does to visitors: it touches deeply rooted (and sometimes deeply buried) cultural and spiritual memories and intuitions. People are awestruck in the Sistine Chapel because, through the frescoes and what they arouse deep within us, this has become another borderland between the human and the divine.

Viewed one by one, in a picture book, Michelangelo's frescoes can seem overwhelming, even frightening, in their sheer physicality. Yet here in the Sistine Chapel itself, this painted architecture, this luminous and brilliant color married to grand and inspiring form, becomes evocative and spiritually transparent. No matter what their religious disposition, or lack thereof, those who visit the Sistine Chapel can't help sensing that its beauty is a kind of window into the truth about the human—and about the yearning for the transcendent that is built into us.

That instinct is right. And that's because this shrine to the beauty of the human body is a privileged place of encounter with the beauty of God. The two go together.

The story of the Sistine Chapel is filled with controversy—not unlike a lot of Catholic history. It began, in 1475, as a combination papal chapel and fortification (as those surprising crenellations on the exterior suggest). It's called the "Sistine" Chapel in honor of its builder, Pope Sixtus IV, a Franciscan member of the della Rovere clan, who sat on Peter's Chair from 1471 to 1484. There's nothing very complicated about the building itself—a rectangular space, 132 feet long, 44 feet wide, and 68 feet high: the dimensions of Solomon's Temple in the Hebrew Bible. The hall is surmounted by a barrel vault; the ceiling is somewhat flattened by lateral vaulting; there are four sail-shaped pendentives in the corners of the ceiling. Twelve windows, six per side, provide natural light. The floor (too often overlooked) is a fine example of inlaid marble in the classic Roman Cosmatesque tradition. About two-thirds of the way down from the altar wall, a marble and iron transenna, a kind of rood screen, separates what would have been the congregation's space from the larger space reserved for the papal chapel—the pope, his cardinals, and sundry prelates of lesser rank.

Sixtus IV had the ceiling painted as a blue sky with golden stars. In fact, Sixtus seems to have been far less concerned about the ceiling (whose topography made it a real challenge for painters) than with the walls, for which he commissioned two biblical fresco-cycles, the life of Moses on the south wall and the life of Christ on the north; as I mentioned a moment ago, these splendid paintings were done by some of the great Renaissance masters. The choice of subject matter was deliberate. Sixtus evidently wanted to show, pictorially, the close connection between God's revelation of himself to the people of Israel and God's self-revelation in Christ.

In 1503, the cardinals chose another della Rovere pope, Sixtus's nephew Giuliano, who took the papal name Julius II. Shortly after his election, Julius had to deal with a structural crisis in his uncle's chapel. Cracks in the vault began to appear in 1504. And as if that weren't enough, the soft soil beneath the chapel was beginning to shift, the south wall had begun to tilt outward, and the whole ceiling was in danger of being pulled to pieces. Iron bars were installed in the ceiling masonry and in the floor to hold the vault together and to steady the foundation. By the end of 1504, the chapel had been stabilized, but the ceiling was a mess.

Julius wanted to commission the brilliant Florentine Michelangelo to replace the starry sky motif on the Sistine Chapel ceiling; he had already hired Michelangelo to sculpt him a colossal tomb. The great Bramante, who served Julius as papal architect, objected, perhaps for political and personal as well as professional reasons. Whatever his motives, Bramante was right in noting that Michelangelo had had no experience in that extremely difficult maneuver the Italians called *di sotto in sù* (from below, upward)—frescoing on a high, curved ceiling so that those standing below can imagine the painted figures to be suspended above them, floating in the air. Julius overruled Bramante. The real problem was that Michelangelo didn't want the commission and refused the Pope, holing up in Florence. Julius II, however, was not a man to take no for an answer; after the cajoling of various intermediaries failed, he simply ordered Michelangelo to return to Rome and submit. Not wanting to risk the papal wrath any further, the stubborn Florentine finally agreed.

Julius's original plan called for the ceiling to be covered with elaborate geometric designs, complemented by portraits of the twelve apostles in the triangular spandrels above the windows. Michelangelo toyed with bringing Julius's design alive, but he wasn't satisfied with it—not least because he wanted to do large-scale frescoes of the human body. Blunt as ever, Michelangelo informed Julius that the Pope's design was *una cosa povera*—a poor thing. For some reason, Julius, who had a very short fuse, didn't explode, but told Michelangelo to make a fresh design.

It was a monumental task. How was Michelangelo to cover 12,000 square feet of vaulted space with fresco, on a surface that combined flat and curved space with large expanses and small corners—and make the entire design hang together? Michelangelo, who dreamed no small dreams, finally decided to create a visual epic of the human drama: the creation of the world and the early history of the human race would march across the vault from west to east in nine epic paintings (three on the creation of nature, three on the creation of humankind, three on the Noah story); ancient prophets and sibyls, heralds of humanity's redemption, would fill the spandrels; and crucial moments in the history of Israel would decorate the pendentives. It took four years for him to execute the plan. When Rome saw it, on All Saints' Day, 1512, everyone from Julius II on down was stunned. Nothing like this had ever been seen before; nothing this magnificent had ever been done before.

Michelangelo, who always insisted that he was a sculptor rather than a painter, may have thought that he was finished with the Sistine Chapel when Julius finally stopped asking about the ceiling—"When will you be done?" Julius II's fourth successor, Paul III, had other ideas, however. In 1535 he asked the Florentine to execute a vast fresco of the

Last Judgment on the chapel's altar wall, replacing several Perugino frescoes and two of the lunettes that Michelangelo himself had painted in 1512. This time, Michelangelo didn't resist. When the work was completed in 1541, all Rome was, once again, awestruck—and some prudes were angry.

The *Last Judgment* is a massive swirl of imagery centered on the triumphant figure of the Risen Christ, who is at once majestic and terrible, decisive and calm. Angels surround the Lord, carrying the instruments of his passion—the cross, the crown of thorns, the pillar of the scourging. The dead who will be saved awake (at the bottom left) and are drawn up by the angels to the glory of heaven; on the right, the damned fall into hell, as Charon, the boatman of the Styx, wields his oar above their fleeing figures. The Virgin Mary is seated at her son's right, her face turned toward the saints. The apostles and martyrs carry the emblems of their suffering; in the folds of St. Bartholomew's flayed skin, Michelangelo painted a self-portrait. (The Florentine wasn't above settling scores through his work, either. The figure of Minos, the Master of Hell, who appears at the bottom right with a snake encircling his torso, bears a not-accidental similarity to Biagio da Cesena, the Pope's master of ceremonies. When da Cesena complained to Paul III, the Pope replied that even he lacked the power of getting someone out of Hell.)

A Vatican guidebook somewhat primly notes that, while the unveiling of the *Last Judgment* aroused "stupor and admiration," it also resulted in "severe and malicious criticism, which has left its mark." It seems that prudes in Counter-Reformation Rome objected to the nudes in the *Last Judgment*; so about forty *braghe* (loincloths) were added to the painting beginning in the late sixteenth century. But that was hardly the end of Sistine Chapel controversy.

By the mid-1960s, the Sistine Chapel was badly in need of restoration. Centuries of smoke, dust, bird droppings (the windows were often left open), the effects of candles and incense, and earlier inept efforts at fresco-cleaning had taken their toll; the ceiling leaked, causing more damage to the paintings. So the roof was fixed and several of the wall frescoes were cleaned between 1964 and 1974. The real brawl began, however, with the proposal to clean Michelangelo's ceiling frescoes and *Last Judgment*. Several forests were sacrificed to provide the paper on which this controversy played itself out over a quarter-century. And while some of the argument involved prudent concerns about the cleaning method and its long-term effects on the frescoes, it seemed as if other art historians and critics just couldn't come to grips with the fact that the dark shadows they had attributed to the repressed Freudian crevices of Michelangelo's mind, or whatever, were in fact . . . pigeon guano and lampblack.

Today, the restoration (which has been complemented by a new lighting scheme) is almost universally considered a tremendous accomplishment. It took nine years to clean the ceiling, a few inches at a time; another four years were required to clean the *Last Judgment*. In both instances, colors that hadn't been seen for centuries were gloriously restored to life. What had once seemed a dark and somewhat forbidding space is now luminously bright. (John Paul II, who authorized the restoration, also had about half the loincloths removed from the *Last Judgment*, leaving the rest in place for historical purposes.)

Stand here, imagine the genius that produced the biblical stories and the genius that brought those stories alive in fresco—and then try to convince yourself that human beings are nothing more than congealed stardust, an accident of evolutionary biology. Here, in this borderland where we can touch and feel the human heart's ardent desire to see God, the burden of proof is on the agnostic and the atheist.

And here, too, the old canard that Catholicism deprecates the material, the physical, and the sexual is revealed for what it is—a lie.

On April 8, 1994, which happened to be Easter Friday that year, Pope John Paul II celebrated a Mass in the Sistine Chapel to mark the completion of the restoration of the Michelangelo frescoes. That Mass was the occasion for one of the most remarkable homilies of a remarkably eloquent pontificate. Pushing hard against the outside of the theological envelope, the Pope proposed that Michelangelo's frescoes were a kind of sacrament—a throbbingly visible reality through which we encounter the mystery of the invisible God. These works of "unparalleled beauty" evoked from those who saw them a passion to "profess our faith in God, Creator of all things seen and unseen," and to proclaim once again our faith in "Christ, King of the Ages, whose kingdom will have no end."

Despite the fact that they were painted decades apart, Michelangelo's two Sistine efforts had a deep theological relationship to one another, the Pope suggested: the *Last Judgment* in fact completes the proto-history of humankind on the ceiling. The beauties depicted in the first six frescoes of the creation cycle—God bringing creation out of chaos, God creating the human world in Adam and Eve—give way to the three paintings of the story of Noah, with its reminder that human beings tend always to make a mess of the gift of the created world. But Noah's betrayal by his sons in his drunkenness (the last of the ceiling's Genesis frescoes and a symbol of enduring human wickedness) isn't the end of the story. For the creation story and the Noah story spill over, on the altar wall, into the story of redemption, synthesized in Michelangelo's stunning portrayal of the *Last Judgment*.

The *Last Judgment* is the "end" of the story in a deeper-than-chronological sense: for the Christ who establishes his Kingdom and brings the righteous into it to reign with him forever thereby brings creation to its "end," in the sense of its purpose and its fulfillment. Life is not random and aimless, these glorious frescoes tell us. *There is purpose in the world, divine purpose.* In the Risen Christ, returned to judge history and the men and women of history, God brings to completion what he began at the far end of the chapel by dividing light from darkness in the first moment of creation.

This Christ of the *Last Judgment*, the Pope continued, is "an extraordinary Christ . . . endowed with an ancient beauty." And that beauty is deeply enmeshed with "the glory of Christ's humanity," for the humanity of Jesus, born of the flesh and blood of Mary, was the vehicle by which God entered the world to set matters aright. Here, the Pope said, we come face-to-face with the Christ, who "expresses in himself the whole mystery of the visibility of the Invisible."

Michelangelo, John Paul suggested, was a man of great Christian conviction and even greater artistic audacity. In his ceiling frescoes, he had had the courage to "admire with his own eyes" God at the very moment of creation, and especially in the creation of man. For Adam, made "in the image and likeness" of God [Genesis 1.26] is a "visible icon" of the Creator himself—and Adam is that icon precisely in his naked physical beauty. But Michelangelo didn't stop here. "With great daring," the Pope continued, the Florentine "even transferred this visible and corporal beauty to the Creator himself"—a bold move that stands just this side of blasphemy. Michelangelo knew where the boundary-line was, though; he has taken us as far as pictorial art can go in representing "God clad in infinite majesty." Then he went no farther, for "everything which could be expressed has been expressed here." And while they must never be confused, the two realities with which Michelangelo's genius wrestled are nevertheless intimately connected: the human body is an icon of God's outpouring of himself to his creation; God himself is the "source of the integral beauty of the body."

In short, John Paul concluded, the Sistine Chapel is the "sanctuary of the theology of the human body." The beauty of man, male and female, created by God for an eternity of communion with the Creator, is completed in the beauty of the Risen Christ, come in glory to judge the living and the dead. Human bodies aren't objects. Human bodies are icons.

Some people, however, just don't get it.

The *New York Times* correspondent who covered that April 1994 rededication Mass was surprised that, preaching before Michelangelo's undraped nudes, John

Paul "seemed not the least embarrassed, despite his frequent affirmations of the Church's conservative teachings on sex." Or perhaps that's what the editors in New York wrote into the reporter's copy. In any event, the *Times* had it exactly backwards.

The Pope didn't celebrate Michelangelo's work as a "testimony to the beauty of man" *despite* the Catholic Church's teaching about sex, but *because* of that teaching. In fact, in a move that takes the argument about the sexual revolution as far beyond prudishness as you can imagine, John Paul proposed that sexual love within the bond of faithful and fruitful marriage is nothing less than an icon of the interior life of God himself. That's right: the Catholic Church teaches that sex, as an expression of marital love and commitment, is another *sacramental* reality on the border between the ordinary and the extraordinary. Which is another way of saying that sex, rightly understood, helps teach us about God, even as it teaches us about ourselves.

Many young Catholics today are fascinated by John Paul II's "theology of the body," which he laid out in 129 general-audience addresses between 1979 and 1984. Those highly compact addresses, dense with biblical, philosophical, literary, and theological analysis, can be a little daunting. Let me give you the briefest outline of the Pope's proposal.

John Paul begins with the Adam and Eve story in the Book of Genesis, which teaches us that our bodies aren't just machines we live in. We *are* embodied, and the body through which I speak, write, play, love, and work is intrinsic to *me*. Remember what I wrote you before about the "gnostic imagination" and its deprecation of the physical? Here's the Catholic counter-bid at its sharpest.

But how are we made, body and spirit, in the "image and likeness" of God, as Genesis describes us? Not only, the Pope suggests, in our capacity to think and choose, but also in *our capacity to live in communion with others—to make a gift of ourselves to others, as our lives are a gift to us.* That means that the "creation of man" wasn't finished until the creation of Eve, for only when there is Eve does Adam discover that the loneliness of the human condition can be overcome in that mysterious process by which we give ourselves to another—and find that we've been enriched by doing so. Love, the creation stories tell us, is not a zero-sum game; neither is life. The only way to find ourselves is to give ourselves away. This *Law of the Gift* is the deep imprint of the "image of God" in us, for that is what God is in Himself: God the Holy Trinity—Father, Son, and Holy Spirit—is a communion of self-giving love, received and returned for all eternity.

So what happened? Why did Adam and Eve start to feel ashamed of their nakedness? When Adam and Eve lived their freedom as a free gift of self, they felt no shame; when they began using each other, they felt shame. The "original sin," John Paul suggests, is the perennial human tendency to ignore the Law of the Gift, the law of self-giving, that has been built into us "in the beginning," as the first verse of the Bible puts it. Adam and Eve "sinned" not because God peremptorily decreed that "x = sin," but because they failed to live the truth built into them. As do we all. So the Adam and Eve stories in Genesis teach a fundamental moral and spiritual lesson about our lives and our loves: *human happiness depends on self-giving, not self-assertion.*

The second part of the "theology of the body" takes up a New Testament text that has puzzled readers for centuries:

Jesus's saying in the Sermon on the Mount that "everyone who looks at a woman lustfully has already committed adultery with her in his heart" [Matthew 5.27–28]. Isn't that an impossibly, indeed insanely, high standard (and for everyone, women as well as men, for the temptation to lust isn't for men only)? On the contrary—John Paul suggests that this puzzling text is in fact a key to understanding our sexuality in a thoroughly humanistic way.

Remember that "original sin" is a corruption of something good: self-giving gets corrupted when it becomes self-assertion. That's what lust does. Lust and desire are two different things. If I'm truly attracted to someone, I want to make a gift of myself to that person for *his* good or *her* good, not just *my* good. Lust is the opposite of that self-giving; lust is the itch for transitory pleasure through the *use* of someone else, even the abuse of someone else. If a man looks lustfully rather than longingly at a woman, or a woman at a man, the "other" isn't a person any longer; the "other" is an object, an object for selfish gratification. There's no giving or receiving or mutual communion there.

The Catholic sexual ethic, John Paul proposes, redeems sexual love from the quicksands of lust. The usual charge is that Catholicism is nervous, even paranoid, about the erotic. The truth of the matter is that *Catholic sexual ethics liberates the erotic by transforming longing into self-giving*, which leads to the kind of relationships that affirm the human dignity of both partners. Does Catholicism blunt desire? On the contrary, *Catholic sexual ethics channels our desires "from the heart," so that desire leads to a true communion of persons, a true giving-and-receiving.* Which, to go back to a point the Pope made earlier, is how sexual love is an image of God in himself and an image of God's relationship to the world.

Catholicism isn't about "self-control," which is a psychological category. Catholic sexual ethics is a matter of growing into *self-mastery*, which is a spiritual and moral category: the mastery of desire that lets us give ourselves to others intimately in a way that affirms the "other" in his or her giving and receiving. That's what Jesus means in the Beatitudes by "purity of heart." Living and loving that way leads to holiness as well as satisfaction; it's a way to sanctify the world.

The third part of the "theology of the body" draws these themes together and teaches us that *marriage is one of those sacramental realities that takes us into the extraordinary that lies just on the far side of the ordinary*. Marriage is an icon of God's creation of the world, which was an act of divine love and self-outpouring; marriage is also an icon of God's redemption of the world, for, as St. Paul taught the Ephesians, Christ's love for the Church is like the love of husband and wife. That creative and redeeming love isn't simply affection, important as affection is. Married love, the Pope suggests, is the human reality that best images the commitment, the intensity, indeed the *passion* of Christ's love for the Church, for which he laid down his life. And that is why John Paul can teach that sexual love within the bond of marriage can be an act of worship.

A t which point you may be saying: this is just too much. But is it? The Church knows that sexual love within marriage isn't always ecstatic; but on a Catholic view of things, ecstasy is what love should aim for, even in our less-than-peak moments of loving. Why? Because a thirst for the ecstatic is built into us—which is another way of saying that the thirst for God is built into us. That's what people sense in the Sistine Chapel. The beauty of the body, mirroring the beauty of God, awakens in us that latent thirst for ecstasy, which is our thirst for communion with others and with God. Don't ever deny that thirst for the ecstatic. Don't be afraid of it.

And don't think you can satisfy that thirst by treating sex as another contact sport, which is about what the sexual revolution has come down to. That's cheating yourself. Sex-as-contact-sport isn't any different than animal sexuality: impersonal, instinctive, a matter of "need." You're made for something far nobler and far more satisfying than that. You've been made for love, for a love freely offered and freely received, a love that includes permanent commitment. That's why, with John Paul II, we can call chastity the "integrity of love." Chastity isn't a laundry list of Thou Shalt Nots. Chastity is the virtue by which I can love another *as a person*. And that's why *chaste* sexual love—the adjective makes perfect sense here—is *ecstatic* sexual love, in the original meaning of "ecstasy": being "transported outside oneself." True sexual love is a matter of putting my emotional center in another's care. You can make that kind of gift, and you can receive a similar gift, because you're free: *your freedom is your capacity to make a free gift of yourself to others*. That's true of all friendship; it's particularly true of the special form of friendship that is marriage, which is sealed with, and expresses itself through, the blessing of sexual love.

And that brings us to another lesson to be teased out of the Sistine Chapel and the "theology of the body" it enshrines: *the Catholic context for thinking about sex is freedom, not prohibition.* Loving, not using—that's the deeply human challenge the Catholic Church poses to the sexual revolution.

Perhaps some of the issues of sexual morality can be brought into clearer focus now. Confronting the tangles and confusions and passions of our sexuality, the first question a serious Catholic asks is not "What am I forbidden to do?" The first Catholic question is, "How do I express my sexuality in a way that affirms my human dignity?" And there's no way to affirm my dignity without at the same time affirming the dignity of the "other." That's the context: dignity. Within that context, there are certain things we don't do, the Church teaches, and we don't do those things because they wound our dignity and corrupt the rhythm of giving-and-receiving that makes for a true communion between human beings.

When we confuse loving with self-pleasuring, our capacity to give ourselves to others atrophies; it can die. This is especially true when sexual solipsism is linked to pornography, which is about as clear an example there is of reducing the "other" to an object for my self-gratification. There's no growth in love in the illusory world of pornographic self-indulgence.

Why does premarital sex violate the integrity of love? Because, as my friend the Lutheran moral theologian Gilbert Meilaender once put it quite neatly, Christians only make love to people to whom they've made promises. Serious promise-making, which is implied by the complete gift of self that sexual love embodies, isn't transitory, and it isn't serial.

Then, within the bond of marriage, there's the question of contraception. You've been bludgeoned, I'm sure, with the claim that Catholicism insists on an ideology of fertility at all costs. That, too, is a lie. The Catholic Church teaches that family planning is a moral responsibility. *The Catholic question is not whether a couple should plan their family, but how they should live that plan.* How do we best regulate fertility and live parenthood responsibly while also safeguarding the dignity of marriage (and especially of women) and honoring the spiritual and moral truth of married love as giving-and-receiving? What the Church proposes is that using the natural rhythms of biology to regulate fertility is a more humanistic way of living procreative responsibility than using chemical or mechanical contraceptives. In a culture in which "natural" has become one of secular society's sacred incantations, that teaching deserves something better than ridicule; it deserves to be engaged thoughtfully, as does the experience of tens of thousands of couples who have found their marriages enriched by natural family planning.

Then there is homosexuality. The gay movement is perhaps the most potent example of what I've been calling the "gnostic imagination" in our culture today. And that perhaps explains why the Catholic Church is a principal target of gay activists. But at least let's get clear on what the debate is about. The Catholic Church teaches that homosexual acts are morally wrong because they cannot embody the complementarity, the rhythm of giving-and-receiving, built into our embodiedness as male and female, and because such acts are intrinsically incapable of being life-generating. The

Church does *not* teach that a homosexual orientation is sinful; it does teach that homosexual desire is a disordered affection, a sign of spiritual disturbance.

Is this "prejudice," as gay activists charge? I don't think so. The Catholic Church flatly rejects the claim—which really is prejudice—that homosexually inclined persons are somehow subhuman. What the Church also teaches is that those homosexually inclined persons are called, *like everyone else*, to live the Law of the Gift built into us "from the beginning." And, when a brilliant young Catholic political commentator like Andrew Sullivan writes that his gay passions are "the very core of my being," the Church says, "No, that can't be right. Your desires can't be all you are; your own talent and political courage and insight testify against that. Give chastity a chance—a chance to remind you what really makes you . . . you."

No one suggests that any of this is easy, for people experiencing same-sex attraction, or anyone else, in today's sex-saturated society. That's why the same Cardinal John O'Connor (the late archbishop of New York), who was frequently attacked by gay activists (who called him, among other things, a "fat cannibal" and a "creep in black skirts"), would regularly visit Church-run hospices to comfort, talk with, and change the bedpans of AIDS patients. It wasn't an act; it wasn't public relations. Cardinal O'Connor did this out of conviction—the same conviction that led him to teach the truth of Catholic faith, even when his critics called his cathedral that "house of walking swastikas on Fifth Avenue."

I think the cardinal's combination of tenacity and humility was a lesson for all of us. The Catholic Church teaches what it believes to be the truth given it by Christ—a truth whose most basic elements were first inscribed on the human heart "in the beginning." At the same time, the Church lives in solidarity with very fallible human beings— all of us—and in matters of chastity as well as in just about everything else, we fall and struggle to get back on our feet.

Jesus stumbled three times on the way to Calvary, according to the Stations of the Cross. We shouldn't expect anything different in our own walks.

St. Mary's Church, Greenville, South Carolina

Why and How We Pray

here are many kinds of "sublime" and many kinds of "transcendent" in the Catholic world. The Sistine Chapel is one obvious example of both. So is a rather different place—St. Mary's Church in Greenville, South Carolina. It doesn't have Perugino or Michelangelo frescoes. Popes haven't been elected there. But you don't need all that to experience the divine touching the mundane in the Catholic world. St. Mary's, Greenville, is as good a place as there is in North America to experience what Catholic worship is and ought to be—and then to think about why and how we pray, as a community and as individuals.

Catholics had been migrating to the Piedmont region of South Carolina since the first days of the American

Republic, but it wasn't until 1872 that a resident pastor settled at Greenville. Missions had been conducted in the surrounding area for the previous twenty years, so the founding of St. Mary's Parish is reckoned to have come in 1852. The first parish church was consecrated in 1876 and dedicated to Our Lady of the Sacred Heart of Jesus, a new Marian devotion that had originated in France in 1854. The church building you see here today was the work of two pastors, Monsignor Andrew Keene Gwynn and Monsignor Charles J. Baum, who, between them, led St. Mary's for seventy-three years. At its sesquicentennial in 2002, St. Mary's included some 2,000 families from a host of racial, ethnic, and economic backgrounds and circumstances, and its school educated 350 youngsters.

When the people of St. Mary's came to church on Sunday morning, July 1, 2001, they noticed that certain things had changed in the previous twenty-four hours. The tabernacle, which had been banished to the side of the sanctuary in 1984, had been restored to its proper place at the end of the long axis of the church, enthroned on the reredos at the rear of the sanctuary. A large icon of Mary had been hung—the first image of the parish patroness to be visible in the church for twenty years. Burlap banners made by second-graders had been removed. The tattered paperback "worship resources" (which is what some confused people call "hymnals") had been removed from the pews and consigned to the parish dumpster; a music program for that Sunday's Mass had been made for every congregant. But these changes were merely a harbinger of what was coming next. For it's safe to say that, in a century and a half, the people of St. Mary's had never heard an inaugural sermon like the one they heard from their new pastor, Father Jay Scott Newman, on the first Sunday of July in 2001:

> I am Jay Scott Newman, and I am a disciple of the Lord Jesus Christ. I am also, by the grace of God, a priest of the New Covenant in the presbyteral order. And by the appointment of Robert, twelfth Bishop of Charleston, I am now the sixteenth pastor of St. Mary's Church. Of these three titles (Christian, priest, and pastor), the most important by far for my salvation is the first: I am a disciple of Jesus Christ. . . .

> My friends, we are here today because the son of Mary is the Son of God: the Alpha and the Omega, the First and the Last, the Beginning and the End. He it is through whom, by whom, and for whom all things were made. Jesus Christ is the answer to which every human life is the question, and only by knowing, loving, and serving Jesus Christ can we fulfill the deepest desires of our hearts.

> . . . I have not always been a Christian. To the horror of my Protestant family, I became an atheist at the age of thirteen, and until I was nineteen I remained sincerely convinced that there is no God, that the cosmos could be explained without a creator. In October of 1981, however, during my sophomore year at Princeton, I discovered my error. The Lord Jesus Christ laid hold of my life on the evening of October 15th, and here I am today to bear witness to the power of his love. Since that moment, the Gospel of Christ has been my consuming passion, and I want it to be yours as well. . . .

> If Jesus Christ is Lord, then he is Lord of everything—of all that we are and all that we have. In the coming years

of my service here, we will explore together the inexhaustible riches of the Incarnate Word who calls us by our baptism to follow him unreservedly. . . .

During all the years of my formation, I struggled to understand how and why God had called me; at length, though, the time of testing and trial came to an end, and on July 10th, 1993, I was ordained to the Priesthood of Jesus Christ for the Diocese of Charleston. Since then I have been a college chaplain, a parish priest, and most recently a seminary professor, and despite the wide variety of work in those jobs, in each of my posts my fundamental duties have been the same: to teach, to sanctify, and to govern. These three duties remain with a priest no matter what work he may be engaged in because they flow not from what he does, but from what he is. Presbyteral ordination configures the man ordained to the Person of Christ the Head and Bridegroom of the Church in such a way that he is able to stand in the Person of Christ and act in his name for the welfare of the whole Church. . . .

. . . [Our] first church was dedicated in 1876 in the month of October; you may recall that my conversion to Christ also occurred in October, 105 years later. [The diocesan] archives revealed to me something more: both events took place on the same day, the 15th of October. My friends, I believe that everything in my life to date has been in some way a preparation for the work I am now beginning here, and words cannot convey the joy I feel to be your pastor. Twenty years ago, the Blessed Virgin Mary, Christ's first and greatest disciple, led me to embrace with faith and love the Sacred Heart of her divine Son, and now she has guided me here to lead a congregation dedicated in her honor on the day of my conversion to the Sacred Heart of her divine Son. There are no mere coincidences in God, and so I am certain that my service here is meant to be a privileged moment of grace in my life. I pray most fervently that it may be the same for you. . . .

I pledge to you today my solemn commitment to love you as a shepherd, to teach you as a father, and to walk with you as a brother in the daily struggle to answer the call of Christ: "Follow me."

At which point, we may safely conclude, the people of St. Mary's Parish in Greenville, South Carolina, knew that it wasn't going to be business as usual with Father Jay Scott Newman.

On June 22, 2003, Corpus Christi Sunday, the parishioners of St. Mary's, Greenville, packed the church for a Solemn Mass. In a little less than two years, the church and its campus had been transformed. The exterior brick had been repointed and the stained glass cleaned; the interior of the church had been completely repainted, the pews had been refinished, and a glorious new golden tabernacle had been installed. A large carved oaken ambo had been built to complement the restored oaken reredos and provide a fitting place for the proclamation of Scripture and for preaching. The baptismal font had been moved to the front door, so that those entering the church could remind themselves, every week—or indeed every day—of who they were and why they were there. The entire parish campus had been re-landscaped. Amidst an economic downtick, the people of St. Mary's cheerfully gave $2 million to have all this, and more, done.

But if you'd been there that day, what would have struck you most powerfully would have been how the congregation itself had been transformed. More than six hundred people lustily sang three classic hymns: "At the Lamb's High Feast We Sing," "Alleluia! Sing to Jesus," and the Latin motet *Adoro Te Devote*; the choir sang Cesar Franck's *Panis Angelicus* and William Byrd's *Ave Verum Corpus*; both congregation and choir were accompanied by organ, trumpet, tympani, violin, and viola. The congregation had also learned to chant its proper parts of the Mass—the *Kyrie*, the *Gloria*, the *Sanctus*, the Memorial Acclamation after the consecration, the Lord's Prayer, and the *Agnus Dei*. Everyone sang the antiphon to the psalm response between the first and second readings, and the priest-celebrant's exchanges with the congregation ("The Lord be with you," and so forth) were also sung. Laymen read the Old and New Testament Scriptures clearly and reverently, and processed the gifts of bread and wine to the altar. Everyone's attention was riveted as Father Newman sang most of the Eucharistic Prayer in a simple chant that underscored the solemnity of this central action of the Mass.

What with a chanted Sequence (a long poem that sets the stage for the proclamation of the Gospel on special feast days and is usually omitted in most parishes), plus an appeal from a visiting missionary, plus the blessing of a seminarian leaving for Rome, the Mass lasted an hour and forty-five minutes. When it was over, everyone present was disappointed that they'd finished so soon.

Why? Because in his brief period as pastor of St. Mary's, Father Newman had restored to his people their baptismal dignity as Christians. Liturgy at many Catholic parishes (as I expect you know) is often a quickie, forty-five-minute affair—"Suburban Lite," as some clerical wags describe it. That's not what happens in Greenville, and there are no complaints. I don't think the reason why can be reduced to the splendid music and the exemplary preaching. Rather, the people of St. Mary's, who are ordinary people (as the world judges these things), have come to understand themselves differently. They now know that they are men and women empowered by Christ in Baptism to offer true worship to the Father.

In 1963, the bishops of the Second Vatican Council taught that the liturgy we celebrate here and now is a participation in "the heavenly liturgy which is celebrated in the Holy City of Jerusalem toward which we journey as pilgrims, where Christ is sitting at the right hand of God, Minister of the holies and of the true tabernacle." The people of St. Mary's, Greenville, might not be able to tell you exactly what that high theological language means. But in a sense they don't have to; they *know* what it means, in their hearts and minds and souls, from their experience. They know that they don't leave church on Sunday morning to return to the "real world." They know that, at Mass on Sunday, they're *in* the real world—the really real world of communion with God. They understand intuitively and experientially what Angelo Scola, the archbishop of Milan and a fine theologian, meant when he said that the sacraments, and preeminently the Eucharist, are where we encounter Christ "as his contemporary."

You know, as every Catholic knows, that the liturgy has been a battleground in the Church since Vatican II. A lot of arguments about the way Catholics worship and pray have to do with tastes and aesthetics. But the deeper arguments have to do with different ideas of what worship is. And that's serious.

As the Catholic Church understands it, the liturgy is God's work, not our work. It's our participation, here and now, in what is already and always happening around the Throne of Grace, where angels and saints sing the praises of God forever. To say that the liturgy isn't "our work" doesn't mean that priests and people don't have a lot to do with what goes on at Mass; they obviously do, and some, like the people of St. Mary's, Greenville, and their pastor, do their parts with great care, reverence, and good taste. But the liturgy at Greenville is such a powerful experience because everyone involved knows that God is the real author of our worship. In the liturgy restored and renewed as Vatican II intended, the people of Greenville have come to understand that it is God who invites us to worship and who empowers us to worship.

Lots of young Catholics complain that they're bored at Mass. I don't blame them. When priests and people forget what's really going on here—when the Mass is another form of entertainment, or therapy, or even therapeutic entertainment—the Mass is not what it's meant to be—*and we're not what we were meant to be, in our baptism.* So here's the basic point, which is a countercultural point: *We don't worship God because it makes us feel good, or relieved, or entertained. We worship God because God is to be worshipped—and in giving God the worship that is his due, we satisfy one of the deepest longings of the human spirit.*

Which means that to participate in the Mass here and now is not a matter of looking down or looking around, but of looking up—it's a taste of what awaits us, through the grace and mercy of God, for all eternity. True worship, like true love, doesn't mean looking into each other's eyes; it means looking together, in love, at the One Who is Love all the way through.

Why is the way we worship—and what we understand our worship to mean—so important? Another Greenville story: In his first few months in St. Mary's Parish, Father Newman went to a coffee in the home of parishioners every Monday night. There, he explained why, as he put it, "I don't believe in living room liturgy." This wasn't a matter of tastes, nor was it a question of power. It was a matter of the right way to worship God—the right way to live the noble calling that is every Christian's by Baptism.

The people of St. Mary's Greenville have learned an ancient theological maxim that you should know: *lex orandi lex credendi*—what we pray is what we believe. Sloppy worship leads inevitably to sloppy theology. Worship-as-entertainment dumbs down the truths that true worship celebrates. In the past forty-five years, according to some serious survey research, more than a few Catholics have begun to lose their grip on the truth that what we receive in the Eucharist is the body and blood of Christ. Can anyone seriously argue that that erosion of belief doesn't have something to do with sloppy liturgy, in which the focal point of worship too often becomes the congregation itself, or the Stephen

Colbert–style priest-"presider" (to use one of the worst tropes in contemporary liturgical jargon)?

My friend Robert Louis Wilken, a distinguished scholar of the early Church, once discussed with a reporter the reasons he had entered into full communion with the Catholic Church in his sixties, after a lifetime as a confessional Lutheran and decades as a Lutheran pastor. For Wilken, a historian and theologian, it finally came down to a question of what preserved the faith over time. What keeps us in touch with, in communion with, the Church's apostolic roots, which we explored in the Scavi of St. Peter's in Rome? The Reformation tradition in which Wilken grew up believed that it could preserve the apostolic faith through a firm adherence to doctrine. The Catholic counter-view, which Wilken finally found irrefutable, was that the community of the Church—the community in which doctrine comes to be understood as doctrine—preserves the faith. One powerful example of that touched this maxim, *lex orandi lex credendi*.

During the controversies of the Reformation and Counter-Reformation, there had been a famous debate between a Lutheran theologian and St. Robert Bellarmine. As Wilken remembered the story, the Lutheran argued against the Catholic practice of Eucharistic reservation and adoration—preserving elements of the Eucharist in a tabernacle before which the faithful would pray—on the grounds that Christ intended the Eucharist to be used, not reserved: "Take and eat," not "Take and reserve," so to speak. Not a bad point. Bellermine's counter was that the Church had been reserving the sacrament for a long time and there wasn't any serious reason to stop the practice. And over time, Wilken admitted, jettisoning the tabernacle and the reserved sacrament had led many Lutherans to a different and diminished Eucharistic theology, uncertain about Christ's real presence in the bread and wine. Catholics kept their tabernacles and sustained the practice of Eucharistic reservation and adoration. Traditional practice—the Catholic community and the way it worshipped—had preserved a key truth of Catholic faith.

Which gives you some sense not only of what *lex orandi lex credendi* means, but of why Father Newman moved the tabernacle back to the center of the sanctuary of St. Mary's, Greenville, fifteen minutes after arriving in the parish.

The Catholic Church has failed its Lord times beyond numbering. "Do this in memory of me" is the commandment of Christ to which the Church has been most faithful. The Eucharist, celebrated at Mass and reserved in order to extend the fruits of the Mass through time, keeps the Church faithful. That's why *lex orandi lex credendi* is so important. And that's why today's liturgical wars are worth fighting. A lot more is at stake here than questions of taste.

While we're on the subject of worship and liturgy, let's think for a minute about what a Catholic priest is. There's more than a little confusion on the subject. Centuries of legalization in the Church, compounded by the bureaucratization that affects just about every aspect of modern life, has led a lot of Catholics, clerical and lay, to think of the priest as a kind of ecclesiastical functionary—a man licensed by the hierarchy to do certain kinds of churchy business. The Second Vatican Council tried to remedy this by reminding Catholics that there is only one High Priest,

Jesus Christ, in whose unique exercise of the priesthood every Christian shares by Baptism—precisely the truth about themselves that the people of St. Mary's, Greenville, have rediscovered through Father Newman. At the same time, the Council taught that the ordained priesthood is not just a set of functions or tasks within what theologians call the "common priesthood" of all the baptized. Nor does the ordained priest "represent" this common priesthood the way, for example, a congressman represents his district—the ordained priest isn't a stand-in for the priestly community that is the whole Church.

Rather, the Catholic Church teaches that *the ordained priest is an icon of the eternal priesthood of Jesus Christ*—someone who, not by his own merits but by the grace of his ordination, *makes Christ present* in his person. That's why an older generation of Catholics were taught that a priest is an *alter Christus*, "another Christ," and that a priest acts *in persona Christi*, "in the person of Christ." Remember our earlier discussion about the difference between a "symbol" and a "sign"? That distinction applies here. The ordained priest is an ordinary man who has been made, by the power of God, into an extraordinary symbol—a "re-presentation"—of Christ the High Priest of his people.

And that brings us to clericalism. Priestly fraternity and fellowship is one of the great goods of Catholic life. Yet when fellowship and fraternity decay into clericalism, and the Church gets divided into castes, something has gone wrong. The Catholic priesthood doesn't exist as a kind of clerical caste for its own sake. In the Catholic Church, the ordained priesthood lifts up and ennobles the "common priesthood" of all the people of the Church. That is what the priest does, as Father Newman put it in his inaugural sermon, by teaching, sanctifying, and governing his people. That governance is a matter of service, not power, because a man is ordained as a servant, not as a petty parochial dictator. At the same time, and by the same token, one service the priest does his people is to exercise pastoral authority—not, again, for its own sake, but to empower the people given into his care. Empower them to do what? To realize in their prayer and worship and daily life the truth about themselves as men and women who have been touched with the fire of the Holy Spirit in Baptism and Confirmation; men and women who can worship God and receive the body and blood of the Son of God in Holy Communion; men and women called and sent into the world as witnesses, servants, and evangelists.

This "iconography" of the priesthood has a body language built into it—which brings us to another thorny issue: Who can be ordained? But perhaps now you can begin to see how this issue, so often positioned as a question of power, is in fact a question that engages some very deep truths about the ordinary and the extraordinary, the visible and the invisible, the mundane and the transcendent.

As we've discussed before, maleness and femaleness are not accidents of evolutionary biology in the Catholic sacramental imagination. Rather, our maleness and femaleness are iconographic—visible, earthy realities through which we learn some important truths about our humanity and about God (just as we saw in the Sistine Chapel). Men and women are radically equal in being images of God. But men and women are not interchangeable icons of God's presence in his creation. The Catholic Church takes our sexual embodiedness as male and female very seriously—far more seriously than those modern gnostics who reduce "male" and "female" to constructs of culture.

In the first and second generations of the Church, Christians came to understand something very important: *Christ's relationship to the Church is spousal, or nuptial.* As Ephesians 5.25 puts it, Christ loves the Church as a husband loves a wife. That complete giving of self is most powerfully evident at Mass, when the priest, acting in the person of Christ, makes the Lord's gift of himself present in a way that we can see and touch and taste by consecrating the bread and wine that become Christ's body and blood.

In a Christian community in which the Lord's Supper is a memorial meal, it makes no difference whether the one who presides at this exercise in table fellowship is a man or a woman; it's simply a question of custom, because here the "ministry" is functional, not sacramental. But that's not what Catholics understand by the Lord's Supper—the Eucharist—or by the priesthood. In the Catholic sacramental imagination, remember, *stuff counts*—including the stuff of being male or female. If the Eucharist is the most intense "making present" of Christ's spousal gift of himself to his bride, the Church, then a priest who can make Christ present precisely in this male donation of self to spouse is required.

Tough stuff in our unisex culture, I know. But consider the possibility that this way of thinking about things takes femaleness and maleness far more seriously than the postmodern academic craziness that reduces our embodiedness to a question of plumbing. When the Catholic Church ordains men to the priesthood, it isn't engaging in misogyny, and it isn't violating anyone's "rights"—no one, from the pope to the humblest parish priest, ever had a "right" to be ordained a priest. Rather, the Church is being serious about embodiedness and what that means. It's living its commitment to the sacramentality of the world.

Thinking about liturgy—the public worship of the Church—leads naturally enough to thinking about prayer. As I've said to you before, Christianity isn't "spirituality" of the sort that you find stocked under that rubric in your bookstore. Christianity isn't about our search for God; Christianity is about God's search for us in history, and our then taking the path through history that God is taking. If that's what Christianity is, then Christian prayer must have something to do with that.

Do you remember the story of Jesus and the Samaritan woman he meets at a well? It's in the fourth chapter of St. John's Gospel, and it's interesting that the *Catechism of the Catholic Church* uses this episode to begin its teaching about prayer. The Samaritan woman comes to Jacob's well to draw water and finds Jesus, a Jew, sitting there. She doesn't expect anything in the way of greeting or courtesy; Jews don't talk to Samaritans. But this Jew does. "Give me a drink," Jesus asks her. Then they begin to talk, and, as the old spiritual has it, "he told her everything she'd ever done." The point here, though, isn't Jesus's insight into the Samaritan woman's tangled personal affairs and spiritual life. It's the way the story is set up.

Jesus's request for a drink, and the woman's final response at the end of the tale—"Come, see a man who told me all

I ever did. Can this be the Christ?"—teaches us something important about the surprising nature of prayer: *Prayer begins with God's thirst for us.* "Give me a drink." Prayer is the meeting place between God's thirst, God's desire, for us and our heart's yearning for God. As the *Catechism* puts it, "God thirsts that we may thirst for him." We can pray because the Spirit is in us, causing us to thirst for God; and the Holy Spirit has been given to us because of God's thirst for us. *Prayer isn't something we initiate.* Prayer is a meeting with the Christ who always takes the initiative, as he did at Jacob's well with the Samaritan woman. For she is all of us: "The wonder of prayer is revealed beside the well where we come seeking water; there, Christ comes to meet every human being. It is he who first seeks us and asks us for a drink. Jesus thirsts; his asking arises from the depths of God's desire for us."

There is a virtual infinity of ways to pray as a Catholic. We've talked at length here about the Mass, and why a place like St. Mary's, Greenville, answers that perennial question, "Why should I go to church?" To which the answer is, "Go to a place like St. Mary's, Greenville, and the question will answer itself." We've talked a bit about the rosary as a way of prayer that embodies Mary's unique role in salvation history as the first disciple who always points beyond herself to her son—"Do whatever he tells you." There are many, many other forms of Catholic devotion, but there's one other major form of Catholic prayer I haven't mentioned—the Liturgy of the Hours, also known as the Divine Office.

Catholicism is about time as well as space, history as well as stuff. In the sacramental imagination, time counts, just as stuff counts. That's why the Church has a liturgy of the *hours*, a daily routine of prescribed prayer—to sanctify time, to take time seriously. The Liturgy of the Hours pivots around Lauds, or "Morning Prayer," and Vespers, or "Evening Prayer." Both Lauds and Vespers are composed of a hymn, psalms and Old Testament canticles, a biblical reading, a gospel canticle, intercessory prayers, the Lord's Prayer, and a concluding prayer, or collect. In the reformed Liturgy of the Hours, the old office of "Matins" or "Vigils," which can be said at any time of the day, has become the "Office of Readings," where lengthier Scripture readings and readings from great theologians and spiritual masters are on tap. There are shorter "hours" at three times during the day, and the whole business concludes with Compline, or "Night Prayer"; after a psalm or two and a very brief reading, the Church's daily prayer ends with the *Nunc dimittis* of aged Simeon in the New Testament ("Now, Lord, you may dismiss your servant in peace, according to your word . . . " [Luke 2.29–32]) and a hymn to the Virgin Mary.

All men in holy orders are obliged to pray the Liturgy of the Hours every day. Cloistered religious women and men make "the office" the structure of their day, and many active religious communities (teachers, health-care workers, and so forth) bind themselves to the Liturgy of the Hours, too—as do a surprising number of laypeople, including younger laypeople. I've made "the office" the basic structure of my daily prayer for thirty years, saying Lauds every morning and Vespers and Compline every evening. When I'm living in a religious house (as when I lived at the North American College in Rome while researching *Witness to Hope*), it's a great pleasure to pray the office in community; but it's also entirely possible to pray it alone, which is what I do most of the time. And while there are certainly dry spells from time to time, I really wouldn't know how to live without that daily routine.

There's a good way to ease yourself into a daily routine of prayer, however, and that's to get a subscription to *Magnificat*, a monthly prayer book that has been one of the astonishing successes in the Catholic Church in recent years. *Magnificat*, which is beautiful as well as handy, is both a missal with all the Mass texts for the month (so that you can join in the Church's reflection at Mass each day even if you can't attend) as well as a shortened form of "the office"—modified Morning, Evening, and Night Prayer. Each monthly issue also includes wonderfully interesting lives of the saints (from a seemingly bottomless treasure-trove of Catholic historical trivia) and brief spiritual readings, some by contemporary authors and others from the Catholic classics. You can fit it into a suit-jacket pocket or a purse. It's simply the best way I know to get some basic structure into daily prayer. A lot of people seem to find it helpful—from a standing start, *Magnificat* (which has editions in several languages throughout the world) has attracted hundreds of thousands of subscribers. You can check it out at www.magnificat.net. It's very much worth a look, as a reminder that beauty and regularity are important elements of worship.

Which reminds us, again, that worship isn't something we make up. To which the only appropriate response is—Thank God.

St. Stanisław Kostka Churchyard, Warsaw /
The Metropolitan Curia, Kraków

How Vocations Change History

here are some important things to learn about what it means to be Catholic—and what being Catholic means to history—in what's arguably the most intensely Catholic country in the world: Poland.

Poland is a land of shrines and pilgrimage. The vast outdoor Holy Land shrine southwest of Kraków, Kalwaria Zebrzydowska, covers hundreds of acres of Galician woodland and draws hundreds of thousands of pilgrims every year, just as it has for centuries. Down in the Tatras, in Zakopane, you can visit one of the newest of Polish shrines, an A-frame church built in Polish mountaineer style and dedicated to Our Lady of Fatima, in thanksgiving for her having spared the life of Pope John Paul II when he was shot in 1981—a Marian intervention that the *Gorale*, the

Polish highlanders, believe is as obvious a fact of history as King Jan III Sobieski's beating the Turks at Vienna in 1683. Then there's Wawel Cathedral in Kraków, magnetic pole of the country's emotional life, where many of Poland's heroes (including Sobieski) are buried. The greatest of Polish shrines is the Jasna Góra monastery in Częstochowa, home of the famous icon of the Black Madonna. On this Polish part of our tour, I hope you'll come to love her as I do. But let's not start, or even end up, at Jasna Góra or any of the other, more obvious places. Rather, let's go to sites that aren't shrines in any formal sense—a parish churchyard in Warsaw; a house and an apartment building, and the bishop's residence in Kraków. In each of these places, young Catholics, not unlike you, made decisions about their vocations.

Those decisions helped change the course of modern history.

It's very hard to find what used to be Warsaw, except in its small Old Town. If you saw the fine movie about the Warsaw Ghetto, *The Pianist*, you know that Hitler ordered the city flattened, building by building and block by block, in retaliation for the 1944 Warsaw Uprising. Having your capital city completely leveled by Nazis is bad enough; having it rebuilt by communists is another form of insult. When I first went there in 1991, Warsaw was a gray, dull place. Unimaginative architecture, shoddy construction, and forty-five years of deferred maintenance had made for almost unrelieved dreariness. Things have changed since then. Downtown Warsaw is lively, even if its new buildings make you think of Dallas or Houston, and the Warsaw Uprising Museum, opened in 2004, is one of the finest historical museums I've ever visited.

I've been to Poland many times, but that first visit, in 1991, was something of a pilgrimage, at least as I think back on it. On a flight back from Moscow in October 1990, I had gotten the idea into my head that the Catholic Church had had something to do with the collapse of European communism—and I came to Poland eight months later to test that intuition by talking with the people who had made the Revolution of 1989. Shortly after I arrived in Warsaw, I felt an irresistible tug drawing me to the churchyard of St. Stanisław Kostka, in the Żoliborz district.

Żoliborz is a fifteen- or twenty-minute tram ride from downtown. Today, as for decades, it's a traditionally bohemian area, leaning to the port side in its politics; in the 1960s and 1970s, I'm told, Żoliborz was one of the few places in Poland where you could find an intellectually respectable Marxist to argue with. The tram lets you off at a roundabout that was known, between 1946 and 1991, by an ungainly communist moniker—Square of the Defense of the Paris Commune. By 1991, and thanks to what had happened in 1989, it had reverted to the name it bore in the 1920s and 1930s: Woodrow Wilson Square. As you walk through the square you can see, off to the left, a steeple. Head in that direction and you'll find yourself, in a couple of blocks, at the Church of St. Stanisław Kostka.

In the churchyard, you'll see a tremendous granite cross, perhaps ten feet long, lying in the ground, its polished surface reflecting the clouds and trees above. The churchyard is rimmed by large, unpolished stones, each joined to its neighbor by iron links. Then you notice that the linked stones are joined to the top of the great granite cross. And suddenly it's clear—this is a rosary.

Buried underneath the granite cross is Blessed Jerzy Popiełuszko.

Father Jerzy (pronounced YARE-zhee), which is "George" *po Polsku*, was thirty-four years old when, in December 1981, Poland's communist government declared martial law in an attempt to crush the Solidarity trade union—which was, as everyone understood and nobody could admit, a political opposition as well as a workers' movement. Popiełuszko (pop-ee-WHOOSH-koe) hadn't had a very distinguished ecclesiastical career up to that point. He wasn't a prodigy in the seminary. He was in chronically poor health, was thin as a rail, and had a weak pulpit voice.

In August 1980, the month that Solidarity exploded into life in the deliciously named "Lenin" shipyards at Gdańsk on Poland's Baltic coast, Cardinal Stefan Wyszyński, the Primate of Poland and Father Jerzy's superior, named the young priest a chaplain to workers at a Warsaw steel mill; the workers were striking in support of what was happening in Gdańsk. Week after week, as the drama of Solidarity played itself out in 1980 and 1981, Father Jerzy celebrated Mass, heard confessions, and counseled with the steelworkers. Then martial law struck on the night of December 12–13, 1981. The Polish state had invaded the Polish nation, using the Polish army as its weapon.

A month later, Father Jerzy Popiełuszko began a monthly "Mass for the Fatherland" at St. Stanisław Kostka, the Żoliborz church where he was assigned as a very junior curate. At those Masses, this previously unassuming, quiet priest found a voice—and perhaps a new depth of meaning in his priestly vocation. There was no rabble-rousing. But Father Jerzy's quiet eloquence soon had hundreds, then thousands, and finally tens of thousands packing into and around St. Stanisław Kostka for the monthly "Mass for the Fatherland." It made no difference whether it was hot or cold, dry or wet, or whether there were feet of snow on the ground. People came. And Father Jerzy challenged them.

He took his theme, relentlessly repeated, from Pope John Paul II: "Vanquish evil with good." He preached nonviolence. But he also preached the moral duty of resistance. In his quiet, urgent way, Father Jerzy was asking his people, "Whose side will you take? The side of good, or the side of evil? Truth or falsehood? Love or hatred?" Father Jerzy wasn't a theological sophisticate, and he wasn't a political theorist. He was something more—a man who could inspire others to the moral heroism he displayed himself. Michael Kaufman, then the *New York Times* Warsaw bureau chief, quickly grasped how utterly, dramatically, defiantly unique all of this was: "Nowhere else from East Berlin to Vladivostok could anyone stand before ten or fifteen thousand people and use a microphone to condemn the errors of state and party. Nowhere, in that vast stretch encompassing some four hundred million people, was anyone else telling a crowd that defiance of authority was an obligation of the heart, of religion, of manhood, and of nationhood."

But the *Times* man in Poland wasn't the only one who understood. So did the SB, the Polish secret police. That's why they decided to kill Father Jerzy Popiełuszko.

On his way back to Warsaw from a pastoral assignment in Bydgoszcz on October 19, 1984, Father Jerzy's car was pulled over by three SB officers, members of a particularly thuggish unit of the secret police. They trussed him up, beat him to death, stuffed his battered corpse into a plastic bag, weighed it down with stones, and then dumped it into the Vistula River near Włocławek. The next day, the state radio announced that Father Jerzy Popiełuszko had disappeared and was presumed kidnapped by "unknown parties." People began flocking to the Żoliborz churchyard by the tens of thousands, from all over the country. Masses were offered every hour, around the clock. This went on for ten days. Then, on October 30, came the news that everyone feared and expected—the body of Father Jerzy Popiełuszko had been dredged out of the Vistula.

The announcement was made in the midst of a Mass at St. Stanisław Kostka. Another of the Żoliborz priests, Father Antonin Lewek, a friend of Father Jerzy, urged the vast congregation to remember Jesus at the death of Lazarus— to cry, but not to strike out in violent anger. Then, Father Lewek later recounted, something extraordinary happened: three times the crowd, in tears, repeated after the priests concelebrating the Mass, "And forgive us our trespasses as we forgive those who trespass against us. And forgive us our trespasses as we forgive . . . "

Normal practice would have called for Popiełuszko to be buried in Warsaw's Powązki cemetery, but 10,000 of Father Jerzy's steelworkers signed a petition to the archbishop, Cardinal Józef Glemp, asking that he allow Father Jerzy to be buried in the churchyard at St. Stanisław Kostka, a few yards from where he had celebrated the Masses for the

Fatherland and called his people to live in the truth. After the slain priest's mother intervened, the cardinal agreed. With several hundred thousand people from all over Poland in the streets that day, Father Jerzy was laid to rest in his churchyard on November 3, 1984.

The churchyard instantly became a shrine—"a little piece of free Poland," as one Solidarity activist put it to me in 1991. This was "Solidarity's sanctuary," a place of prayer and reflection that carried on the work Father Jerzy had begun from the pulpit inside the church. In his sermons, he had told his people that "one cannot murder hopes." Five years after his death, his hopes, and those of millions of other Poles, were vindicated in the Revolution of 1989. No one who had ever been to the churchyard in Żoliborz could doubt that Father Jerzy was watching those epic events, if from a different vantage point.

Father Jerzy Popiełuszko was beatified in June 6, 2010, at a Mass in Warsaw's Piłsudski Square attended by 150,000 people, including the murdered priest's mother and siblings. That ceremony, and the process that preceded it, confirmed what many people who knew him, and many more who didn't, believed—this was a saintly man. There are many different kinds of sanctity in the Church. Hans Urs von Balthasar once wrote that some saints are "God's prime numbers," men and women who blaze new trails in holiness or who have utterly unique Christian personalities: Francis of Assisi, for example. Other saints lead exemplary lives that run along more conventional spiritual tracks. In either case, the "prime numbers" or the exemplars, it's important to understand that the Church doesn't make saints; God makes saints. The Church recognizes publicly the saints that God has made.

Father Jerzy Popiełuszko's sanctity unfolded in very distinctive circumstances. In the ninth decade of a century of lethal lies, he embodied the sanctity of integrity. Father Jerzy was in no sense a born revolutionary. But when the moment came, he knew how to speak truth to power, and he knew how to do it in ways that summoned others to a similar truth-telling—without violence, but without compromise, either.

Things were very, very dicey in Poland in the early 1980s. The situation could easily have gotten out of hand; if it had, the Soviet Union might have invaded, with untold consequences in Europe and around the world. But events didn't spiral out of control. Solidarity changed Poland (indeed, Solidarity helped change all of Central and Eastern Europe) through means other than the usual twentieth-century method of large-scale social change—mass slaughter. That was due in no small part to the courage and the conviction of people like Father Jerzy Popiełuszko. Without him, and others like him, things could have been very different indeed, for all of us.

So we come here to honor a man of courage. But we also come here because Father Jerzy's story teaches us several other important things about Catholic faith and its practice. *Faith has consequences.* At the personal level, those consequences are vocational—What is it that I am called to do? How do I live the truth of who I am? When he entered the seminary, young Jerzy Popiełuszko hadn't the slightest idea of becoming a world figure, much less a martyr. He was a quiet, retiring, pious lad who may well have seen the priest-hood as a place to be, well, quiet and retiring and pious. Yet he lived out, to the very end, the truth of what he had been ordained to be. And that had consequences, not only for him personally but for the people whose lives he touched—people through whom he helped change history. Faith has consequences for history, too.

That's an old Catholic idea, nowhere more clearly ex-pressed than by the great English historian Christopher Dawson, who reflected on the fact that one of the most de-cisive moments in European history was completely ignored by the historians of the time:

> When St. Paul, in obedience to the warning of a dream, set sail from Troy in AD 49 and came to Philippi in Macedonia, he did more to change the course of history than the great battle that had decided the fate of the Roman Empire on the same spot a century earlier, for he brought to Europe the seed of a new life which was ultimately destined to cre-ate a new world. All this took place underneath the sur-face of history, so that it was unrecognized by the leaders of contemporary culture . . . who actually saw it taking place beneath their eyes.

"Underneath the surface of history"—that's where Cath-olic faith has its deepest consequences. Yes, the Catholic Church appears time and again on the "surface" of history. But what's often of more enduring consequence is taking place below-the-radar-screen, as it were. It's happening in minds and hearts and souls, in vocational choices and decisions.

And that brings us south, to a much lovelier city, Kraków, ancient capital of royal Poland and the center of the country's cultural life for hundreds of years. Here, from 1939 through 1946, things were also happening "underneath the surface of history"—things that eventually changed the course of the late twentieth century.

Pope John Paul II was the first pope in a long time to tell us that he'd had a hard time making a vocational decision for the priesthood. Yet he did. When Karol Wojtyła moved to Kraków with his pensioner father in 1938 to begin his studies in Polish philology at the Jagiellonian University, he didn't think he was going to be a priest; he thought he was going to be an actor, a man of the theater, with perhaps a parallel career in academic life. As he put it in a memoir published in 1996, he was "completely absorbed by a passion for literature, especially dramatic literature, and for the theater." It wasn't simply a question of that passion leaving little or no room for a priestly vocation; young Karol Wojtyła's passion for literature and the theater seemed to him to be his vocation.

Then things changed. And so did Karol Wojtyła.

The brutal German occupation of Poland from September 1939 through January 1945 was the biblical fiery furnace in which Karol Wojtyła's vocation was clarified and purified. The long-term German strategy for Poland was simple: the Poles were to be erased as a race of subhumans. In the interim, they were to work for the greater glory of the Third Reich, subsisting on a minimal diet. Hitler knew that the Poles wouldn't truckle quietly; alone, the Poles in 1939 held out against the Wehrmacht for three weeks longer than the French would manage to do, with British air and ground support, in 1940. So Poland was divided. Its eastern regions were handed over to Stalin (his reward for the cynical Molotov-Ribbentrop Pact of August 1939); western Polish areas were annexed to the German Reich (thus the Polish town of Oświęcim was renamed "Auschwitz"); and the great center of the country became what historian Norman Davies called "Gestapoland." Styled the *Generalgouvernement* and run from Krakow's Wawel Castle by a political gangster named Hans Frank, it was an area in which the rule of law ceased to exist and a reign of terror ensued. This was where Karol Wojtyła lived from age nineteen through age twenty-four.

In Hans Frank's Gestapoland, the initial occupation strategy was to decapitate any possible Polish resistance by decapitating Polish culture. So the Nazis shut down the Jagiellonian University and shipped 184 of its professors off to the Sachsenhausen concentration camp. Polish cultural life went underground; it was a capital crime to be caught playing Chopin, and Poles of courage and conviction defied the German effort to destroy their cultural memory at the daily risk of their lives. Young Wojtyła was one of them. He took clandestine courses as the Jagiellonian reorganized itself as an underground school. He helped found a theatrical group that believed in resistance-through-drama: the Rhapsodic Theater, which worked to keep Poland's memory alive by performing the classics of the Polish stage and of Polish poetry. At the same time, young Karol was a manual laborer, first in a stone quarry, later in a chemical factory, walking to work in freezing winter weather in denims and clogs, trying to scrounge something to eat for his father and himself on his way home in the evening.

If you walk through Kraków's Old Town toward Wawel Castle and Cathedral and then turn right, you'll find yourself walking, like Karol Wojtyła did, along the embankment of the Vistula River. Cross the first bridge you come to and you'll be in the working-class neighborhood, Dębniki, where young Karol Wojtyła wrestled with the question of what he was supposed to do with his life. Tyniecka Street borders the embankment on the Dębniki side of the Vistula; if you walk a few hundred yards down the street, you'll come to 10 Tyniecka Street, a three-story house where Karol lived from 1938 to 1944. Here, in the dark and damp basement apartment his friends called "The Catacomb," the Rhapsodic Theater was launched and held some of its rehearsals. Here, Karol's father died on February 18, 1941; here young Karol spent a night in prayer beside his father's body, remembering later that "I never felt so alone." Here, he asked himself a question he remembered a half-century later: "So many people of my own age are losing their lives, *why not me?*"

And here he read the works of the great Carmelite mystics St. John of the Cross and St. Teresa of Avila. They had been lent to him by a surprising character, a man he came to call the "unexpected apostle"—Jan Tyranowski. Tyranowski, a forty-something bachelor who was a tailor by training, lived a few blocks away, at 11 Różana Street. He spent the early hours of each day at his trade, and the rest of the day in a life of meditation and prayer more rigorous than that led by many monks or nuns. When the Gestapo arrested most of the Salesian fathers at the Dębniki parish, the remaining priest asked Tyranowski to take over what we would now call the parish's "youth ministry" to young men.

Tyranowski began forming the young men of Dębniki into what he called "Living Rosary" groups, fifteen to a group, with a more mature youngster as the group leader, or "animator." Karol Wojtyła was one of the first "animators" of the Living Rosary. Tyranowski, who must have sensed that this literarily inclined young man would be attracted to the poetry of John of the Cross and the drama of Teresa of Avila's rambunctious life, introduced him to the basic works of these sixteenth-century Spanish mystics: St. Teresa's *Autobiography*; St. John's *Dark Night of the Soul, Spiritual Canticle, Ascent of Mt. Carmel*, and *Living Flame of Love*. Carmelite mysticism is a spirituality of abandonment focused on the crucified Christ, who died in complete self-abnegation and abandonment to the will of his Father. Reading St. John and St. Teresa under the tutelage of Jan Tyranowski, it's not hard to imagine Karol Wojtyła saying, as Edith Stein had in the 1920s when reading Teresa's autobiography, "This is the truth."

Back in "The Catacomb," and while lugging buckets of lime during the night shift at the Solway chemical plant in the Borek Fałęcki district, Karol wrestled with that truth, with himself, and with God for several months after his father's death. According to the Carmelite mystics, we can only know God in himself when we give up all our human attempts to "reach" God by our own striving—when we, like Jesus, abandon ourselves in an act of complete self-surrender, which is a radical act of love. It would be hard to imagine a way of thinking more different from the Nazi exaltation of the "triumph of the will," which was then killing Karol's friends and colleagues, day by day, on the streets of Kraków.

As 1941 gave way to 1942, something was happening in the soul of Karol Wojtyła. Abandoning himself to the will of God was slowly becoming the defining characteristic of his discipleship. Like carbon deposits deep beneath the earth, he was being hard-pressed by turbulent forces. And, as sometimes happens with carbon, those powerful forces were forming him into a diamond, something brilliant and hard, able to cut through the seemingly impenetrable.

He made his decision in the fall of 1942. It wasn't a matter of choosing the priesthood, as he would have chosen the theater or the academic life. It was a question of coming to recognize that he had been chosen—and to that choosing there could only be one answer. Karol's decision led him to the great house and diocesan office complex at 3 Franciszkańska Street in Kraków's Old Town. This was the longtime residence of the archbishops of the city, known formally as the "Metropolitan Curia" and usually called by its street number, "Franciszkańska Three." The Nazis had shut down the seminary shortly after seizing power; the courageous archbishop, Adam Stefan Sapieha, had reconstituted the seminary underground. Karol Wojtyła now became a clandestine seminarian, working at the Solway plant, studying on the side, and quietly slipping in and out of Franciszkańska 3 for reading assignments, exams, and spiritual direction. (Looking across Franciszkańska Street from the Metropolitan Curia today, you can see a statue of Cardinal Sapieha that Karol Wojtyła, then archbishop himself, commissioned in the 1970s. The cardinal seems to be looking down into hell, and the inscription on the stone base of the bronze statue describes him as "the archbishop of the long, dark night of Occupation." The Carmelite allusion isn't accidental.) Karol would also come to Franciszkańska 3 to serve the archbishop's early morning Mass, usually with another clandestine seminarian. One day in April 1944, his fellow-server, Jerzy Zachuta, didn't show up. After Mass, Karol ran to the Zachuta home to see what had happened; Jerzy had been arrested the night before and was shot a few days later. One was taken, another remained—"So many young people of my own age are losing their lives, *why not me?*"

On August 6, 1944, the Nazis swept the city, trying to arrest all its young men in order to forestall a possible repeat of the Warsaw Uprising, which had begun five days earlier. Karol hid in "The Catacomb," and it was there that he got his orders: Sapieha was calling all the clandestine seminarians in. They would now live with the archbishop, underground and hidden, at the Metropolitan Curia. So, with the help of a friend's mother, Karol worked his way across town, dodging the German patrols, and disappeared into Franciszkańska 3, which would be his home until the following summer. The archbishop's drawing room was the underground seminary's dormitory; other rooms in the residence became classrooms. Every night, the seminarians could watch the elderly archbishop go into his chapel to lay the day's problems and trials before the Lord.

Cardinal Sapieha ordained Karol Wojtyła to the priesthood in that chapel on November 1, 1946. Forty-five years later, I came to Poland to find out what had caused the Revolution of 1989. Like all epic historical events, this singular revolution was a complex affair and I wasn't interested in one-size-fits-all explanations. What I did want to know was when the Revolution of 1989 had been ignited. So I asked people, "When did this really get started?" And without exception, believers and unbelievers, Catholics and Jews, agnostics and atheists, conservatives, liberals, and radicals *all* said the same thing—it began during Pope John Paul II's nine-day pilgrimage to Poland in June 1979. Which was one, powerful answer to the question the man who would become pope had asked himself in "The Catacomb": Why had he been spared? *"Why not me?"*

One year after Mehmet Ali Ağca shot him down in his front yard, St. Peter's Square, Pope John Paul said that "in the designs of Providence, there are no mere coincidences." That's the truth about vocation, and obedience, and abandonment that his remarkable story illustrates. Chance is for card games. God doesn't work that way.

What do the stories of Blessed Jerzy Popiełuszko and of young Karol Wojtyła, who became St. John Paul II, have to do with you and your questions?

I hope they encourage you to think vocationally, rather than in terms of "career." A career is something you have, and if those ubiquitous "career-planners" are right, you may have two, three, or four of them in a lifetime. It's much more important, though, to think about vocation. For *a vocation is something you are.*

I hope these two stories encourage you to find and get to know men and women who are living vocationally—husbands and wives, professionals and workers, priests and consecrated religious. Becoming a good person isn't just a matter of convincing yourself about certain moral truths, important as that is. It's also a matter of finding virtuous people and learning from them how to live like them. The same goes for vocation. You may not find people whose vocational dramas are quite so intense and public as Father Jerzy's or Pope John Paul II's. That's fine. The drama is there to be discovered, if you look hard enough.

Being here in Poland, breathing the air of these remarkably ordinary places where extraordinary things happened, and thinking about how Poland-the-state has died and risen and died and risen again, should also help you understand a bit more about how history really works.

According to the conventional wisdom of the 1980s, Poland's communists had all the cards: they controlled politics, they controlled the economy (such as it was), they controlled the army, and they controlled the media. The resistance Church in Poland—men like Father Jerzy, inspired by John Paul II—didn't believe that. With the Pope (who had learned this in underground resistance efforts like the Rhapsodic Theater), they were convinced that *culture is what drives history over the long haul.* A people in possession of its culture, a people that owns the truth about itself, has weapons of resistance that totalitarianism can't match. People determined to live the truth of who they are—*people determined to live vocationally*—are the most dynamic force in history.

This is, once again, countercultural Catholicism—at least in terms of how Western high culture today thinks about how the world and history work. It's much more fashionable today to think of history as the product of economics, or politics, or some combination of politics-and-economics, than to think of history as the product of culture. But that's what this stop on our tour suggests—that "history" (which certainly includes politics and economics) is even more the product of friendship and love and commitment and faith and the great artifacts of literature and music and painting and sculpture to which those deepest yearnings of the human spirit give birth. For friendship and love and commitment and faith are the deepest aspirations of the human spirit. That's why, to return to an image I've used before (and which I first learned from philosopher Peter Kreeft), history is *His*-story, the story of God at work in the world, often "underneath the surface of history," in a drama of salvation that *is* the human story, read in its proper depth.

Catholics can't think of history as flat. Catholics can't think of history as the exhaust fumes of the "means of production." Catholics can't think of history as politics, period. Catholics have a craggier view of the way things work. The world may consider it crankier, rather than craggier. Consider the possibility that it is, in fact, the far more humane view.

The obedience of faith has consequences—not only for individuals, but for societies and for history. The obedience of faith is profoundly countercultural. It's also, as we learn here, a difference that can make a lot of difference.

The North American College Mausoleum, Campo Verano, Rome

The Hardest Questions

very Roman knows Campo Verano, although it's a bit off the typical tourist track. Originally the estate of Lucius Verus, co-emperor with Marcus Aurelius from 161 to 169, Campo Verano was designated as Rome's municipal cemetery when Napoleon and his minions were running things Italian in the early nineteenth century. It took decades to build; the idea, a grandiose one, was that, after its opening on July 1, 1836, everyone who died in Rome would be buried there. This being Italy, it took a while to complete the original plans—the great gates to the cemetery were only finished in 1878.

Campo Verano occupies an enormous tract of land, some three times the size of Vatican City, in the Tiburtino District near Stazione Termini, the main train station. The gated entrance is a good stone's throw from the Basilica of St. Lawrence Outside the Walls; Blessed Pius IX is buried there in a memorial chapel whose mosaics are well worth a look. Once you're a few hundred yards inside Campo Verano, you can't see the cemetery's boundaries in any direction.

As you walk past the flower vendors and through the entrance gates to begin exploring Campo Verano's various "neighborhoods," you quickly get the impression that the Italians handle death about the same way they handle everything else—dramatically. Monuments, mausoleums, family tombs, and even individual gravesites vie for splendor and *bella figura*. As you walk along a seeming infinity of paths, up and down hills and through small valleys, you'll notice that there's a very mixed population here—anticlericals and militant atheists share Campo Verano with squadrons of cardinals and other high-ranking clerics. According to one story, possibly apocryphal, students from Rome's Pontifical Gregorian University used to come here the night before exams to pray at the Gregorian faculty mausoleum—presumably to make sure that certain demanding professors . . . stayed put. Politicians, movie stars, literary people, and ordinary Romans long forgotten to history are all here; you can actually get to know many of them from the photos or etchings on their tombstones.

I first visited Campo Verano on All Souls' Day, November 2, 2001, when I went there with several faculty members and students from the Pontifical North American College for a memorial Mass at the college's mausoleum. In the first half of the twentieth century, American seminarians who died in Rome were buried in this three-story stone building;

the annual memorial Mass is a college tradition, and as I was staying at the college while working in Rome, I was invited to come along. After Mass, while exploring the inscriptions on the vaults inside the mausoleum, I came across the name *Franciscus Parater.* One of the seminarians asked whether I had read "Frank Parater's Prayer" in the college *Manual of Prayers.* I had to admit that I hadn't. "Don't miss it," was my young friend's advice.

Frank Parater came to Rome in November 1919 to study for the priesthood as a seminarian of the Richmond diocese. Twenty-two years old at the time, he had been one of the Virginia capital's most impressive young men in his day, a model student and exceptional Scout leader whose character and courtesy cut through the genteel anti-Catholicism of that time and place. He had first felt attracted to a monastic vocation and began his studies at Belmont Abbey Seminary College in North Carolina, with an eye to becoming a Benedictine. During his two years at Belmont Abbey, though, Frank Parater decided that, whatever his own personal inclinations toward a more contemplative life, he really ought to dedicate himself to the diocesan priesthood in a more active ministry.

A month after arriving in Rome, Frank Parater wrote the prayer to which my young friend at Campo Verano had referred. The prayer—which he called "An Act of Oblation to the Sacred Heart of Jesus"—was in fact a spiritual last will and testament. Parater had left it in an envelope with instructions that it was only be opened in the event of his death. In his prayer, he offered himself for the conversion of his beloved state:

I have nothing to leave or give but my life and this I have
consecrated to the Sacred Heart to be used as He wills. I
have offered my all for the conversion of non-Catholics in
Virginia. This is what I live for and in case of death what
I die for. . . . Since my childhood I have wanted to die for
God and my neighbor. Shall I have this grace? I do not
know, but if I go on living, I shall live for this same purpose;
every action of my life here is offered for the spread and
success of the Catholic Church in Virginia. . . . I shall be
of more service to my diocese in Heaven than I can ever be
on earth.

In late January 1920, after just two months in Rome,
Frank Parater contracted rheumatism, which developed into
rheumatic fever. On January 27 he was taken to a hospital
run by the Blue Nuns, where he suffered intense pain for two
weeks. When the college spiritual director came to the hospital to give him the Last Rites, Frank Parater wanted to get
up from his deathbed to receive his last Holy Communion
kneeling; the doctors wouldn't permit it, so he knelt on the
bed to receive the Viaticum, the "food for the journey." The
college rector offered the votive Mass of the Sacred Heart for
Frank Parater on February 6. He died the next day. His prayer
was found in his room when a fellow-student was gathering
up his belongings. Pope Benedict XV and Pope Pius XI both
asked for copies of "Frank Parater's Prayer."

Then the world and the Church seemed to move on—
although the few who remembered were convinced that
Frank Parater was keeping an eye on the Diocese of Richmond from a distance, so to speak. It took another Richmond seminarian, studying in Rome in the 1970s, to bring

the Frank Parater story back to life. Having become fascinated by this striking tale during his own studies, Father J. Scott Duarte kept the story in mind after his own ordination and during his graduate studies. Years of Father Duarte's patient research paid off in January 2002, when the Diocese of Richmond officially opened the cause for the beatification of The Servant of God Frank Parater, Seminarian. Thousands of Catholics around the United States are now linked to this cause through a great chain of prayer, asking Frank Parater's intercession for their needs and asking God to bless the cause for his beatification with a miracle.

Frank Parater's story isn't an Everyman story. He died very young; he died heroically, away from home; and in some sense he not only embraced his premature death but anticipated and welcomed it as the best gift he could make of his life. There aren't a lot of us who are going to die that way. Yet for all its singularity, Frank Parater's story is a powerful one, particularly for a generation that often finds commitment difficult. In any case, here we are at Campo Verano, at Frank Parater's tomb, which is as good a place as any to think about two questions this young son of Virginia seems to have had answered, to his own satisfaction, before he died eight months short of his twenty-third birthday: Is there any meaning in suffering? Is death the final absurdity?

Once upon a time—indeed, as recently as the mid-twentieth century—those were assumed to be two of the enduring questions of the human condition. No longer. Advances in medicine, and the promise of even greater progress through the application of our new genetic knowledge to curing disease, have led some doctors, geneticists, and bio-tech engineers to speak quite bluntly about the immortality project—not merely ending suffering, but making us virtu-ally immortal, here on this earth.

All of which led my friend Cardinal Francis George of Chicago to a sobering observation. "Do you realize," the cardinal asked me in the early years of the new millennium, "that we're going to spend the rest of our lives trying to con-vince people that suffering and death are good for you?" It's hard to imagine something that cuts more deeply against the grain of contemporary American culture, so absorbed as it is by the pleasure principle. Yet that's what Catholics are going to have to do. And the first step in convincing others is con-vincing ourselves.

L et's start with suffering. The first thing to notice about suffering is that it's something uniquely human. Dogs and cats and cows and sheep feel pain; only human beings suffer. That's because our suffering is not simply physical, but mental and spiritual. Physical suffering can, of course, lead to spiritual anguish. But we can also suffer morally and spiritually without any physical pain, and the less tan-gible forms of suffering are often the worst. If you've ever had a broken arm or leg, you've known one kind of pain; if a friend has betrayed you, you've known another, and likely worse, pain. Love spurned, plans frustrated, the in-comprehension of parents, the indifference or cruelty of teachers—these are forms of moral and spiritual suffering that wound more deeply and ache more sharply than bro-ken bones.

That suggests that suffering is telling us something important about ourselves as human beings: *Suffering tells us that we have souls, that the "me" that makes me a unique person isn't just a bundle of neurons.* Suffering is another of those human experiences that points us beyond the ordinary to its near far side, where we meet the extraordinary—which in this case means the human soul and its capacity for endurance, courage, and self-sacrifice. Suffering isn't just a problem; it's part of the mystery, the transcendence, of the human experience.

The second thing we might notice about suffering is that *suffering has something to do with freedom.* As you've doubtless found out, a lot of very bright people find it easier to reconcile suffering with a purpose-free universe than to reconcile suffering with the idea of a good God. And, truth to tell, some conventional religious answers haven't been very helpful here. To say that God "permits" suffering, for example, seems to make God into a blundering fool or a sadist. The biblical answer to this quandary, which informs the Catholic answer, is that suffering, like evil, is one of the implications of freedom—at least as men and women have lived their freedom since the stories recorded in the Book of Genesis. God created a world of freedom because, among other things, God wishes the love of men and women who freely choose to love him, as they freely choose to love one another. And a world of freedom is a world in which things often go wrong, with suffering as one result.

The third thing to be said about suffering, from a Catholic perspective, is this: at the bottom of the bottom line, *suffering isn't a problem to be "solved" but a mystery to be engaged, in love.* When the Church says that something is a "mystery," it doesn't mean "mystery" in the sense that solving a crime is figuring out a "mystery." Rather, by "mystery" the Church means some essential truth that can be grasped only in an act of love. We don't get the Catholic "answer" to the mystery of suffering by completing a syllogism; the Catholic "answer" to the mystery of suffering comes through an encounter with Jesus Christ.

God's creation of the world was a free act of divine love, a love that spilled out of the inner life of God himself. God's love, therefore, is what gives true meaning to whatever exists—including suffering. God gives his answer to the world's question about the meaning of suffering through a demonstration. And the dramatic climax of the demonstration of God's love for the world, and the capacity of that love to give meaning to the most intense suffering, is the cross of Christ. On the cross, in the suffering of Christ, God cleared out "all the refuse of the world's sin by burning it in the fire of suffering love," as Hans Urs von Balthasar once put it.

When the Son takes all the world's evil and sin and suffering upon himself and offers it to the Father in a perfect act of obedience, and when God vindicates that act of radical obedience and love in the Resurrection, suffering itself is transformed. When Christ redeems us by his suffering, suffering itself is redeemed. The Christ who died for all offers a share in his redemption to all—and offers us the possibility that, by identifying our suffering with his, we, too, can participate in his redemptive suffering for the world. That's what Frank Parater knew, intuitively. When Christ made himself a sharer in human suffering, he enabled us to share in his work of redemption. When we identify our suffering with Christ's, our suffering becomes redemptive, because our suffering, like his, is thereby linked to love. Offering our suffering for the good of others is sharing in the redeeming work of Christ. Offering our suffering for the good of others is one way we help the Church extend the saving work of Christ in history.

I had been taught these things in school, but it was years later that I saw the truth of redemptive suffering at work in a life. I had gotten to know Congressman Henry Hyde and his wife Jeanne over the years, and I visited, talked, and prayed with Jeanne in the hospital when she was being treated for cancer in the early 1990s. In her last illness, Jeanne Hyde offered her suffering for the great cause for which she and Henry had fought so long and nobly; and in doing so, it seemed to me, she was doing more good than she imagined. Who knew, I once wrote her, how many desperate, lonely young women had found the courage not to abort their children because of Jeanne's offer of her suffering for their sakes? I was out of the country when Jeanne Hyde died. One of her sons told me a few weeks later that his mother's death had been peaceful, even happy, because of her conviction that in identifying her suffering with Christ's, she was somehow helping young women affirm the gift of life.

"No cross, no crown," is the maxim that sums up St. Paul's entire message in his second letter to those cantankerous and confused Corinthians—suffering, he says, prepares us for "an eternal weight of glory, beyond all comparison" [2 Corinthians 4.17]. Transformed by the cross of Christ, our suffering is no longer an absurdity, but rather another way to become the kind of people who can live with

God forever. Suffering helps us learn to be comfortable in the blazing light of the God whose Son enters the world to suffer and die for it, and for us. Frank Parater knew that, in his heart. So did Jeanne Hyde. That's why they died happily, and ready for life in the Kingdom of God.

All of which suggests that, for Catholics, suffering is a vocation. It's another way of making ourselves into the gifts for others that our own lives are to us. It's a way of growing into compassion—which, in its Latin root, means the capacity to "suffer-with." Like the Good Samaritan, we learn through suffering, our own suffering and others', that you can't just "pass by" on the other side of the road of life. Suffering, our own and others', teaches us a fundamental human solidarity.

Like everything else in life, suffering looks different when we experience history as *His*-story, as Christ's story—the story of redeeming love burning its way through the world. Peter Kreeft puts in nicely: when we look at history as *His*-story, suffering becomes the bass note "in a harmony whose high notes are lost in heaven." So don't think of suffering as spiritual castor oil. In the mystery of human life, suffering makes us the kind of people who can live in an eternity in which every tear has been wiped away, death will be no more, and there is neither mourning nor crying nor pain [Revelation 21.1–5]. Suffering is what makes us the kind of people who can live with Love itself without suffering from it, or getting bored by it.

You're going to live your Catholic life in a world in which death is increasingly seen as a disease to be cured. Hormonal therapies, the possibility of "replacement parts" being grown out of stem cells, and research into the genetic basis of aging all suggest the possibility that the human life-span can be expanded a very long way, and perhaps indefinitely. What does a "pro-life" Church say about that?

One of our wisest guides here is Leon Kass, whom President George W. Bush appointed chairman of the President's Council on Bioethics in 2001. Kass, a brilliant reader of both the Bible and the Great Books of the Western tradition, suggests that the immortality project has been built into modern science from its beginnings. Francis Bacon and René Descartes were quite open about the purpose of the new kind of experimental science they were launching in the seventeenth century—it was to "relieve man's estate," by which they meant nothing less than reversing the sentence of death that had hung over every human being since Adam and Eve. That project now stands on the threshold of success. What should we think of that?

Kass, who's not arguing as a Catholic but as a man of reason, suggests that we should look at the immortality project with robust skepticism—not because it might not "work," in the technical sense, but because it would be lethal for humanity if it did work. Like Cardinal George, Leon Kass believes that death is good for us, in a deeply human if mysterious sense. In a brilliantly provocative article ("L'Chaim and Its Limits: Why Not Immortality?"), Kass suggests that we reverse the question and ask, Is mortality a blessing? He then offers several reasons why the answer to that is emphatically "yes."

Would an infinite life-span (or even a life-span extended twenty-five or fifty years) really increase our satisfaction? It's very unclear, Kass argues, that doing more of the same things for a much longer time, or even doing the occasional extraordinary things during a vastly expanded life-span, would add to the sum total of human happiness. Then there's the question of human striving, and what virtual immortality would do to that essential human quality: "Could life be serious or meaningful without the limit of mortality? Is not the limit on our time the ground of our taking life seriously and living it passionately?" When the Psalms enjoin us to "number our days" so that we may "get a heart of wisdom," the Psalmist is teaching us a very large truth. Even pagans once understood this, Kass suggests. In the *Iliad* and the *Odyssey*, it's the immortals who are silly, frivolous, aimless; Homer's mortals, by comparison, are full of striving, passion, courage, and fellow-feeling.

Then, Kass reminds us, there are beauty and love. There is nothing beautiful, and there's no real love, in the brave new world—and that, in itself, is a warning. Then there's what Kass calls "the peculiarly human beauty of character," which brings us to the relationship between our mortality, on the one hand, and the virtues, on the other. Living life as the gift it is to us would be far more difficult without mortality, Kass proposes: "To be mortal means that it is possible to give one's life, not only in one moment, say, on the field of battle, but also in the many other ways in which we are able in action to rise above our attachment to survival"— or, I'd add, our attachment to our self-assertion, which is something we all cling to. Immortals, Kass argues, "cannot be noble." The only kind of people who can reach genuine nobility of character are those willing to spend "the precious coinage of the time of our lives for the sake of the noble and the good and the holy."

Yet, as Leon Kass frankly notes, "our soul's reach exceeds our grasp," and people will continue to seek an answer to the mystery of death. One answer is the immortality project. As Kass teaches us, though, that project is an ultimately dehumanizing enterprise. "To argue that human life would be better without death," he writes, is "to argue that human life would be better off being something other than human." So what's the Catholic counterproposal? It's the Resurrection, and the eternal life with God that the Resurrection of Christ has made possible for us.

K ass suggests that what our souls are really longing for is not deathlessness but "wholeness, wisdom, goodness, and godliness—longings that cannot be satisfied fully in embodied earthly life." Catholics propose that these are precisely the longings that are satisfied in the resurrected, transfigured, and transformed life of the saints—of those who have become the kind of people who can live with God forever. That's our Christian destiny and our human destiny. Kass has it exactly right when he argues, against the immortalists, that "mere continuance will not buy fulfillment." But transfiguration can. And transfiguration is what we are promised in the resurrection of the dead in the Kingdom of God.

And it won't be the bore that "immortal life" here would almost certainly be. Perhaps without intending to, Leon Kass himself supplies the answer to why heaven won't be boring when he reminds us that "some activities . . . [may not] require finitude as a spur." The quest for understanding is one; we can imagine that continuing without the prod of mortality, for there is always something more to under-stand, to grasp more deeply. Friendship and love are two others; they seem capable of growing infinitely. *And that is exactly what awaits us in the Kingdom of God*: an eternity of unfolding understanding and friendship and love.

There's one more reason—and it's the most urgent rea-son—why Catholics think that death is good for us: and that's because our dying is what gives us the opportunity to configure our lives most radically to the life of Christ. It's not just a question of a final deathbed offering-of-self in union with Christ, although when we pray for a "good death," that's what we're praying for. Our dying is some-thing that should live in us every day, not morbidly, but as part of our prayer. Knowing that we are to die—even if that death is, on the odds, far down the road—we should ask every day that our dying in small things, just as our dying to this life, will be configured to the sacrifice of Christ, which redeems all suffering and death.

Our old friend G. K. Chesterton once said that, while man has always lost his way, "modern man has lost his ad-dress." That address is the Kingdom of God. Knowing that gives us directions for navigating the roads of this life, and gives our travel along those roads its ultimate human meaning.

The Hill of Crosses, Šiauliai, Lithuania / The Basilica of St. Bartholomew on Tiber Island, Rome

The New Martyrs and Us

he custom of bringing homemade wooden crosses to the Jurgaičiai mound, some seven miles outside the city of Šiauliai in north central Lithuania, seems to have begun in the nineteenth century. It was one expression of traditional Lithuanian piety; as a way of sealing a vow or giving thanks for a favor received, Lithuanian Catholics would "plant a cross," as the local phrase had it. And in the often mysterious ways of the Catholic world, the prayerful care put into crafting these emblems of faith created a mystical link between this small country on the Baltic seacoast and the Holy Land far away even as it prepared the Lithuanian people for their own experience of the Passion.

The Hill of Crosses outside Šiauliai traces its origins to a local villager who, gravely ill, recovered his health while setting up a cross on the Jurgaičiai mound while praying for a cure. As the news of his healing spread throughout the countryside, other crosses were erected, so that there were more than two hundred on the hill before World War I. The war took its toll on Šiauliai's now-famous shrine, and in 1920 only fifty crosses were left. By 1923, though, the count was up to four hundred, and the Hill of Crosses had become a major pilgrimage site: in addition to erecting a small forest of crosses, each of a unique size and character, the people of Lithuania participated in the celebration of Mass there, and amidst the crosses they began to leave rosaries and religious pictures on the hill.

Lithuania's brief period of independence following the Great War ended abruptly in 1940, when the Soviet Union absorbed its small neighbor. What had been the Republic of Lithuania became the Lithuanian Soviet Socialist Republic. Under the communist regime, the Hill of Crosses became what one Lithuanian guide calls a *locus non gratus*, a kind of geographical persona non grata: something unwelcome—indeed, something to be shunned. The Hill of Crosses atrophied. Many Lithuanians were deported to other parts of the USSR, including the Siberian slave-labor camps, and the Second World War raged throughout the region after Nazi Germany invaded and occupied the Lithuanian SSR in 1941. After the defeat of Germany, the Soviet secret police kept an iron grip on Lithuania, and the communists did everything in their power to eradicate Lithuanian culture. In 1956, however, Lithuanians began bringing crosses to Šiauliai again, carving stories of their wartime hardships and their current persecution into the wood of the crosses they erected on the Jurgaičiai mound. Three years later, the Hill of Crosses included a thousand of these handcrafted votive offerings.

It was all too much for the communists, who began their war against the Hill of Crosses by forbidding anyone to erect a new cross there and by removing "the crosses having no artistic value"—a supremely ironic judgment from a regime that specialized in ugliness. Yet those restrictions didn't seem to have the desired effect, as the people still came on pilgrimage to Šiauliai. So the communists opted, as they usually did, for raw brutality: on April 5, 1961, the Hill of Crosses was bulldozed, and 2,179 crosses destroyed.

The battle for the Hill of Crosses continued for three decades. Lithuanian Catholics would come by night and erect crosses on the Jurgaičiai mound; the communists destroyed the crosses, year after year. In 1977, the government tried to isolate the shrine by creating a nearby pond; in 1982 they tried again to quarantine the Hill of Crosses by turning it into an inaccessible island in that pond. And still the people came. On one memorable occasion in July 1979, a procession of several hundred Catholics from the village of Meškuičiai came to the Hill of Crosses, joined along the way by a barefooted priest, Father Algirdas Mocius, who carried a large cross for almost five miles.

Lithuania refused to accept the naked public square—the religious desert—that communism demanded. In 1972, a remarkable underground journal, *The Chronicle of the Catholic Church in Lithuania*, was launched; it eventually became the longest-running uninterrupted *samizdat* publication in the history of the USSR. In 1978, the Lithuanian Committee for the Defense of Believers Rights was formed; three of its leading figures—Father Sigitas Tamkevičius, SJ, Father Alfonsas Svarinskas, and Sister Nijolė Sadūnaitė—did hard time in the Gulag camps as a result. Yet the Catholic underground refused to be crushed, and as Lithuania began to reassert its religious and cultural identity during the late 1980s, the Hill of Crosses underwent a remarkable revival. Pilgrim groups came to Šiauliai from all over the country, often on foot, bringing their specially crafted crosses to the hill as a distinctively Lithuanian sign of their Catholic faith. And by the turn of the millennium, there were almost 100,000 crosses on the Jurgaičiai mound.

Lithuania reclaimed its independence as the Soviet Union crumbled in 1990–1991. In September 1993, Pope John Paul II—who, shortly after his election, had expressed his solidarity with persecuted Lithuanian Catholics by sending his cardinal's red zucchetto to the shrine of Our Lady, Gate of the Dawn, in Vilnius—came on pilgrimage to the Hill of Crosses. There, in a powerful homily that linked the Lithuanian people's sacrifices to the sacrifice of Christ—and, finally, to the Resurrection—he commemorated the battle for this unique center of pilgrimage and lifted up the memory of those who had paid dearly for Lithuania's religious and political freedom:

We have come here, to the Hill of Crosses, to remember all the sons and daughters of your land, including those persecuted and condemned to prison, to concentration camps, those deported to Sibera . . . and those condemned to death. . . .

Condemned among the innocents. In your Fatherland, where a terrible, violent totalitarian system raged. A system that trampled and humiliated man.

Those who were subjected to these horrors of violence and death, knew that, before their eyes, among their friends and in their families, there was being repeated and completed that which had already been undergone at Golgotha, where the Son of God "taking on himself the condition of a slave, humbled himself and became obedient unto death" [Philippians 2.7–8], for every man.

And thus the drama of the Cross was experienced by many of your compatriots, for whom Christ crucified represented an unfailing source of strength of spirit in the moment of deportation and in the moment of condemnation to death.

The Cross has been for all nations and for the Church a providential font of blessing and a sign of reconciliation among men. It has given meaning and value to suffering, to illness, to sorrow. And today, as in the past, the Cross continues to be a part of the life of man.

But the Cross, at the same time, is also an "exaltation." . . . And that, for us, constitutes an annihilation of death, for the sacrifice of the Cross reveals divine power: the power of the redemption, of saving power. "It is necessary that the Son of Man be lifted up, that those who believe in him may have eternal life" [John 3.14–15].

Christ himself thus assures us that, in his Cross, on Golgotha, the possibility of eternal life opens up for the world and for man, who lives on this earth under the unavoidable law of death. And this is how Jesus assures us: "God so loved the world that he gave his only-begotten Son, that whoever believes in him will not perish but have eternal life" [John 3.16]. The sons and daughters of your land carried to this Hill crosses that were similar to those of Golgotha, on which the Redeemer died. And they proclaimed in this way their firm conviction that those of their brothers and sisters who had died—and above all those who were murdered in various ways—"had eternal life."

The 100,000 crosses erected at Šiauliai, in personal and communal acts of piety that continue to swell the number of votive offerings there, make this hill one of the most striking places in the Catholic world. For the resurrection of the Hill of Crosses from under the rubble of the communist system embodies in a unique way the relationship between Good Friday and Easter, between the Cross and the Resurrection—between seeming catastrophe and the ultimate triumph of God's saving purposes for the world and for history.

When I was in the third grade, I was given a one-volume abridgment of a Catholic classic, *Butler's Lives of the Saints*. As I began to read it, I was immediately drawn to the lives of the martyrs: my patron, St. George; the boy-martyr Tarcisius, who died defending the Holy Eucharist; the North African women Perpetua and Felicity (whose Acts I would later be assigned to translate in high school Latin classes); Lawrence the deacon and the pope he served, Sixtus II. But for me then, as for many Catholics of the Western world now, "martyrdom" was something that typically happened a long time ago. Curiously, in my school days, we knew nothing of the martyrs of Mexico, who died during the Cristero rebellion against an aggressively secular Mexican regime in 1926–1929; or the many martyrs of Spain who were brutally executed by Republican forces during that country's bloody civil war in 1936–1939; or the martyrs killed by the Nazis during World War II, such as Father Alfred Delp, SJ, and the young people of the anti-Nazi "White Rose" movement; or the 108 Polish martyrs of World War II who would be beatified by John Paul II on June 13, 1999. We knew a little about the martyrs under communism, but I had no sense that I was living in the greatest century of martyrdom in Christian history—as had my parents and grandparents.

But John Paul II knew. He knew because, unlike sheltered Americans, he had lived the drama of twentieth-century martyrdom in Poland, both during the World War II Nazi occupation and under communism. And throughout his epic pontificate, he lifted up the witness of modern and contemporary martyrs, beatifying and canonizing them by the dozens (and in some cases, hundreds), adding some of them to the universal Church's liturgical calendar, and dedicating a special day of remembrance to an ecumenical array of Christian martyrs, which he celebrated with other Christian leaders at the Roman Colosseum on May 7, 2000. The choice of locale was clearly intended to link the experience of the early Christian martyrs to the martyrs of the twentieth century—and to remind the whole Church that *martyrdom is both a permanent feature of Christian life and the most perfect form of Christian witness.*

Why is that? I think it's because of that Law of the Gift we've discussed before. If a law of self-giving is hardwired into us as the very structure of our spiritual and moral lives, then the most radical form of self-giving, of liberating obedience to that law, is the giving that is literally "unto death." The martyr is the Christian most fully conformed to the crucified Christ. The martyr is also the Christian witness who can, in his or her death, make the most radical, complete gift of self.

Pope Paul VI once observed that "modern man listens more willingly to witnesses than to teachers, and if he does listen to teachers, it is because they are witnesses." John Paul II, for his part, believed that the blood of the twentieth-century martyrs—those most compelling teachers of the faith—had prepared the ground for a new season of sowing: the season of what he called the New Evangelization. It was a conviction as old as the second-century Church Father Tertullian ("The blood of martyrs is the seed of the Church") and as contemporary as the morning newspaper's headlines. John Paul II quoted Tertullian's maxim in his Spiritual Testament; yet the truth to which Tertullian gave expression remains rather detached from the spiritual and intellectual experience of twenty-first-century Catholics in the West.

There is a place I'd like to take you next, however, where something is being done about that.

As its name suggests, Tiber Island lies in the midst of the river that traverses Rome and that once made the city a great, rowdy port. In the heyday of the Roman Empire, Tiber Island was home to a temple dedicated to the Roman god Aesculapius, who, in the regnant mythology of the day, was one of the divine representatives of medicine, and especially of healing. Thus his temple on Tiber Island became a place where the city's sick—who were not usually well cared for, except by Christians—came to seek remedies for their ills. The island's shape suggests a boat, and the Romans eventually "carved" the island to resemble a ship: travertine stone was installed on the island's banks, walls were built around the periphery, and an obelisk (suggesting a mast) was erected in the center of the island, which was connected to the city by two ancient stone bridges you can still walk across today.

In 998, Emperor Otto III built a basilica on the site of the Temple of Aesculapius to house the relics of his compatriot St. Adalbert, who was martyred while on a mission in what is now Poland. The apostle Bartholomew was later made the basilica's co-patron; over time, the basilica came to be known simply as St. Bartholomew on Tiber Island. In 1584, the tradition of Tiber Island as a place of healing was revived when the Hospitaller Order of St. John of God (known in Italian as the *Fatebenefratelli*, the "Do-Good Brothers") built a hospital near the basilica, which they served from the monastery they also built on the site.

St. Bartholomew on Tiber Island houses many fine works of art, including a thirteenth-century facade mosaic depicting Christ blessing the multitude, and interior fresco cycles by Antonio Caracci and Giovanni Battista Mercati. The visual centerpiece of the basilica in the twenty-first century, however, is a new work: the Icon of the New Martyrs, mounted above the high altar.

In preparation for the Great Jubilee of 2000, John Paul II established a Commission on the New Christian

Martyrs of the Twentieth Century. The commission did its research at St. Bartholomew's, assembling some 12,000 files on those who had borne heroic witness to the faith all over the world. After that work had helped shape the ecumenical Jubilee commemoration of the New Martyrs at the Colosseum, John Paul wanted the momentum generated by the study to continue, so he asked that the witness of the twentieth-century martyrs be especially memorialized at St. Bartholomew's. In response to the Pope's request, the Icon of the New Martyrs was written, drawing on symbols from the Book of Revelation. It was solemnly dedicated in October 2002 at an ecumenical service led by Cardinal Francis George of Chicago (whose Roman "title," or parish, was St. Bartholomew's) and Patriarch Teoctist of the Romanian Orthodox Church.

The Icon of the New Martyrs bears artistic witness to the ecumenical nature of twentieth-century martyrdom, as it honors Christians of different confessions who made the ultimate sacrifice for fidelity to Christ. Just as impressive are the basilica's side chapels, which the St. Egidio Community (which has had its second Roman home at St. Bartholomew's since 1993) has converted into a Memorial of the New Martyrs arranged by period and region. The artifacts collected in these chapels are deeply moving.

Here is one of the stones the Polish secret police used to bludgeon to death Blessed Jerzy Popiełuszko, whom you met in another letter; the stone was recovered from the plastic bag in which his battered body was found on the bed of the Vistula River. Here, in another memorial, is the Bible of Shahbaz Bhatti, the Pakistani Christian parliamentarian and minister of minority affairs, an advocate of tolerance and religious freedom who was murdered in 2011 after protesting his country's legal concessions to Islamist extremists. Here are small crosses and rosaries, patens and chalices, made out of concentration camp and slave-labor camp detritus by the martyr-victims of Nazism and communism. Here is the crozier, the shepherd's staff, of Cardinal Juan Jesús Posadas Ocampo, archbishop of Guadalajara, killed by Mexican narcotraffickers on May 24, 1993. Here are the rosary and paten of a Russian Orthodox priest, ecumenist, and martyr, Father Alexander Men, axe-murdered on May 9, 1990. Here is the pectoral cross of Father Josep Maria Noguer i Tarafa, parish priest of Santa Pau in Catalonia, executed on August 9, 1936. Here is the stole of Father Giuseppe Puglisi, a parish priest in Sicily, killed by the Mafia on September 15, 1993.

And here are mementos of Father Christian de Chergé, one of the Trappist monks of Tibhirin in Algeria who were martyred in 1996. Father Christian's last testament—written, as its closing lines indicate, with the murderer who would cut his throat in mind—is one of the great documents of contemporary Catholicism:

> If it should happen one day—and it could be today—
> that I become a victim of the terrorism which now
> seems ready to engulf all the foreigners living in Algeria,
> I would like my community, my Church, and my
> family to remember that my life was given to God and
> to this country. I ask them to accept the fact that the
> One Master of all life was not a stranger to this brutal
> departure.
>
> I would ask them to pray for me: for how could I be
> found worthy of such an offering?

I ask them to associate this death with so many other equally violent ones that are forgotten through indifference or anonymity.

My life has no more value than any other. Nor less value. . . . I should like, when the time comes, to have a moment of spiritual clarity that would allow me to beg forgiveness of God and of my fellow human beings, and at the same time forgive with all my heart the one who would strike me down . . .

Obviously, my death will appear to confirm those who hastily judged me naïve or idealistic: "Let him tell us now what he thinks of his ideals!" But these persons should know that finally my most avid curiosity will be set free. This is what I shall be able to do, God willing: immerse my gaze in that of the Father to contemplate with him His children of Islam just as He sees them, all shining with the glory of Christ, the fruit of His Passion, filled with the Gift of the Spirit, whose secret joy will always be to establish communion and restore the likeness, playing with the differences.

For this life lost, totally mine and totally theirs, I thank God, who seems to have willed it entirely for the sake of that joy in everything and in spite of everything. In this thank you, which is said for everything in my life from now on, I certainly include you, friends of yesterday and today, and you, my friends of this place, along with my mother and father, my sisters and brothers and their families—You are the hundredfold granted as was promised!

And also you, my last-minute friend, who will not have known what you were doing: Yes, I want this thank you and this goodbye to be a "God-bless" for you, too, because in God's face I see yours.

May we meet again as happy thieves in Paradise, if it please God, the Father of us both.

The relics of the New Martyrs on Tiber Island are a powerful and sobering reminder of the depravity to which hatred and evil can and do lead. Yet the Memorial is ultimately a place of comfort and a place of joy: comfort, because we are reminded here that ordinary men and women, people just like us, are capable of heroic virtue under extreme circumstances; joy, because, as the Icon suggests, this great multitude of witnesses and heroes, who have "washed their robes in the blood of the Lamb" [Revelation 7.14], now live in the radiant presence of the Thrice-Holy Trinity, their every tear wiped away and their every longing satisfied, interceding for us that we might remain faithful to the gift of Baptism and to friendship with the Lord Jesus Christ.

And here, on Tiber Island, you can hear echoes of their song, as given us by the Apostle John and set to music by Georg Friedrich Handel in one of the great chorales of his *Messiah*: "Worthy is the Lamb who was slain, to receive power and wealth and wisdom and might and honor and glory and blessing!"

Šiauliai and Tiber Island are also places to reflect on one of the titles of Mary in the Litany of Loretto: Queen of Martyrs. The litany, of course, also addresses Our Lady as Queen of Angels, Patriarchs, Prophets, Apostles, Confessors, Virgins, and indeed, All Saints. So is Mary "Queen of Martyrs" simply because she is Queen of All Saints? St. Bernard of Clairvaux, a doctor of the Church, suggested that there's more to the title than that. Mary, he teaches, is "Queen of Martyrs" because she herself was a martyr, although in a unique way. St. Bernard put it like this, in a twelfth-century homily that the Church reads every September 15 on the Memorial of Our Lady of Sorrows (which follows immediately after the September 14 Feast of the Exaltation of the Holy Cross):

> The martyrdom of the Virgin is set forth both in the prophecy of Simeon and in the actual story of our Lord's passion. The holy old man said of the infant Jesus, "He has been established as a sign which will be contradicted." He went on to say of Mary: "And your own heart will be pierced by a sword."
>
> Truly, O blessed Mother, a sword has pierced your heart . . . for the violence of sorrow has cut through your heart, and we rightly call you more than martyr, since the effect of compassion in you has gone beyond the endurance of physical suffering.
>
> Or were those words, "Woman, behold your son," not more than a sword to you, truly piercing your heart, cutting through to the division between soul and spirit? What an exchange! John is given to you in place of Jesus, the servant in place of the Lord, the disciple in place of the master; the son of Zebedee replaces the Son of God.

And in that exchange, the Church was born. Catholicism has long understood that, in the climax of the Passion, the Church was born from the water and blood that flowed from the pierced side of Christ—symbols of Baptism and the Holy Eucharist. Yet we can think of that "sacramental" birth as a sign or confirmation of the birth of the Church that took place when the dying Jesus entrusted Mary to John: Mary, mother of the incarnate Word, is now Mother to the companions of the Word-made-flesh, his disciples and friends. Thus from the cross, the Lord Jesus made Mary the Mother of the Church, the title solemnized by Pope Paul VI in 1964 when he promulgated the Second Vatican Council's Dogmatic Constitution on the Church, *Lumen Gentium* (Light of the Nations).

Mary is "Queen of Martyrs" because her complete offering of self to the will of God—the silent "Be it done unto me according to your word" at the foot of the cross—was a perfect act of discipleship. And because of that, as Bernard of Clairvaux explained, the Passion of Christ and the passion of Mary are intimately connected: "He died in body through a love greater than anyone had known. She died in spirit through a love unlike any other since his."

There are very few regions of the world where Christians are not being persecuted and martyred in the first decades of the twenty-first century. Other religious believers suffer for their religious convictions; the ancient plague of anti-Semitism seems to be crawling out of the gutter in various parts of the world (including Europe); yet, by the numbers, it is Christians who are being most relentlessly persecuted in the first decades of the third millennium. Thus in 2009 the International Society for Human Rights estimated that 80 percent of the acts of religious persecution on this planet in the early twenty-first century were aimed at Christians, while the Pew Forum, in 2012, identified anti-Christian persecution (of varying degrees of severity) in 139 countries. Among the worst offenders were, in order of awfulness, North Korea, Afghanistan, Saudi Arabia, Somalia, Iran, the Maldives, Uzbekistan, Yemen, Iraq, Pakistan, Eritrea, Laos, and Nigeria: places where, as my friend John Allen wrote, "simply being a Christian on a routine level—owning a Bible, going to church, having religious symbols in one's home, and so on—is, all by itself, dangerous."

The worst persecutors, moreover, make no distinctions between ordinary Catholics and their religious leaders. In Sudan, a knife-wielding Muslim tried to assault Cardinal Gabriel Zubeir Wako, the archbishop of Khartoum (and the tallest member of the College of Cardinals by many inches), while he was celebrating Mass; in that same country, Mariam Yehya Ibrahim was sentenced to death for apostasy when she was eight months pregnant, although she was eventually allowed to leave Sudan following mass international protests. Ibrahim's release underscores one crucial point about solidarity with the persecuted: in these extreme situations, the only protection our fellow Catholics have is the protection provided by international publicity. Young Catholics might well make the support of their persecuted brethren a priority, especially through the new technologies of social media.

While Christians are being martyred in many places in the twenty-first century, the hard fact is that most of the New Martyrs are dying at the hands of jihadist or Islamist fanatics. Those same fanatics are also driving entire Christian communities from their ancient and ancestral homes throughout the Middle East—in some cases, from Christian settlements that can trace their histories back to the days of the Apostles and the decades immediately following. The response to this persecution has not been impressive throughout the comfortable world of Christians in the West. And that is a grave defect in our living out the virtue of solidarity.

In 2006, Pope Benedict XVI tried to identify the roots of this wave of persecution—and a possible path beyond it—in a lecture he gave at his old university in Regensburg, Germany. Widely pilloried by an ignorant world media as a grave insult to Islam, the Regensburg Lecture was in fact a brilliant reflection on the fact that all great questions are, ultimately, theological. The Pope developed that theme by suggesting that there were two great questions that history had put before Islam in the third millennium.

The first question was about religious freedom: Could Muslims find, within their own spiritual and intellectual resources, Islamic arguments for religious tolerance (including tolerance of those who convert to other faiths, like Mariam Yehya Ibrahim)? That desirable development, Benedict suggested, might lead over time (meaning centuries) to a more complete Islamic theory of religious freedom.

And the second question was about the structuring of Islamic societies: Could Muslims find, again from within their own spiritual and intellectual resources, Islamic arguments for distinguishing between religious and political authority in a just state? That equally desirable development might make Muslim societies more humane in themselves and less dangerous to their neighbors, especially if it were linked to an emerging Islamic case for religious tolerance.

Pope Benedict went on to propose that interreligious dialogue between Catholics and Muslims might well focus on these two linked questions. The Catholic Church, he freely conceded, had had its own struggles developing a Catholic case for religious freedom in a constitutionally governed polity in which the Church played a key role in civil society, but not directly in governance. But Catholicism had finally done so: not by surrendering to secular political philosophy, but by using what it had learned from political modernity in order to reach back into its own tradition, recover elements of its thinking about faith, religion, and society that had gotten lost over time, and develop its teaching about the just society for the future.

Was such a process of retrieval-and-development possible in Islam? That was the Big Question posed by Benedict XVI in the Regensburg Lecture; it is a tragedy that the question was, first, misunderstood, and then ignored. The results of that misunderstanding and that ignorance—and a lot of other misunderstanding and ignorance—are on grisly display throughout the Middle East: in the decimation of ancient Christian communities; in barbarities that have shocked a seemingly unshockable West, like the crucifixion and beheading of Christians; in tottering states; in the shattered hopes that the twenty-first-century Middle East might recover from its various cultural and political illnesses and find a path to a more humane future.

If the conversation about Islam's future that Benedict XVI proposed is to take place, Christian leaders must help prepare the way by naming, forthrightly, the pathologies of Islamism and jihadism; by ending their ahistorical apologies for twentieth-century colonialism (lamely imitating the worst of Western academic blather about the Arab Islamic world); and by stating publicly that, when innocent people are being murdered by bloody-minded fanatics, armed force, deployed prudently and purposefully by those with the will and the means to defend innocents, is morally justified.

Perhaps, in the years ahead, you can help advance the conversation for which Benedict XVI prophetically called at Regensburg in 2006.

In 2010, Cardinal Francis George of Chicago, trying to underscore what the consequences of an aggressively secular society might be, proposed a bold hypothetical: "I expect to die in bed, my successor will die in prison, and his successor will die a martyr in the public square." That certainly got his audience's attention, and thanks to someone's smartphone, the comment quickly went viral on the Internet.

Cardinal George's hypothetical was not, he later wrote, a prediction, but an illustration of what might happen if certain trends in the contemporary West played themselves out to their logical conclusions. And whether the ninth archbishop of Chicago dies in prison and the tenth is publicly shot as a cautionary lesson to others is really not the point: the point is *that faithful discipleship today has its costs.*

Perhaps the cost already familiar to you as a young Catholic is the incomprehension or mockery of peers who mistake the Church's moral teaching for a set of shackles, when in fact it's a program of liberation, if a challenging and demanding one. I've had personal experience of young Catholics who, in prestigious universities, have been given grades below what their work deserved because they had the temerity to challenge the politically correct "answer" required by the tenured bigots teaching them. Catholics in the healing professions are under intense pressure to conform to dubious, even death-dealing, "medical" practices prescribed for reasons of confused "compassion" or economic efficiency. Catholics in politics are counseled to trim their moral convictions to fit the prevailing winds if they want to attain or retain public office.

When these pressures are brought to bear on you, there's another piece of advice from Cardinal George that's worth remembering:

> God sustains the world, in good times and in bad. Catholics, along with many others, believe that only one person has overcome and rescued history: Jesus Christ, Son of God and Son of the Virgin Mary, savior of the world and head of his body, the Church. Those who gather at his cross and by his empty tomb, no matter their nationality, are on the right side of history. Those who lie about him and persecute or harass his followers in any age might imagine they are bringing something new to history, but they inevitably end up ringing the changes on the old human story of sin and oppression. There is nothing "progressive" about sin, even when it is promoted as "enlightened."
>
> The world divorced from the God who created and redeemed it inevitably comes to a bad end. It's on the wrong side of the only history that finally matters.

Through friendship with Jesus Christ and incorporation into his body, the Church, you've put yourself on the right side of history. And not only in some ultimate sense (although that is, finally, the most important sense). For even if Catholics in the West are entering a season of persecution like that described in Cardinal George's hypothetical, it's important to remember what the cardinal said about the *eleventh* archbishop of Chicago, after the eighth had died in bed, the ninth had died in prison, and his successor had been executed: the next in that episcopal line, the cardinal concluded, "will pick up the shards of a ruined society and slowly help rebuild civilization, as the Church has done so often in human history."

CELL 18, BLOCK 11, KL-AUSCHWITZ

The Mystery of Evil

he modern railroad station in the town center welcomes visitors to *Oświęcim Miasto Pokoju*—Oświęcim, the City of Peace. That was not the case here for four and a half years in the 1940s, when the Polish town that had been incorporated into the Third Reich and renamed "Auschwitz" became the home of *Konzentrationslager Auschwitz*, a complex of labor and extermination camps. In KL-Auschwitz, industrialized mass murder, motivated by racial hatreds and demonic nationalism, took the lives of well over a million human beings, who were systematically slaughtered not for what they had done, but for who they were.

The Nazis were not political modernity's only practitioners of genocide in service to a warped, satanic ideology. Large swaths of Siberia are a vast cemetery of unmarked graves where millions died in slave-labor camps, islands in what Aleksandr Solzhnitsyn called the "Gulag Archipelago." Millions of Ukrainians were deliberately starved to death in the *Holodomor*, another act of Stalinist genocide. Mao Zedong's "Cultural Revolution" killed tens of millions of Chinese, as did his insane attempts to collectivize Chinese agriculture. The killing fields of Pol Pot's Cambodia witnessed the murder of 2 million more. Jihadist Islam does not cavil at mass slaughter, and has introduced to the twenty-first century the brutalities of beheadings filmed for YouTube.

But in a world deeply confused about good and evil, the word "Auschwitz" retains a singular resonance, evoking the *mysterium iniquitatis*, the mystery of evil, in an unmistakable way and reminding humanity of the depth of wickedness into which men and women can sink. The twenty-first century is uncomfortable with the notion of hell; the twentieth century built hell, here.

Almost three millennia before German industrialists competed for the contracts to produce the lethal Zyklon-B crystals, the gas chambers, and the crematoria of Auschwitz, the Psalmist grappled with the darkest recesses of the human condition, and the relation of God to all that, in words the Catholic Church prays at Compline, or Night Prayer, every Friday:

> Lord my God, I call for help by day;
> I cry at night before you.
> Let my prayer come into your presence.
> O turn your ear to my cry.

For my soul is filled with evils;
My life is on the brink of the grave.
I am reckoned as one in the tomb:
I have reached the end of my strength,

like one alone among the dead;
like the slain lying in their graves;
like those you remember no more,
cut off, as they are, from your land.

You have laid me in the depths of the tomb,
in places that are dark, in the depths.
Your anger weighs down upon me:
I am drowned beneath your waves.

You have taken away my friends
and made me hateful in their sight.
Imprisoned, I cannot escape;
my eyes are sunken with grief.

I call to you, Lord, all the day long;
to you I stretch out my hands.
Will you work your wonders for the dead?
Will your wonders be known in the dark
or your justice in the land of oblivion?

As for me, Lord, I call to you for help:
in the morning my prayer comes before you.
Lord, why do you reject me?
Why do you hide your face?

Wretched, close to death from my youth,
I have borne your trials; I am numb.
Your fury has swept down upon me;
Your terrors have utterly destroyed me.

They surround me all the day like a flood,
they assail me all together.
Friend and companion you have taken away:
My one companion is darkness.

[Psalm 88]

Few places on this planet so graphically embody the Psalmist's lament—"You have laid me in the depths of the tomb / in places that are dark, in the depths"— as Block 11 of Auschwitz I, the first of the camps in the Auschwitz-Birkenau complex. Block 11 was the punishment block, where prisoners were tortured in a variety of ingenious ways, one crueler than the next. The basement of Block 11 was reserved for special horrors, including the "standing cells," where four prisoners were made to stand all night in a small concrete box before being returned to work the next day. Block 11's basement also includes the "dark cells," which had minute windows and solid doors: the prisoners slowly suffocated as they exhausted the available oxygen; the Nazis sometimes lit a candle to burn the oxygen faster.

Then there is Cell 18 of Block 11: the starvation bunker. Here, prisoners condemned to death were left without food or water until they perished. Some managed to live on in agony for extended periods before dying.

One of them was a Conventual Franciscan friar named Maximilian Kolbe. A paschal candle, placed in Cell 18 of Block 11 by John Paul II in 1979, bears silent witness to Kolbe's martyrdom—and symbolizes the Christian response to the *mysterium iniquitatis*.

Raymund Kolbe was born in Zduńska Wola, in the Russian-ruled section of partitioned Poland, on January 8, 1894, the son of an ethnic German father and a Polish mother. When he was twelve, he experienced a vision of the Blessed Virgin Mary that he later described in these terms: "I asked the Mother of God what was to become of me. Then she came to me holding two crowns, one white, the other red. She asked me if I was willing to accept either of these crowns. The white one meant that I would persevere in purity, and the red that I should become a martyr. I said that I would accept them both."

Kolbe entered the novitiate of the Conventual Franciscans in 1911 and was given the religious name Maximilian. When he professed final vows in 1914 he took the additional religious name "Maria," such that he was known in religious life as "Maximilian Maria"; he was ordained a priest in 1918. After his doctoral studies in Rome, where he earned degrees in philosophy from the Gregorian University and in theology from the Seraphicum (the Pontifical University of St. Bonaventure), he returned to Poland, where he did seminary teaching, organized a Marian movement known as the Militia Immaculata, and founded a new monastery in Niepokalanów, which became a major publishing center for a variety of projects, including Kolbe's monthly magazine, the *Knight of the Immaculate.*

Kolbe went on missionary journeys to Asia in the 1930s, during which he founded a monastery in Nagasaki and earned the nickname "Mad Max" for the fervor of his evangelism. Returning to Poland in 1938, he amplified his efforts by starting Radio Niepokalanów, which was both another vehicle for his evangelization efforts and a stern critic of the Nazi regime in Germany. During the Nazi occupation, the Niepokalanów monastery sheltered Polish Jews and published anti-German materials; it was eventually shut down by the Germans on February 17, 1941, the day Kolbe was arrested. On May 28, he was transferred to KL-Auschwitz and tattooed with the prisoner number 16670.

Two months after Kolbe arrived at the camp that would be known to history as Auschwitz I (after the extermination camp at Birkenau, Auschwitz II, was built to accelerate the "Final Solution" and the extermination of European Jewry), three prisoners escaped. In retaliation, the deputy camp commander, SS-Hauptsturmführer Karl Fritzsch, selected at random ten men during the morning roll call; all were summarily condemned to death in the starvation bunker. When one of them, Franciszek Gajowniczek, cried, "My wife! My children! I will never see them again," Prisoner 16670 volunteered to take his place, declaring himself a Catholic priest. Thus Father Maximilian Maria Kolbe, OFM Conv., was stripped naked and taken with nine other men to Cell 18 in Block 11.

There, Father Kolbe led the prisoners in prayers and hymns until, one by one, they died of starvation, dehydration, or both. Kolbe alone remained alive after two weeks, when, wanting to clear the cell, a guard injected Kolbe with a lethal dose of carbolic acid. His remains were cremated the following day, August 15, the Solemnity of the Assumption of Our Lady, who had promised him two crowns and had kept her promise.

Maximilian Kolbe's sacrifice became widely known in Poland shortly after the war, and a cause for his beatification and canonization was quickly introduced. He was beatified as a confessor by Pope Paul VI in 1971, but was only given the honorific title "martyr of charity" at the time, for Kolbe's death did not seem to have satisfied the traditional criterion for martyrdom, death *in odium fidei* (in hatred of the faith).

John Paul II, however, had a different idea (as did many Poles and Germans, who hoped that Kolbe would be venerated as a martyr). John Paul commissioned a study of Kolbe's death in anticipation of his canonization, and that commission came to the same conclusion as Paul VI: Kolbe had died a death of heroic charity, but he had not died *in odium fidei*. Yet on October 10, 1982, when John Paul II processed into St. Peter's Square for the Mass at which Maximilian Maria Kolbe would be declared a saint—a Mass attended by Franciszek Gajowniczek, the man for whose life he had sacrificed his own—the Pope was wearing the red vestments used to honor a martyr. And in his homily, he underscored the point symbolically represented by that choice of vesture: "In virtue of my apostolic authority, I have decreed that Maximilian Maria Kolbe, who following his beatification was venerated as a confessor, will henceforth be venerated also as a martyr."

Temptations to regard this decision as Polish special-leading should be stoutly resisted, for John Paul II was making an important theological point, which bears on our visit here to KL-Auschwitz.

Catholicism teaches the dignity of the human person; Nazism and communism denied that dignity—indeed, lived (and murdered) in denial and hatred of it. To persecute others in hatred of their human dignity is to persecute Christ and his Church, for Christ is the embodiment of the dignity of the human person and the Church is his Body. And therefore, John Paul II seemed to suggest, systematic *odium hominis*—systematic hatred of the human person—is a contemporary equivalent to the traditional criterion for martyrdom, *odium fidei*. The truth of the dignity of the human person is not peripheral to the Catholic faith; it is an integral part of the faith. Anyone who hates that truth hates, implicitly, the faith—and hates the Church's Lord. Modern totalitarianism, in its Nazi or communist forms, was an exercise of *odium fidei*, because it demeaned and degraded human beings, reducing people to things in the name of racial or class abstractions.

John Paul's decision to honor Maximilian Kolbe as a martyr took an important lesson from the twentieth century for the Church's third millennium: *ultramundane ideologies hate the faith in principle, and thus must be resisted.* Ideas have consequences, and bad ideas can have lethal consequences. If the twentieth century should have taught humanity anything, it should have taught us that, and John Paul II wanted to underscore the point.

Yet to walk through the gravel pathways of Auschwitz I, or along the infamous railroad tracks of Auschwitz II–Birkenau, is to be reminded that more was at work in these modern hells than ideology.

In Martin Amis's novel *The Zone of Interest*, various Nazi officials are depicted having dinner at the home of a concentration camp commandant. Thanks to the novelist's craft, their table-talk and its casual blindness to evil is as subtly revealing as it is horrifying. One of the guests is bragging about the educational credentials of the men present at a recent meeting: "Of the fifteen attendees? *Eight* doctorates . . . Strength in depth. *That's* how you get the optimal decisions."

The meeting in question was held in a villa at #56–58 Am Broßen in the Berlin suburb of Wannsee on January 20, 1942. Chaired by SS-Obergruppenführer Reinhard Heydrich, those fifteen officials present, eight of whom had earned coveted German doctoral degrees in fields including law, planned what became known as the "Final Solution" to the *Judenfrage*, the "Jewish Question." That "solution" was the deliberate, systematized mass murder of all European Jews, to be undertaken in special extermination camps that would be built in the parts of Poland that had been absorbed into Germany or in the Nazi-administered part of occupied Poland known as the *Generalgouvernement*—better described by the historian Norman Davies as "Gestapoland." In the *Generalgouvernement*, as in KL-Auschwitz, there was no "rule of law." Random, violent death awaited any Pole whose attitude struck an SS officer, Gestapo agent, or Wehrmacht soldier as insolent or insubordinate. Systematized death—murder undertaken as an industrial process—awaited those transported to the new camps: Auschwitz II–Birkenau and Chelmno in the Third Reich; Belzec, Majdanek, Sobibor, and Treblinka in the *Generalgouvernement*.

The table-talk in Martin Amis's novel is chilling in its portrayal of the effects of evil on putatively civilized human beings, and in its reminder that learning detached from wisdom and morality can lead to wickedness and brutality. So are the grainy photos of the "selection process" at Auschwitz II–Birkenau, which are displayed in one of the old prisoner blocks in what is now the State Museum at Auschwitz I. There are the train tracks, along which trainload after trainload of doomed men, women, and children arrived at their destination, the Auschwitz II camp, having been shuttled like cattle across Europe. There, standing along the sidings and platforms, are the arbiters of death-now or death-later: the uniformed servants of the Third Reich, choosing which prisoners would be sent immediately to the gas chambers, which would be temporarily housed in the wooden huts, whose brick chimneys still dot the landscape of Birkenau, and which would be the subjects of hideous medical "experiments" by Dr. Josef Mengele. The photos, as I say, are grainy and black-and-white, but the Nazi officials can be seen clearly enough, and there is no sense of horror or shame on their faces: some are smoking peacefully while they consider the sight before them; others seem to be joking with their Nazi colleagues.

As you walk along the platforms where the "selection process" at Auschwitz II–Birkenau was carried out, the *mysterium iniquitatis* ceases to be an abstraction. "Evil" and "sin" are not theoretical constructs here, in the sense of "evil" construed as the absence of good, and "sin" being defined intellectually as a failure to conform to the divine will. Evil and sin are very real here, and they are lethal in the last degree.

That reality, I suggest, means taking seriously the reality of the Evil One and his impact on the human condition, from that difficult afternoon in the Garden of Eden until today. The appeal to Satan and his minions as a causal factor in great historical events should be deployed with great care. But at Auschwitz, wrestling with that possibility is virtually unavoidable, at least to anyone with a biblical sense of the world and of history.

A s Jeffrey Burton Russell points out in his book *Mephistopheles: The Devil in the Modern World*, "the fact that most people today dismiss the idea [of Satan or the devil] as old-fashioned, even 'disproved,' is the result of a muddle in which science is called upon to pass judgment in matters unrelated to science. . . . [It] is certainly true that the Devil cannot exist in a scientific sense. But he can exist in a theological sense, in a mythological sense, in a psychological sense, and in a historical sense; and these approaches are, like science, capable of fixing a course on truth." Denying the reality of the Evil One is another way of walking through history wearing heavily tinted Enlightenment spectacles, which not only filter out a lot of light but also obscure the depths of darkness in the world. For in an ultramundane, hyper-secular worldview, Satan makes no sense, and "satanic" is reduced to an adjective describing someone exceptionally odious, like Adolf Hitler or Joseph Stalin.

In a biblical view of the world, however, in which "history" is the great contest between God's love and all that would frustrate God's love (an optic that informs the last book of the Bible, Revelation), Satan is entirely real, and so are his effects in history. You can see those effects at work here in what John Paul II called the "Golgotha of the modern world." Just as at Golgotha, where Satan must have tempted the crucified Jesus to despair and apostasy, here, when we walk the paths trod by men and women who imagined themselves civilized, but who had become instruments of satanic hatred, we can be tempted to abandon the faith, and the hope to which the faith gives birth.

The now almost forgotten "Death of God" movement, which was trendy enough to garner the first *Time* magazine cover ever composed of letters alone (*Is God Dead?*), took at least some of its inspiration from Auschwitz, and the claim that here, the God of the Bible, by abandoning the children of Abraham with whom he had entered into covenant, "died" as a plausible subject of belief. That quandary—"Where was God at Auschwitz?"—shaped some of the most powerful literature of the Holocaust. And for many years a story circulated that, at Auschwitz, a trio of rabbis had in fact put the God of Abraham, Isaac, and Jacob on trial, finding him guilty. The story was largely regarded as apocryphal until Nobel laureate Elie Wiesel, in a 2008 interview with the *Jewish Chronicle*, gave the story a fascinating new twist. Confronted with skepticism about the story, Mr. Wiesel replied, "Why should they know what happened? I was the only one there. It happened at night;

there were just three people. At the end of the trial they used the word *chayav*, rather than 'guilty.' It means 'He owes us something.' Then we went to pray."

There is no blinking the reality of Satan when one confronts the reality of Auschwitz. Nor is there any blinking the reality of evil and its power in the world. But as Elie Wiesel's novels suggest, and as Jeffrey Burton Russell would likely agree, these are matters best approached through the arts, rather than through abstractions and logic-chopping. One such effort produced one of the great religious paintings of the twentieth century, a reproduction of which has hung over the desk in my study for twenty-five years.

Marc Chagall (known in childhood as Moishe Shagal) was born in 1887 to Jewish parents in what is now Belarus. His career, in which themes from the Jewish folk culture of Eastern Europe and various modernist influences combined to produce remarkable art, took him all over Europe, although he lived in the United States from 1941 to 1948. His stained-glass compositions are at least as well known as his paintings, and include the magnificent windows depicting the twelve tribes of Israel in the synagogue of the Hadassah Medical Center in Jerusalem, his "America windows" at the Art Institute of Chicago, and the windows of St. Stephen's Church in Mainz—all of which illustrate Pablo Picasso's point that, "when Matisse dies, Chagall will be the only [artist] left who understands what color really is." Chagall's religious paintings evoked controversy (some of it fictionally re-created, albeit in a wholly different setting, in Chaim Potok's novel *My Name is Asher Lev*); one of his boldest efforts is the painting that has looked over my work for a quarter-century, the *White Crucifixion*.

In an earlier letter, I introduced you to the great historian Jaroslav Pelikan. It was his book *Jesus Through the Centuries* that first drew my attention to Chagall's *White Crucifixion* and its remarkable Jewishness, so permit me to cite his description of it here:

> The crucified figure in Chagall's painting wears not a nondescript loincloth, but the *tallith* of a devout and observant rabbi. His prophecy, "They will put you out of the synagogues; indeed, the hour is coming when whoever kills you will think he is offering service to God" [John 16.2], is seen as having been fulfilled, in a supreme irony, when some who claimed to be his disciples regarded the persecution of Jews as service to God. And the central figure does indeed belong to the people of Israel, but he belongs no less to the Church and to the whole world—precisely because he belongs to the people of Israel.

Chagall's painting puts the Crucified One at the very center of the twentieth century's genocides. Painted in 1938, shortly after *Kristallnacht*, the Nazi pogrom of November 9–10, 1938, *White Crucifixion* shows Christ surrounded by fleeing Jews and burning synagogues; yet Chagall's understanding of the *odium hominis* involved in the great twentieth-century totalitarianisms included communists as well as Nazis, as a mob flying the Red Flag careens across the rubble of the century from the top left corner of the painting. The mourning angels typically deployed in renderings of the Crucifixion are replaced here by three Jewish patriarchs and a matriarch, while a ceremonial candelabrum burns beneath the feet of the Crucified One, whose head is surrounded by a halo, across which is written, in Hebrew, the inscription Pilate ordered placed on the cross of Christ.

It is an altogether startling work of art, remarkable in its rendering of the inhumanity of which humanity is capable, and striking in its theological insight: for here, the Christian believer would say, is the answer to the question so many posed at, and after, Auschwitz, "Where is God?"—the answer is, God is right here, transforming the suffering of his people through the Son, who was sent into history by the Father to transform history so that fear, and hatred, and death do not have the final word.

Go back to Psalm 88 a moment and recall the biblical songwriter's heartrending lament: "You have laid me in the depths of the tomb / in places that are dark, in the depths. . . . Friend and companion you have taken away / my one companion in darkness." The Church prays that psalm every week because the Psalmist's cry from the heart resonates with the Church's cry each Friday as the Lord is taken from the cross and laid in the tomb. From there, the Apostles' Creed tells us, he "descended into hell." But what does that affirmation, which we typically breeze through when reciting the ancient baptismal "symbol" or creed of the Church of Rome, really mean? And what might that affirmation say to us today?

There has been an interesting theological debate over the "descent into hell" in the late twentieth and early twenty-first centuries, initiated by Swiss theologian Hans Urs von Balthasar's argument that the "descent" means that Jesus experienced total God-forsakenness between his death and the Resurrection. Critics of Balthasar's theology of the descent point out that hundreds of years of Christian preaching and art have depicted the "descent" in quite a different way: as Christ's triumphant march into the netherworld, where he frees those in darkness to accompany him into the light of the Kingdom of God, which was inaugurated by his ministry and, above all, by his Resurrection.

Thus each Holy Saturday, as it awaits the Easter Vigil, the Church ponders an ancient homily in the Office of Readings: "Something strange is happening—there is a great silence on earth today, a great silence and stillness. The whole earth keeps silence because the King is asleep." But though he is asleep in the tomb, he is not inactive. No, as the anonymous Greek preacher of that ancient sermon puts it, he has "gone to search for our first parent, as for a lost sheep." Then, exercising the Church's imagination, the preacher describes the message the King brings to Adam in what the Psalmist called "the depths":

Awake, O sleeper, and rise from the dead. . . . I am your God, who for your sake have become your son. Out of love for you and your descendants I now command by my own authority all who are held in bondage to come forth, all who are in darkness to be enlightened, all who are sleeping to arise. I order you, O sleeper, to awake. I did not create you to be a prisoner in hell. Rise from the dead, for I am the life of the dead. Rise up, work of my hands, you who were created in my image. Rise, let us leave this place, for you are in me and I am in you; together we form one person and we cannot be separated. . . .

Rise, let us leave this place. The enemy led you out of the earthly paradise. I will not restore you to that paradise, but I will enthrone you in heaven. . . . The throne formed by cherubim awaits you, its bearers swift and eager. The bridal chamber is adorned, the banquet is ready, the eternal dwelling places are prepared, the treasure houses of all good things lie open. The kingdom of heaven has been prepared for you from all eternity.

I don't know whether Maximilian Kolbe, dying in Cell 18 of Block 11 at Auschwitz, meditated on that text while ministering to those who were condemned to an agonizing death with him. But the Christian conviction expressed by that ancient homilist is surely what sustained Kolbe in his slow-motion martyrdom: the conviction that love is stronger than evil and stronger than death. That is why the Catholic and Christian answer to the *mysterium iniquitatis* is not, finally, an argument, but an event: the Paschal Mystery of the Cross and Resurrection, in which Christ, "obedient even unto death" [Philippians 2.8], by taking the whole world's fear upon himself, immolated that fear in the fire of divine love, such that we, the members of his Body, are now empowered to live beyond fear.

One of the greatest theologians of the twentieth century, Joseph Ratzinger, unpacked this article of faith in these terms:

Yes, Jesus died, he "descended" into the mysterious depths death leads to. He went into the ultimate solitude where no one can accompany us, because "being dead" is above all loss of communication. It is isolation where love does not penetrate. In this sense Christ "descended into hell" whose essence is precisely the loss of love, being cut off from God and man. But wherever he goes, "hell" ceases to be hell, because he himself is life and love, because he is the bridge which connects man and God and therefore also connects men among themselves. And thus the descent is at the same time also transformation. The final solitude no longer exists—except for the one who wants it, who rejects love from within and from its foundation, because he seeks only himself, wants to be from and for himself.

God does not condemn anyone to hell. Hell is chosen by those who choose to ally themselves with the Evil One— and who, in doing so, obliterate, utterly, their identity.

It all comes back, as always, to Easter. Easter faith, which comes from meeting the Risen Lord and becoming his friend and disciple, is the faith that allows us to see Christ's death as transformative—transforming death from oblivion to Passover, from ultimate slavery to final liberation. Easter faith allows us to look on Chagall's *White Crucifixion* and know that the haters do not have the last word, even as we are fully cognizant of the horrors the artist masterfully depicts. Easter faith allows us to stand at those railroad tracks in Auschwitz II–Birkenau and realize, even as we shudder and weep, that this is not the end of the line of the human story.

CHARTRES CATHEDRAL, FRANCE

What Beauty Teaches Us

et's now travel from the depths of ugliness to the summit of beauty.

In an earlier letter, I was reckless enough to suggest that the Sistine Chapel is the most extraordinary room in the world. Let me crawl out even farther on the comparative limb and propose that Chartres Cathedral is the most extraordinary building in the world. I've been in the Dome of the Rock in Jerusalem; it's magnificent, but it isn't Chartres. I've not been to the Taj Mahal, but I very much doubt that it could rival Chartres. Chartres is stone and glass into which have been poured the obedience of faith and a passionate, transforming love for Christ, for Mary, for the world, and for the beauty of the human. The result is what its builders imagined it to be—an antechamber to heaven.

It's a good thing to come here when you're young. I was forty-six, alas, before I finally got to Chartres, thanks to my friend Jean Duchesne. Jean had been deeply involved in preparing the 1997 World Youth Day in Paris, during which I'd stayed with his family in their Parisian flat. After a busy week, we had all gone to the Duchesnes' country place in Normandy to rest up, and it was from there that Jean and I drove to Chartres for the day. After a fine ramble through the French countryside, there it was, on the near horizon, without much warning: a great stone ship, massive yet ethereal, silhouetted against the sky. Imagine how a medieval pilgrim must have felt after days of trudging the dirt roads and pre-harvest fields of France when that vision came into sight.

The contemplative is not my natural cast of mind. But there was something about the cathedral of Chartres that rendered me, quite literally, speechless. Looking through and studying a great building for the first time, I usually like to talk about it with friends or a knowledgeable guide. Not here. Here, I just wanted to look, and admire, and absorb. Absorb what? It's not easy to say. Perhaps I'll simply call it the beauty of the place—the beauty of Chartres' stained glass. I didn't want to talk about it; I simply wanted to let the luminous splendors of that incomparable glass wash over me in great waves. I had the sense of praying, without words. Like the eleventh and twelfth stations of the Church of the Holy Sepulcher in Jerusalem, although for very different reasons, Chartres invites us to "practice the presence"—to rest and just *be*, in the beautiful, turbulent, peaceful presence of God.

Which is what I did for the better part of three hours before my practical French friend suggested that it was time for lunch.

While we were eating, we talked about the Gothic and its peculiarities. You've read about the ways in which the vaulting, the height, and the flying buttresses of Gothic cathedrals evoke a sense of transcendence. So, obviously, do those extraordinary glass "walls" framed by intricately chiseled stone. The Gothic creates a sense of suspension, of floating in space, about itself; and when we're "inside" the Gothic it's not hard to get a similar sense of weightlessness. But all that's familiar to you. My friend Duchesne suggested a few other reasons for the Gothic's unique permeability to the transcendent.

Jean pointed out that Gothic is a particularly successful form of Christian architecture because it's cranky. Things aren't uniform. In fact, Chartres displays a settled determination *not* to be uniform. The great towers don't match—one is intricately decorated with stone webbing; the other is plainly roofed. Then there are those three great rose windows. Each is structured by a different geometric form, with circles dominating the South Rose window, squares the North Rose, and circles within asymmetrical ellipses the West Rose. This jumble, Jean suggested, was quite deliberate: God didn't make a one-size-fits-all world, and the builders of Chartres wanted that to be reflected in their design.

The Gothic also manages to combine the majestic and the personal in ways that other styles don't quite match.

The majesty of Chartres is obvious; you have to look a little more closely for the personal, but it's there. For the people who made Chartres possible by their generosity—its donors large and small—are recognized in that extraordinary glass. Ploughmen, priests, nobles, drapers, bakers, butchers, bankers, fishmongers, vintners, farriers, apothecaries, haberdashers, wheelwrights, carpenters, shoemakers, and pilgrims had all contributed to the building of Chartres; and they're all memorialized, not by name but by luminous image in over a hundred scenes scattered throughout the windows. Some of them gave fortunes; others undoubtedly gave little more than the biblical widow's mite. They're all there, and they all count, in the democracy of receiving-and-giving that is the Church.

Which is appropriate enough, because the building of Chartres, which certainly involved enormous skill and craftsmanship, was also something of a populist enterprise. Today's Gothic masterpiece was built out from an earlier structure, which had been badly damaged in a fire that destroyed much of the city and left only the crypt, the tower foundations, and the west facade of the twelfth-century cathedral. Once it was clear that the town's most famous relic—the *Sancta Camisia*, a garment believed to have been worn by Mary during the birth of Christ—had been spared, the people immediately demanded that a new cathedral be built. Thousands of townspeople went voluntarily to the quarry at Berchères, singing hymns and chanting. There, they loaded wooden-wheeled carts with great blocks of stone and pushed, pulled, and dragged the stone five miles back to Chartres, singing and chanting all the way.

The entire Chartres project seems, in fact, to have been accompanied by an exceptional outpouring of generosity. The great fire was in 1194. By 1223, less than thirty years later, much of the structure we know today had been completed, thanks to the philanthropy of the donors and the enthusiasm of the builders and craftsmen. The cathedral wasn't consecrated until 1260 (at which point the idea of building nine steeples was, happily, abandoned). But the bulk of the work had been done in a breathtakingly short period of time, in a world without electricity or steam engines or gigantic cranes of the sort you now see at every major building site in the world.

Why? I think there were several reasons, and they're all interesting. The *Sancta Camisia* was a famous relic that attracted large numbers of pilgrims. The local people thought of its home, the Chartres Cathedral, as "the earthly palace of the Queen of Heaven," according to the great Chartres scholar and guide Malcolm Miller. And if the Queen's home burned down, her loyal subjects ought to build her another one even more splendid than the last. That was certainly one driving force behind the rapid construction of Chartres.

Then there was the sense of expectation that permeated medieval life. The people of the Middle Ages took the idea of Christ's Second Coming very seriously. But as the Lord himself had said, "of that day and hour no one knows, not even the angels in heaven, nor the Son, but the Father only" [Matthew 24.36]. So it was best to be prepared—and by "prepared," medievals meant more than attending to their own souls. They meant preparing places appropriately glorious to welcome Christ at his return. You can't really understand the fantastic burst of creativity that resulted in the great Gothic cathedrals without wrestling with that fact: people were quite convinced that they were preparing a guest room, so to speak, for Christ himself. That was a powerful spur to energy, creativity, and generosity.

Those convictions also explain why the world-famous glass of Chartres is organized the way it is. You've probably been told that Gothic stained glass is didactic, its images intended to teach the basics of the biblical story and of Christian faith to illiterates. That's true as far as it goes, but to appreciate the imaginative genius involved in a place like Chartres means widening the lens of our understanding a bit. For the men who designed the Chartres windows, and the master craftsmen who executed those designs, intended the cathedral's glass walls to be nothing less than a comprehensive account of salvation history—the world's story read as *His*-story. That intention neatly coincided with the windows' didactic purpose: For what would be a more fitting reception room for Christ returning in glory than one that told the whole story that had brought the world to this climactic point—the point where it could recognize and welcome its redeemer?

That's why the first stunning quartet of windows over the Royal Portal to the cathedral, the West Rose and its three accompanying lancets, are a summary of the great narrative that unfolds throughout the rest of Chartres cathedral. The central and largest window in the triptych of lancets is the Incarnation window—central because it depicts the chief dynamic of history: God's love for the world manifest in God's Son come in the flesh for the world's salvation.

The left lancet is the window of the Passion and Resurrection, equally stunning in its evocation of the central act in the drama of redemption. The West Rose itself is dedicated to the Last Judgment—the climax of history as *His*-story. It's the right lancet below the West Rose that perhaps best expresses the richness of medieval faith and imagination, however, through the use of a favorite medieval image—the Jesse Tree. Let me give you a brief excerpt from Malcolm Miller's description of it:

> Jesse, the father of David, reclines at the bottom of the window upon a bed of white linen. He is wrapped in a bright red, yellow-bordered blanket. . . . His feet are bare, like those of prophets and evangelists. . . . Above him a lamp hangs on a golden chain and a curtain flutters from a red semicircular arch, beyond which, in the spandrels, spreads the royal city of David, Bethlehem.
>
> From Jesse's groin, the source of life, springs not a rod, but the trunk of a tree, in the center of which the sap can be clearly seen rising through a succession of four kings of Judah, richly clad in red and green, yellow and purple, against a background of intense blue. . . . Although they carry neither attribute nor inscription, the four crowned figures probably represent David, Solomon, Roboam, and Abia, the first in Matthew's long list of twice-fourteen kings of Judah, Christ's royal ancestors. . . .
>
> Christ is seated at the summit of the tree . . . surrounded by doves that symbolize the seven gifts of the Holy Spirit. . . . Contained within red half-circles on either side of the figures in the tree, and turned towards them, are twice-seven Old Testament prophets bearing scrolls on

which their names are written. . . . Thus Christ's spiritual forebears frame His ancestors of the flesh and prepare for the narrative of the Incarnation, the temporal fulfillment of the prophecies, in the adjacent central lancet window.

Chartres is inconceivable without the obedience of faith. The people who built Chartres thought they were building an earthly representation of the New Jerusalem—but perhaps "representation" isn't quite the right word. Those who built Chartres and those who gave of their substance to make Chartres possible believed that, in this place, they were in the antechamber of heaven. Chartres is a uniquely permeable "border" between the mundane and the transcendent, the visible and the invisible, the ordinary and the extraordinary, the human and the divine: *and that's exactly what it was meant to be.* That's why Chartres has the awe-inspiring effect it has. That's why Chartres renders us speechless. To pass through the Royal Portal into this privileged space is, in Malcolm Miller's words, as if one were passing "through the gates of Paradise into the heavenly city itself, with its walls opened and set with glittering jewel-like stained glass windows which diffuse a mystic and divine essence: light."

Chartres is both a powerful expression and a powerful confirmation of the Catholic sacramental imagination. Here is where you can experience, through brilliantly luminous color, the permeability of this world to the really real world.

The experience of Chartres' incomparable beauty is our primary reason for coming here. At the same time, as you fix this beauty in your mind's eye, let me suggest that there are some things to be learned here—things that are important for your Catholic life.

Chartres powerfully reinforces our old friend G. K. Chesterton's claim that tradition is the democracy of the dead. Do we want to give the people who built Chartres "votes" in the forming of our humanity and our faith today? I certainly hope so. To cut ourselves off from the civilization that produced something as beautiful as this is to lobotomize ourselves culturally. When I was a boy, intellectually assertive Catholic youngsters were urged to read a book with the in-your-face title *The Thirteenth, Greatest of Centuries*. It's not an argument I'm all that eager to defend, particularly as I'd prefer a thirteenth (or any other) century that included modern dentistry, indoor plumbing, antibiotics, anesthesia, single-barrel bourbon, and baseball. But that kind of unapologetic medievalism does raise a question you ought to consider—and that's whether the Middle Ages have gotten a bad rap that's damaging to us, and to the human project, here and now.

"Medieval" has become an all-purpose putdown word in American high culture, a synonym for "obscurantist," "undemocratic," "primitive," "unenlightened." That's a *very* hard case to sell here at Chartres, though. There's nothing obscurantist about a human artifact that uses light to create powerful visual and emotional experiences of transcendence; far from being "obscurantist," the medieval world as embodied by Chartres Cathedral is almost blindingly luminous. As for "undemocratic," look at all those workers and tradesmen memorialized in Chartres' donor windows—there's a lot more democratic sensibility here than in, say, early American Protestant churches with their class-stratified pew rents and balconies reserved for servants and slaves.

"Primitive"? Quite the opposite. The unity of design and the iconographic integrity of Chartres speak to us of people with a coherent and rationally defensible idea of who they were, what the world was, and how things fit together. That's a rather different atmosphere from that of the contemporary university world, where very few of the best and brightest are prepared to claim that *anything* is "true"—and thus end up believing the most preposterous things about what makes for human happiness. (Remember your Chesterton again: people who have stopped believing in God don't believe nothing; they believe anything.)

"Unenlightened"? This is a place built of and for light and enlightenment. Chartres' resolute insistence on the Catholic *both/and*—visible *and* invisible, nature *and* grace, material *and* transcendent—seems ever so much more human and humane, so much more enlightened and enlightening, than the flat, windowless, locked-down world of the modern secular materialist.

So if coming to Chartres teaches you what Mr. Jefferson would have called a "decent respect," in this case for the rich human and spiritual experience of the medieval world, it's been worth the journey.

Chartres also teaches us about the importance of beauty and the beautiful for Catholic faith. The sad fact is that a lot of contemporary Catholicism is ugly: ugly buildings, ugly furnishings, ugly decorations, ugly vestments, ugly music. There are exceptions, huge exceptions, to be sure. But the general Catholic drift in the United States since the 1960s has not tended toward the beautiful. That's not just an aesthetic problem. It's a serious religious and theological problem.

Why? *Because beauty helps prepare us to be the kind of people who can be comfortable in heaven—the kind of people who can live with God forever.* Beautiful things and beautiful music draw us out of ourselves and into an encounter with a truth that's beyond us, yet accessible to our senses. We've talked a lot in these letters about self-giving, not self-assertion, as the royal road to human happiness and spiritual growth. Well, there are few greater obstacles to self-giving than self-absorption—and the beauty that, by its very nature, draws us out of ourselves is an antidote to self-absorption. The beauty of Beatrice drew Dante out of himself and into Paradise, and into an encounter with the beauty that is Love itself. The same experience is available to us, in our encounters with the beautiful.

The joy of beauty is another anticipation of the Kingdom, and another way that we're prepared for the Kingdom. How are we to become the kind of people who can be happy forever—especially those of us who are congenitally, well, grouchy? Beauty, by giving us experiences of unalloyed joy here and now, prepares us for that dimension of life with God. So does beauty's inexhaustibility—the fact that we never tire of a beautiful painting, sculpture, building, poem, or piece of music. I've written you about friendship and the quest for understanding as human realities that we could imagine "growing" indefinitely, even infinitely. The same applies to the inexhaustibility of beauty, which is another reason why beauty prepares us for, even as it anticipates, life in the Kingdom, life with God forever. As Hans Urs von Balthasar once wrote, the more we know and love and understand a great work of art, the more we recognize that we can't, in the final analysis, "grasp" its genius. That's why we never "outgrow" a beloved work of art. And that inexhaustibility prepares us to "contemplate God in the beatific vision, [when] we will *see* that God is forever the ever-greater."

So beauty helps deepen in us a sense of our human and spiritual destiny, which is life forever in the light and love of the Holy Trinity. Beauty has one other link to faith, though, that I'd like to mention briefly. Beauty is something that even the most skeptical moderns can *know*. Balthasar once wrote that people who doubt they can say what's good or what's true can't be similarly skeptical about the meaning of beauty, once they've experienced it. People *know* that they *know* what's beautiful. Thus beauty is one way we can introduce our doubting friends and colleagues to something they often deny: *there is truth and we can know it*. Once they've crossed the bridge of radical skepticism, the results can be dramatic and surprising. You'll remember Father Jay Scott Newman from an earlier letter. It's worth noting that the Gothic beauty of the Princeton chapel played a considerable role in breaking him free of the rationalistic atheism he had adopted as a teenager and bringing him to Christ.

All of which takes us back to the great theological mentor of the Middle Ages, St. Augustine, and his *Confessions*. In perhaps the most famous and lyrical moment in this first of true autobiographies, Augustine takes himself to task for his resistance, and then exults in his surrender, to the God who is Beauty itself:

> Late have I loved thee, O Beauty ever ancient, ever new,
> late have I loved thee! You were within, but I was outside,

and it was there that I searched for you. In my unloveliness I plunged into the lovely things which you created. You were with me, but I was not with you. Created things kept me from you; yet if they had not been in you they would not have been at all. You called, you shouted, and you broke through my deafness. You flashed, you shone, and you dispelled my blindness. You breathed your fragrance over me; I drew in my breath and now I pant for you. I have tasted you, and now I hunger and thirst for more. You touched me, and I burned for your embrace.

The Catholic spirit can't live without beauty; the *human* spirit can't live without beauty. Sometime when you're in Florence, I hope you'll go to the Convent of San Marco. As you come up the stairway, you'll find yourself looking down, as we all do when climbing stairs; then, at the top, you'll look up and meet the gossamer beauty of Fra Angelico's famous fresco of the Annunciation. But that's not the only thing to be pondered in San Marco. Several dozen cells—the Dominicans' modest rooms—have been restored and preserved, from the days when Girolamo Savonarola ruled the community. The cells are small, there is (obviously) no indoor plumbing, and you can imagine the austerity in which these Dominicans lived, even without the prod of Savonarola's passion for penitence. Then you notice something else. Each of these plain cells, utterly lacking in what we imagine as creature comforts, has a small Fra Angelico fresco in it—a biblical scene from the life of Christ or the life of Mary. From the prior to the humblest monk, *everyone* had a beautiful Fra Angelico fresco is his cell. Because everyone needs beauty. We need it for our souls. We need beauty to prepare our souls, and the rest of us, for what lies ahead, when we come home at last.

The builders of Chartres knew that. The prior who commissioned Fra Angelico to fresco a small portion of every single friar's cell knew that. We should know it today.

Let me close this letter by pulling a few of the threads of our conversation together, through an observation about icons. Icons have always been an integral part of the piety of the Eastern Catholic Churches—those local churches with a Byzantine liturgy that have remained in full communion with Rome. Icons have not been a significant part of the Catholic Church of the West, however—until very recently. Now, many parish churches display icons; icons are readily available in Catholic bookstores and religious goods shops; and an increasing number of Catholics pray with icons in their homes. Why?

In part, I suspect, because of a reaction to the not-infrequent ugliness I mentioned a moment ago. Even the most sterile cinderblock "worship space" (another of those awful AmChurch neologisms) is ennobled by an icon. Post-Vatican II Catholics may also be discovering the power of icons after too many preconciliar decades of religious "art" that was, in fact, shlock. But whether it's in response to modern AmChurch ugliness or a reaction to old-fashioned Catholic bad taste, the new interest in icons is instructive for the same reason that Chartres is instructive—it tells us that beauty and prayer go together.

When Chartres invites us out of ourselves into a realm of luminous beauty, it's inviting us, however gently, to pray.

The brilliant craftsmen who put those extraordinary blues and reds into the glass of Chartres intended their work as an offering to the Queen of Heaven, patroness and protector of their city. At the same time, the glass they made was an invitation to a wider and deeper vision of the human estate, a vision that necessarily leads to praise and thanksgiving, intercession and contrition—in a word, to prayer. The same is true of icons. I think that's what so many people who now buy icons or applaud the erection of icons in their churches intuitively understand.

As we've discussed before, we don't merely look *at* icons; we look *through* them and discover ourselves engaged with the Truth the iconographer has written. We meet the truth of Christ through the *Christos Pantokrator*, as we meet the truth of Mary in the Black Madonna and the truth of the Trinity in Andrei Rublev's famous evocation of the angels' visitation to Abraham. All of these encounters are invitations to prayer. Beauty is an invitation to pray. The God who is Augustine's "Beauty ever ancient, ever new," pours beauty into the world as one facet of his thirst for us. God asks us to drink at the wellsprings of beauty here and now in order to drink, finally, of his own ineffable and inexpressible and inexhaustible beauty in the New Jerusalem.

Through the beauty of a Chartres we encounter what the early Greek Fathers of the Church called the "divinization" of man. Cardinal Christoph Schönborn, OP, reminds us that this "divinization" of man is made possible by what the cardinal calls "the *humanization* of God"—the Incarnation. When God enters history in the flesh, history isn't the only thing radically transformed; so are the possibilities of the human. Through the Incarnation, human nature is led to its fulfillment, its completion.

That's the truth shining through the ineffable blues of the Chartres windows. That's the truth that makes every icon possible. That is grace at work—God's outpouring of his superabundant life into the world and into our lives. Like Augustine, we, too, burn for the embrace of the Beauty that is always the same and always new. That burning, which God himself has built into us, is the beginning of every prayer.

King's College Chapel, Cambridge / Ely Cathedral

The Secularization Puzzle

he summer of 1961 sticks in my mind for four reasons: my crush on my fourth-grade lay teacher at Baltimore's Cathedral School, over whom I had swooned for the previous nine months, continued unabated; my tonsils were surgically removed (unpleasant), which led to a two-day diet of ice cream (pleasant); the Baltimore Orioles, to whom I had plighted my baseball troth years before, struggled to repeat their prodigies of the previous summer, when they came within a hair's breadth of taking down the mighty New York Yankees; and Robert Twynham arrived at the Cathedral of Mary Our Queen as organist and choirmaster.

Until the hormones kicked in, I sang soprano for Bob Twynham for four years, in a fine choir of men and boys he

trained in the English choral style, perfected in the twentieth century by the longtime director of music at King's College in Cambridge University, David Willcocks. Bob was a
holy terror in those days, but he became a lifelong friend for
whose tutelage in matters musical I remain deeply grateful.
Through him, I got some basic understanding of the rudi-
ments of good liturgical music, and it was under his baton,
and accompanied by his mastery of the organ, that my lifelong love affair with hymns began.

U.S. Catholic hymnody in the 1950s was pretty dreadful. A lot of it reflected the most saccharine forms of Marian piety: to anyone with either musical or poetic sense,
the stuff we sang at the annual May procession was an
aesthetic nightmare. (For example: "Bring flowers of the
fairest / bring flowers of the rarest / From garden and
woodland and hillside and dale / Our full hearts are swell-
ing / Our glad voices telling / The praise of the loveliest
flower of the vale!"—which my brother and I, in a fit of
boyish impiousness inspired by disdain for the crotchety
neighbors who wouldn't let us retrieve baseballs that fell
into their protectorate, rewrote as "Bring flowers of the
fairest / Bring flowers of the rarest / From garden and hillside and your neighbor's back yard . . . "). Happily, Bob
Twynham's arrival in Baltimore coincided with the first
phase of liturgical renewal before and during Vatican II,
when a lot of the treacle was jettisoned and Catholics in
America began to discover the great hymn traditions of
Germany and England, both Catholic and Protestant.
Well do I remember the thrill—there's no other word for
it—that I felt when I first heard the Ralph Vaughan Wil-
liams hymn "For All the Saints," sung with gusto by a

massive adult choir under Bob's direction in the Baltimore Civic Center during the 1965 Liturgical Week.

At Christmas 1964, Bob introduced Baltimore to the King's College tradition of "A Service of Lessons and Carols," now a common and beloved custom in many parishes, but then something daringly new in a Catholic setting. If memory serves, about eighty or a hundred people (most of them the choir boys' parents) showed up in the 2,000-seat cathedral for that inaugural service; today, you've got to get there very early if you want a seat. We sang from a book, *Carols for Choirs*, edited by the aforementioned David Willcocks, and it must have been that experience that planted in me the idea that, one day, I'd like to hear what the boys sounded like on the banks of the Cam, singing in that clean, crisp, no-warbling-allowed English choral style, a musical universe removed from the caterwauling of the Sistine Choir.

It took almost forty years for that aspiration to bear fruit, but it eventually did when I took a daytrip to Cambridge and visited King's College Chapel hoping to hear Evensong, the Anglican version of Vespers in the Roman Rite. It was my lucky day, for I got not a mere Evensong, but the King's College Choir singing an entire memorial service in honor of the college's founder, King Henry VI. It was supernal; after I left, I called my wife back in the United States and said, "Now I know what I was supposed to sound like when I was eleven years old."

It must have been a few months later that I bought a two-volume CD of hymns sung by the Choir of King's

College and, as is my wont, started playing it loudly in my car. One of the hymns is "Christ Is Made the Sure Foundation," the seventh-century Latin text translated by John Mason Neale and set to music by the great Henry Purcell:

> Christ is made the sure foundation,
> > Christ the head and cornerstone,
> Chosen of the Lord and precious,
> > Binding all the Church in one;
> Holy Zion's help forever
> > And her confidence alone.
>
> Founded on the Lord victorious
> > Christ the everlasting Rock,
> Stands the Church in heav'nly places,
> > Dreading not the storm of shock;
> Built with life divine she ever
> > Stands against attack and mock.
>
> Though the gates of Hades frustrate,
> > Yet the Church still stands for God,
> Overcoming evil spirits
> > By her Lord's victorious blood;
> And at Christ's return in triumph
> > All her foes will then be trod.

And then, hearing those crystalline English choirboy voices once again, a thought occurred: Do any of these kids have the faintest idea what those words *mean*?

The question must have been lurking in the back of my mind since that first visit to King's College Chapel. It's a magnificent building, arguably the finest example of the Perpendicular Gothic, a uniquely English style. King's Chapel boasts the world's largest fan-vaulting in its sixteenth-century ceiling, built by the master mason John Wastell; its stained glass is also splendid. But on that first, long-anticipated visit to King's, I was struck, even stunned, by something else: the visual focal point of the chapel is not a tabernacle or high altar but a painting, Peter Paul Rubens's 1634 *Adoration of the Magi*, which was installed in the chapel in 1968. And then the contemporary (and tragic) circumstance of King's College Chapel came into focus for me: this is a museum, a basilica of the real absence. Christian services continue; the magnificent choral tradition flourishes; but both seem effectively detached from a vibrant Christian community. They continue as a matter of cultural heritage, not as an expression of the life-transforming conviction that Jesus, raised from the dead, has been constituted Lord and Savior, changing history and the cosmos forever.

All of which took me back more than a decade, to Moscow, where I visited several of the magnificent churches within the Kremlin with my friend Brad Roberts and a young Russian, a man of twenty-four or so who'd been hanging about in our hotel lobby and button-holing guests, obviously looking to practice his English. This kind and intelligent young man helped Brad and me navigate our way through the famous Moscow subway and the vastness of the Kremlin complex, chatting knowledgeably about this and that. But when we were walking through one of the Kremlin churches (newly restored for the 1988 millennium of Christianity among the eastern Slavs), he stunned us with a question.

We had come around a corner and were facing a very large fresco of the Last Supper, done in the Byzantine style. There was no question it was the Last Supper; it couldn't possibly have been anything else. Yet our guide, after looking at it for some time, turned to Brad and me and said, in complete earnestness: "Please tell me: Who are those men and what are they doing?"

That's what seventy years of communism had done: it had obliterated the cultural memory of a nation, such that a very bright and well-educated young man hadn't the faintest idea of what was happening in one of the most familiar scenes in the history of Christian art.

But as I learned when visiting another Cambridgeshire church, right after my second visit to King's, a decade after the first, the secularization of the European mind could produce bizarre contemporary effects even in countries that had been spared a state-inflicted spiritual lobotomy.

My friend Pauline Stuart and I were motoring back to London from a visit to several of the Cambridge colleges when Pauline suddenly said, "Have you ever seen Ely Cathedral?" I hadn't, so off we went. It's another architectural, decorative, and engineering marvel, rising out of the rolling English countryside much like Chartres emerges from the French country landscape. First built by the Norman conquerors of England between 1081 and 1189, the original cathedral featured a large stone central tower in addition to the great west tower you see today. But the weight of the central tower was too much, and it fell on

February 13, 1322; the noise was so shattering that the monks, who had just finished Matins, thought there had been an earthquake. Miraculously, no one was hurt. The rubble was removed, and the stone central tower was replaced by a shorter octagonal tower and lantern, much of which is wood covered in lead. The interior of the Octagon is magnificently decorated with polychrome figures evoking the heavenly choirs of angels. Just as striking is Ely Cathedral's extraordinary nave ceiling, a Victorian-era masterwork by two artists, Henry Styleman le Strange and Thomas Gambier Perry, who covered the vast space with twelve painted panels that tell the story of Jesus's ancestors, from Adam and Abraham through Mary. The painted ceiling, a unique, yet strikingly effective accompaniment to the familiar arches and rib vaulting of the Gothic design, draws the eye up into the Octagon.

Pauline and I were shown some of the remaining bits of early medieval sculpture surrounding one of the doors by a knowledgeable and friendly gentleman of advanced years who seemed grateful to meet visitors who treated Ely Cathedral as a Christian building. And with reason, as Pauline and I may have been among the few to come to Ely Cathedral as Christian pilgrims that day. For on entering the cathedral on a late spring Saturday afternoon, we had discovered, to our amazement, that Ely Cathedral had been turned into a vast platform for a local flower show.

Virtually everything in the cathedral was covered with (admittedly impressive) floral arrangements. In fact, under the circumstances, it was impossible to get much sense of Ely as a place of Christian worship. As for the dead, well, it was also impossible to tell who was who beneath the complex displays of flowers, ferns, and other forms of floral decoration that obliterated the distinctiveness of the individual tombs. Local connoisseurs of the world of flowers and their display wandered about the cathedral (for a price); but despite the painted ceiling and the interior of the Octagon, there was little sense of what Rudolf Otto called the *mysterium tremendum et fascinans*—the holy—in Ely Cathedral that day. What its builders had intended to be a portal to heaven had become, on this day at least, another basilica of the real absence: in this case, a vast Gothic greenhouse.

Christian services are conducted at Ely Cathedral, and the small guidebook invites visitors wanting to talk with a priest of the Church of England to approach one of the welcomers, guides, or staff members so that a meeting can be arranged. But on that particular Saturday, Ely Cathedral seemed to have been detached from the purpose for which it was built: to be a place of encounter between this world and the real world, the world of transcendent truth and love opened up through the Eucharistic worship of the Church. Its painted ceiling told the story of salvation history, as understood by men and women who cherished the Bible, not because it was entertaining, but because it was true. Now, I wondered whether, in the not-too-distant future, Britons of a certain age would find their way into Ely Cathedral, look up at that painted ceiling, and ask, as my young friend had in religiously deracinated Moscow in the last years of communism, "Please tell us: 'Who are those people and what are they doing?'"

All of which made for a very sobering conversation on the drive back to London. What on earth had *happened*?

The simple answer is that something usually called "secularization" happened—and then the Church of England, like many other Christian communities in the Western world, acquiesced in its own transformation into a community of cultural museum-keepers. Why the supine surrender? Because from the late nineteenth century on, secularization seemed an inescapable fact of modern life. The churches, it was argued, had to cut their jib to the prevailing cultural winds. The net result of all that was the answer that an Anglican archbishop gave to my friend Father Richard John Neuhaus in the 1990s, when Neuhaus asked him what the Church of England was for: "Well, we like to keep alive the religious option for those interested in that sort of thing."

In this case, however, the simple answer is unsatisfactory. The path from King's College Chapel and Ely Cathedral as centers of vibrant Christian worship to basilicas of the real absence was not determined by irresistible historical and cultural forces. And the de-Christianization for which King's College Chapel and Ely Cathedral may stand as reference points is most certainly not universal; it seems confined to one part of the world. It's worth pausing on that fact for a moment.

Fifty years ago, the claim by the founders of modern sociology that modernization inevitably and ineluctably led to "secularization," i.e., the withering-away of traditional religious belief and practice, seemed set in analytic concrete—something as true as "true" gets in the social sciences. What some called "demystification" and others called "demythologization," and the great social theorist Max Weber called "the disenchantment of the world," seemed encoded in the DNA of modernity. Rigorously empirical natural science, with its mechanistic concept of the world and its scorn for such strange metaphysical notions as the "final cause" or purpose of things, would be humanity's new tutor. And as science brought humanity to a new maturity, beyond our childish enthrallment to pious myths and fables, the work of "maturing" the world and its people would be aided by developments in the study of history that would, in time, call into question virtually every truth-claim Christians had ever made.

You could bet the ranch on it, according to a lot of the common wisdom among Western intellectuals: modernization equaled secularization, and the more modern a people got, the less religious they would become. Like the state in the utopia envisioned by Marx and Engels in the *Communist Manifesto*, religious conviction and practice would fade away as the world grew up. Many of the best and brightest welcomed this; a few lamented it. But just about everyone agreed that this was the way things were going, and the way things in the future would be.

Then it didn't happen.

In the early twenty-first century, at least among those paying attention to the data, the secularization hypothesis is dead. It's been empirically falsified over and over again, and the only rational conclusion is that it's just not true. Modernization has not ineluctably led to secularization in most of the world, although it surely has in a lot of the North Atlantic world, including more than a few U.S. zip codes. But in the early twenty-first century, it seems, the bastions of deep-set (and sometimes quite aggressive) secularism are the outliers. Religious conviction and practice are flourishing in most of the world, including rapidly modernizing parts of the world like India and South Korea; and religions that late nineteenth-century sociology couldn't imagine getting any traction (Pentecostalism and Mormonism) have become the fastest growing religions in the world. As my friend Peter Berger has often put it, what needs explaining from a sociological point of view is not the Haj to Mecca, or the Catholic pilgrims who flock to Rome and Guadalupe and Lourdes, or the pious Jews who pray at the Western Wall of the Temple in Jerusalem, or the tens of millions of Hindus who participate in the Maha Kumbh Mela, a pilgrimage to the Ganges that takes place every twelve years. What needs explaining is the Harvard Faculty Club, the *New York Times* editorial board, and all the other redoubts of what seems, literally, God-forsakenness.

So the first thing to be said about "secularization" is that it's not inevitable. Neither was the transformation of great Christian churches into basilicas of the real absence. *Those things have happened, not because of some irresistible cultural tidal wave, but because too many Christians ceased to believe that the Gospel is true: and not just "true for me," but true in the sense that this-is-the-truth-of-the-world; this is the world's story read truly.*

And that brings us to another often-unremarked complication to the simple-minded claim that modernization inevitably leads first to secularization, and then to aggressive secularism: some Christian communities have actually grown and flourished even as their historical irrelevance was being proclaimed in the lecture halls of many of the world's greatest universities. And which were the communities that didn't just survive, but flourished? The Christian communities that took care to keep an eye on their boundaries: the communities that had a clear idea of what was orthodoxy (true belief, formed by both revelation and reason) and what was orthopraxis (righteous living according to revealed truths).

Which suggests, in turn, that there is a law built into the relationship between modernity and Christianity—although it's not the "law" confidently proclaimed by several generations of secularization theorists. It's what I've called the Iron Law of Christianity in Modernity: Christian communities that have a firm grasp on their doctrinal and moral boundaries survive, and can flourish, under the conditions of modernity; Christian communities whose notion of their doctrinal and moral boundaries become so porous that they can't tell you who's inside and who's out wither and ultimately die. And that, I suggest, is the "law" that explains why King's College Chapel and Ely Cathedral have become basilicas of the real absence: the doctrinal and moral boundaries of Anglicanism became unrecognizable, to the point where the Anglican Church's purpose was obscured. No persuasive answers were offered to culturally affirmed, establishment secularism by cowed bishops, priests, and theologians; and so, bereft of faith in Jesus as Lord and its life-transforming power, people stopped coming, save for the beautiful music or the county flower show.

There's another question left on the table, though, and it involves the indisputable fact that there *was* a great abandoning of traditional biblical religion in large swaths of the North Atlantic world. So, again, *What happened?*

There have been numerous attempts to find an answer in the world of ideas. Classical sociology held that the empiricism of the scientific method, philosophy's inability to get itself unstuck from explorations of subjective consciousness, evolutionary theory, and advances in our historical understanding of ancient texts and civilizations had combined to "disenchant" the world: to draw our minds and hearts out of the heavens and down to earth. Think back to how Charles Ryder described the view of Christianity espoused in his prep school in *Brideshead Revisited* and you'll get the idea.

More recently, some daring scholars have begun to suggest that the seeds of Western secularism were first planted, quite inadvertently, by the Reformation. As this line of argument goes, the great Protestant Reformers, intent on purifying the Christian Church, set loose a stream of unforeseen consequences that eventually undid Christianity's accustomed place in Western civilization and dislodged a biblical view of our lives and their meaning from the consciousness of the West. How?

In *The Unintended Reformation: How a Religious Revolution Secularized Society*, historian Brad Gregory suggests that one fatal move was made in the seventeenth century, when, in the desperate search for an idea of God that would free them from the theological debates that had played a considerable role in turning post-Reformation Europe into chaos, philosophers and scientists adopted the view that God was detached from the world—which was then readily understood as a mechanical system whose secrets could be pried loose by the empirical method, absent any notion of divine causes or a divine end to the human story. Thinkers who accepted Francis Bacon's notion that science, and it alone, could come to "the relief of man's estate" were not going to be very open to theological explanations of the human condition; as Bacon famously put it, theology was "barren of works" (that is, it provided no dividends in "the relief of man's estate").

Yet if Gregory is on to something important here—and I think he is—the conclusion he suggests has important implications for the twenty-first century: the entire religion vs. science argument of the past three and a half centuries has been misconstructed. For the naturalists and secularists (not to mention the down-market New Atheists) have been fighting a concept of God—in popular terms, God the Divine Watchmaker who builds the watch, sets it going, and steps aside—that is simply not the God of the Bible.

Gregory finds other unintended consequences in the Reformation. Luther's principle of *sola Scriptura* (Scripture alone as the final authority for the Church) led, in actual practice, to sectarianism that divided the Church again and again; to the principle of "private judgment" (rejected, as you'll remember, by John Henry Newman); and, by a long and winding road, to what Gregory calls "hyperpluralism"— the "enormously wide range of incompatible truth claims pertaining to human values, aspirations, norms, morality, and meaning" that defines the culture of postmodernity. Seeking to ground the Church's authority in the authority of the Bible, *sola Scriptura*, on Gregory's argument, ended up demolishing all authorities, except the authority of the imperial autonomous Self. *Sola Scriptura* became (if I may butcher Latin grammar for the sake of a good rhyme) *sola mea*: "Scripture only" became "Me only."

As these confusions worked themselves out in history over the past three hundred years, they led, in turn, to the widespread notion that Christianity is a matter of lifestyle choice, not of revealed truths that make for happiness and human flourishing when they're lived out. Or, to come back to a sloppy trope we've talked about before, religion became "spirituality."

Gregory doesn't pull any punches in describing the effect all of this has had on higher education in the West. "Intellectually sophisticated expressions of religious worldviews," he writes, "have not been 'left behind' or 'overturned' by 'modernity' or 'reason.' They have been institutionally excluded [from high-end Western academic life] and ideologically denounced, not disproven." And that, Gregory concludes, has led to the "modern charade," according to which the phenomenon we've been calling the "disenchantment of the world" is something "demonstrated, evident, self-evident, ideologically neutral . . . [and clear] on the basis of impartial inquiry." But that, Brad Gregory charges, is "ideological imperialism masquerading as an intellectual inevitability."

Which means that the secularist hegemony in the high culture of the West is a dangerous thing: a threat to that respect for truth that has always been a hallmark of our civilization.

My colleague Mary Eberstadt offered a different take on the puzzle of secularization in a fascinating book called *How the West Really Lost God*.

Mary's book began, in a way, with my 2005 polemic on the subject of European godlessness, *The Cube and the Cathedral*, which argued that throwing the God of the Bible over the side of history, as the atheistic humanism of nineteenth-century European high culture did, had produced (among many other results) a culturally engrained selfishness that impedes us from creating the human future in the most elemental sense: that of creating future generations. Mary turned my proposition inside out and asked whether declines in family life didn't accelerate the turn from the God of the Bible—and, according to a lot of data, it did, and does.

Or, as her book puts it, family decline and religious decline have gone hand in hand in the West, such that "family" and "faith in the God of the Bible" are "the double helix of society, each dependent on the strength of the other for successful reproduction." The sociological record, she argues, "suggests that family decline is not merely a *consequence* of religious decline, as conventional thinking has understood that relationship. It is also plausible . . . that *family decline in turn helps power religious decline.*"

In brief: one strand in the double helix of family and faith in the God of the Bible is only as strong as the other. It's a provocative thesis, and the data Mary Eberstadt marshals in support of it is impressive. Her book is one you should put on your must-read list.

The arguments over the secularization puzzle will doubtless continue for a long time. One immediate question for you is, How do I live a Catholic life when I'm constantly being challenged by what Brad Gregory called the "modern charade"? One possible answer to that question can be found in a small Polish village in the hill country southeast of Kraków. You can call that answer "living inside the Bible."

The village is called Pasierbiec, and its church, the Basilica of Our Lady of Consolation, is full of *votum* gifts testifying to favors received through the intercession of the basilica's namesake. Outside the church, the priests and people of Pasierbiec have done something quite remarkable: they've constructed a stunning contemporary *Via Crucis*, a Way of the Cross, in which figures from modern Polish Catholic history are "inserted" into the traditional fourteen stations. The bronzes themselves are well-done, but what is particularly striking about the Pasierbiec *Via Crucis* is the idea that animates these sculptures—the idea that we can, and should, imagine ourselves living *inside* the biblical story. Or, if you prefer, the Pasierbiec *Via Crucis* is a powerful invitation to look at the world around us, including recent history, through lenses ground by biblical faith.

Some examples of this optic at work in the Pasierbiec Stations of the Cross:

In the depiction of the fifth station, St. John Paul II, not Simon of Cyrene, helps Jesus carry the cross.

At the sixth station, Blessed Jerzy Popiełuszko, the martyr-priest of Solidarity, relieves Jesus of some of the weight of the cross while Veronica wipes the Holy Face; the message Father Jerzy preached during martial law in Poland—"Overcome evil with good"—is inscribed on the cross.

At the seventh station, the second fall, the Lord is supported by Father Franciszek Blachnicki, founder of the Oasis youth movement, in which tens of thousands of young Poles, subjected to atheistic propaganda in communist-run schools, were catechized during holiday camping trips.

At the eighth station, where Jesus traditionally meets the women of Jerusalem, he now meets Stanisława Leszczyńska and Stefania Łacka, prisoners who rescued children born in the Auschwitz concentration camp.

At the ninth station, the third fall, the priest comforting the Lord is Blessed Roman Sitko, rector of the seminary in the Polish city of Tarnów, who (like several thousand Polish priests) was another concentration camp prisoner, dying at Auschwitz in October 1942.

At the tenth station, Cardinal Stefan Wyszyński, intrepid leader of Polish Catholicism for thirty-three years of communist rule, holds the clothes being stripped from Jesus—an image that evokes memories of the cardinal being stripped of his freedom and his dignity during three years of house arrest.

Viewed close-up, the soldiers nailing Jesus to the cross at the eleventh station are obviously Roman; from a distance, their helmets are eerily reminiscent of the familiar SS helmets of World War II.

And at the fourteenth station, two contemporary Polish martyrs witness the entombment of the Crucified One: Father Jan Czuba, martyred in the Congo, and Father Zbigniew Strzałkowski, martyred in Peru.

The dedication of this shrine, which reflects a thoroughly contemporary biblical faith, was led by the archbishop of Cologne, Cardinal Joachim Meisner, who once told me that the witness of the German martyrs of the twentieth century, not the speculations of German theologians, would be the foundation on which Christianity in twenty-first-century Germany would be rebuilt. Meisner's presence at the dedication was a powerful sign of the German-Polish reconciliation sought by Wyszyński and Karol Wojtyła, the future John Paul II, at the end of the Second Vatican Council: a reconciliation demonstrating that what seems impossible can appear not-quite-so-immune to change, and new possibilities can come into focus, when viewed through the lens of biblical faith.

In its hyper-secular regions, the postmodern world is a wilderness of mirrors in which nothing is stable: even maleness and femaleness, two "givens" throughout recorded human history, are now regarded as "cultural constructs." Reason alone seems unable to offer a powerful antidote to either the "modern charade" or postmodernism's gnostic culture of unreality. To see the world around us from "inside" the biblical story, and from "within" the Bible's depiction of the human condition, can be a reality-check. And that reality-check can lead us deeper into the mystery of God's providence—the mystery of salvation history unfolding within history.

Having begun with hymns, let's finish with another.

> And did those feet in ancient time
> Walk upon England's mountains green
> And was the holy Lamb of God,
> On England's pleasant pastures seen!
> And did the Countenance Divine
> Shine forth upon our clouded hills?
> And was Jerusalem builded here
> Among these dark Satanic Mills?
>
> Bring me my Bow of burning gold;
> Bring me my Arrows of desire:
> Bring me my Spear: O clouds unfold!
> Bring me my Chariot of fire!
> I will not cease from Mental Fight,
> Nor shall my Sword sleep in my hand:
> Till we have built Jerusalem,
> In England's green & pleasant Land.

Americans know William Blake's poem, set to music by Hubert Parry, from the film *Chariots of Fire*. When it's sung at a memorial service for the great runner Harold Abrahams at the end of the movie, it's intended to sum up the aspiration that led Abrahams, the son of a Lithuanian Jewish father, to reach the apex of British athletics while studying at Cambridge, hard by King's College Chapel and not so far from Ely Cathedral. It's a splendid hymn, and I love listening to it on that CD by the King's College Choir I mentioned at the beginning of this letter. Sung in the twenty-first century, however, its promise to build Jerusalem—a City of Man that reflects the nobility of the City of God—has something of a hollow ring to it, at least in contemporary Great Britain and other parts of the English-speaking world that have abandoned the biblical view of the world and of us.

It didn't have to be that way. It doesn't have to be that way. Your generation can bring the truth back to "Jerusalem," the hymn—but only by recovering, deepening, and then sharing the faith in the God of the Bible that inspired Blake, and that once inspired the choirboys of King's College and the builders of Ely Cathedral.

THE BASILICA OF
OUR LADY OF GUADALUPE,
MEXICO CITY

Inculturation and the New Evangelization

y friend Mario Paredes has been the instigator of many of my adventures in the past fifteen years or so.

In 2001, he arranged for me to give several lectures in Bogotá, Colombia, then considered the most dangerous city in the Western Hemisphere. The trip was pleasant and uneventful, and as I drove out of Newark International Airport on my return to the United States, I saw the World Trade Center's Twin Towers, golden in the sunset—and the thought occurred to me that several friends had seriously overestimated the dangers of the moment in warning me about Bogotá. It was the evening of September 9, and less than forty-eight hours later, the dangers of our age made themselves horribly clear when the Twin Towers, which I had just admired in the gloaming of a brilliant fall evening, crumbled into dust, thousands of innocents died because of jihadist fanaticism, and the course of the twenty-first century was changed.

Twelve years later, Mario arranged for me to give a series of lectures in various cities in Argentina. We had a grand time, and toward the end of our week we visited the archbishop of Buenos Aires, who had turned seventy-five the previous December. During our conversation, he told us that he had submitted his letter of resignation to Rome and was looking forward to retirement and the life of a simple parish priest. Ten months after that, Jorge Mario Bergoglio, SJ, was elected Bishop of Rome, taking the papal name Francis.

Mario Paredes was also the instigator of my first visit to Mexico City, where I arrived on March 9, 2000, for a program of lectures and interviews built around the first volume of my biography of Pope John Paul II, *Witness to Hope*, the Spanish edition of which had been published a few months earlier. After he and I rendezvoused at our hotel, Mario called me and said, "Let's go see Mother." So we hopped into one of the then-ubiquitous green-and-cream-colored Volkswagen Beetles that dominated Mexico City's cab fleet and headed off to the Basilica of Our Lady of Guadalupe—and my abysmal ignorance of Mexico City was quickly revealed.

From all that I had read about the "Hill of Tepeyac"— where Juan Diego, an Indian convert to Catholicism, had encountered the one who styled herself the "Perfect Virgin Holy Mary of Guadalupe"—I assumed that the shrine was somewhere outside the city, perhaps in a country setting.

What I quickly learned was that, in the megalopolis that is Mexico City (which then had a population of 18 million), *nothing* is outside the city, unless you drive a very long way. Thus I discovered that the shrine of Guadalupe and the Hill of Tepeyac are right in the midst of the sprawl of Mexico City—which, on further reflection, seemed exactly right. For the icon of Our Lady of Guadalupe teaches us important things about what has come to be called the "inculturation" of the Church: the way the Gospel is proposed in different environments, and the way Catholic faith subsequently shapes those environments.

The Basilica of Our Lady of Guadalupe is located on a plaza in the northern part of the city; Mexicans call the entire complex La Villa de Guadalupe or, more familiarly, La Villa. The older structures on the Plaza de las Americas include the original basilica, which dates to 1531, the Pocito Chapel, the chapel of the Capuchin nuns, and the Capilla del Cerito, built on the site of the Hill of Tepeyac and the apparitions of Our Lady to Juan Diego. The old basilica, always threatened by the marshy terrain on which it was built, suffered many trials over the centuries, including a bombing by anticlericals in 1921; it has now been structurally restored and hosts perpetual adoration of the Blessed Sacrament. Adjacent to the old basilica is the new basilica, which was completed in 1976. A circular structure of a decidedly Bauhaus sensibility, it's spacious enough for 50,000 people to attend services inside. The interior of the new basilica is two-tiered, and an electronic walkway guides pilgrims beneath the gold frame enclosing Juan Diego's *tilma*, the rude

Indian cloak on which is imprinted the miraculous image of Our Lady of Guadalupe.

I have to confess to being a bit off-put, at first, by the new basilica's blandly modernist architecture and by the walkway. But those sentiments quickly faded when I first saw the icon of Our Lady of Guadalupe. I'm not sure just what I had expected, but I certainly hadn't expected something quite so large and quite so luminously colorful. It's extraordinarily beautiful. And perhaps that beauty underscores the answer the basilica's rector gave to U.S. Secretary of State Hillary Clinton when she asked, on her visit to the shrine, "Who painted it?" To which the rector replied, "God."

The story of Our Lady of Guadalupe is quite as extraordinary as the miraculous *tilma* of Juan Diego.

The sixteenth-century Christian mission in Mexico got off to a difficult start, in part because of the ferocity with which the Spanish conquistadores demolished the shrines of the native religious deities after their victories in 1520–1521. From the vantage point of the twenty-first century, one might have thought the natives would have welcomed liberation from gods who demanded, and got, human sacrifice. But as Carl Anderson and Eduardo Chávez put it in their study *Our Lady of Guadalupe: Mother of the Civilization of Love*, the Spanish Conquest shattered the very foundations of the natives' apprehension of reality:

> The drama of Cortés's campaign of conquest was more than the collapse of Mesoamerican military, social, economic,

and political structures. By prohibiting sacrifices and other religious practices, he deprived their gods of their necessary sustenance, and the Indians anticipated an apocalyptic end of the world. Instead, they saw that, though the human sacrifices to the gods had ceased, the cycle of life around them continued. The result was increasing doubt among the Indians about their worldview. But doubt is not enough for conversion, especially in the face of the violence of those who practiced the religion of their conquerors. As the Aztec priests told the Franciscans [who had come to the New World to evangelize the Indians]:

> *What are we to do then,*
> *We who are small men and mortals;*
> *If we die, let us die;*
> *If we perish, let us perish;*
> *The truth is that the gods also died.*

In these circumstances, evangelization could not come from the top down, as it had in, say, Poland, where the baptism of the Piast prince Mieszko I in 966 led to the conversion of his people, or in Rus', where the baptism of Vladimir and Olga in 988 led to the mass conversion of the eastern Slavs, who would later be known as Belarussians, Russians, and Ukrainians. Linking religious conversion to political authority was not working in New Spain; and by 1530, one of the Franciscans who would play a large role in our story, Father Juan de Zumárraga, had just about abandoned hope of converting the native peoples of Mexico.

Something more, something different, something deeper was needed.

That "something" was Our Lady of Guadalupe and her encounter with Juan Diego, whose native name, Cuauhtlatoatzin, means "the eagle who speaks."

In 1524, when Cuauhtlatoatzin was fifty, he and his wife were baptized by one of the missionary Franciscans who had come to Mexico with the conquistadores. Given the Christian names Juan Diego and María Lucía, our visionary and his wife were one of the first Catholic married couples of the New World. María Lucía died in 1529, and after her death, Juan Diego lived with his uncle, another convert, Juan Bernardino, near Mexico City.

Juan Diego was an eager neophyte, it seems, and every week he walked a considerable distance to attend Mass and receive catechetical instruction in Tlaltelolco. That weekly journey took him past the Hill of Tepeyac, where, on December 9, 1531, he heard singing and went to investigate. A woman's voice called to him in the native diminutive form of his Christian name; when he went to the top of the hill in response, he found a beautiful woman clothed "like the sun," standing upon stones that shimmered like jewels. She asked him where he was going, and when he replied that he was headed for "your little house in Mexico, Tlaltelolco, to follow the things of God," she introduced herself in his native language, Náhuatl, using phrases drawn from the native religious vocabulary: "I am the ever-perfect holy Mary, who has the honor to be the mother of the true God by whom we all live, the Creator of people, the Lord of the near and far, the Lord of heaven and earth."

And then she made a request: "I want very much that they build my sacred little house here, in which I will show Him, I will exalt Him upon making Him manifest, I will give Him to all people in all my personal love, Him that is my compassionate gaze, Him that is my help, Him that is my salvation. Because truly I am your compassionate Mother, yours and that of all the people that live together in this land, and also of the various other lineages of men, those who love me, those who cry to me, those who seek me, those who trust in me."

Juan Diego, she continued, was to deliver this request to Father Juan de Zumárraga, the Franciscan leader of the Catholic Church in Mexico City, then bishop-elect. Zumárraga, who boasted of having destroyed 20,000 pagan idols and who was skeptical of visions, which he believed to be vestiges of the natives' old religious ways, received the convert, but with considerable reserve: Why would the Virgin Mary appear to someone like Juan Diego, when a bishop-elect was available? So Zumárraga sent Juan Diego away, telling him he'd listen more carefully another time. The dejected Indian returned to Tepeyac, reported his failure, and asked the Lady to send a nobleman to the Franciscan with her request. The Lady, reflecting one of the themes of the Magnificat ("He has put down the mighty from their thrones and exalted those of low degree" [Luke 1.52]), wasn't having any of this, and sent him back to the friar, who received him the next day and questioned him more closely. At the end of the interview, Father Zumárraga asked for evidence that the apparition was not a phantasm or a dream.

Juan Diego dutifully went back to Tepeyac and told the Lady of the bishop-elect's wish for a confirming sign, which she promised him she would provide the following day. Juan Diego intended to return, but his uncle was taken ill, so he skirted Tepeyac in the hopes of avoiding the Lady and getting help for his uncle from Mexico City. But the Lady met him, asked what was going on, and when told of Juan Bernardino's illness, promised Juan Diego that his uncle would be cured. Then she sent him to the rocky summit of Tepeyac to pick flowers—in December—that she would arrange in his *tilma*, the rough Indian cloak Juan Diego wore. Juan Diego did as he was told, and then the Virgin Mary said: "My youngest son, these different kinds of flowers are the proof, the sign that you will take to the bishop. You will tell him for me that in them he is to see my wish and that therefore he is to carry out my wish, my will; and you, you who are my messenger, in you I place my absolute trust."

Juan Diego returned, as instructed. When he opened his *tilma* to show Father Zumárraga the flowers he had picked on the barren, wintry summit of Tepeyac, the petals fell out onto the floor and there, on the *tilma*, was the image we now know as Our Lady of Guadalupe.

A library of books have been written about the image of Our Lady of Guadalupe; let me make a few basic points about the image here.

First, the Lady on the *tilma* is the "woman clothed with the sun, with the moon under her feet," described by the visionary John in Revelation 12.1. She is pregnant, as the purple-shaded ribbon above her waist—another expression of Indian culture—demonstrates. The woman of Revelation is thus Our Lady of Advent—the Madonna of hope who teaches us to wait for her Son, who makes all things new. The angel beneath her feet evokes memories of the Indian eagle, who in the old religion carried human sacrifices to the gods; here, the angel-eagle witnesses to Christ, the sacrificial victim of the New Covenant, who is the liberator of the native peoples from their old habits of appeasing bloodthirsty gods. The Virgin's reign over sun and moon in the image is another indicator that these celestial objects are not divine, but are subject to the reign of the one true God. The positioning of the feet of the Lady suggests an Indian dance step, and for Mexican natives, dance was the highest form of prayer.

And then there is her complexion: Our Lady of Guadalupe is clearly a mestiza who combines in her flesh the Old World and the New, and yet lifts up the New World by bringing its mestizo people to her Son.

Some scholars regard the image of Our Lady of Guadalupe as a kind of catechetical codex, in which symbols from the Náhuatl language are used to convey basic Christian themes. As Anderson and Chávez wrote, "only recently has Náhuatl and Guadalupan scholarship uncovered the reason for the flowers to take the particular shape and position they have on the *tilma*: each flower represents the pictographic writing, or glyphs, found in Náhuatl codices. . . . [T]he flowers are more than flowers; they are symbols, words and concepts," and they are the reason why what seems at first blush a strikingly beautiful image is in fact a catechism.

One such glyph is the four-petaled jasmine flower on the Virgin's tunic, a cosmological symbol of the universe in Náhuatl; and the flower's fifth "point," its center, symbolically represents what Indian wise men knew as Ometéotl, the one true God. And because the jasmine flower is positioned over the womb of the Virgin, just below the belt indicating her pregnancy, the one, true God is identified with Mary's Son. As Anderson and Chávez wrote, "the four-petal jasmine shows the Indians that the omnipotent God is reachable by any human being; and not only is he interested in them but he delivers himself to them. . . . [T]his omnipotent God, the deeply rooted God, now comes to find and deliver himself to mankind through his mother."

Another glyph with biblical resonance is an eight-petaled flower, which to the Indians represented Venus, the "morning star" and "evening star." Aligned with the sun on the *tilma*, it suggests harmony and peace, expressing in Náhuatl symbols Luke's gospel narrative of the birth of Christ during Augustus's *Pax Romana*—"when all the world was at peace," as the Roman Martyrology for Christmas Day puts it.

There are many other such glyphs in the image of Our Lady of Guadalupe, but perhaps the point made by Pope John Paul II in his apostolic exhortation *Ecclesia in America* (The Church in America) has now come into clear focus. Here in Our Lady of Guadalupe, the Pope wrote, is a "perfectly enculturated evangelization" in which the *semina Verbi*—the "seeds of the Word" of which Vatican II spoke— were taken from native culture and made into instruments of evangelization and catechesis: purified of falsehood and grafted into the Gospel message of the inbreaking of the Kingdom, as proclaimed by the One borne by the Lady who called Juan Diego from obscurity to eternal glory as a saint.

The story of Our Lady of Guadalupe had an extraordinary effect on the evangelization of the Mexican Indians. Where once the Franciscans had met resistance, they now found widespread and enthusiastic acceptance. Top-down evangelization on the old altar-allied-to-throne model had failed. Evangelization "from below," using purified images and concepts familiar from the old culture, was such a success that, some seven years after Father Zumárraga was pondering the abandonment of the Mexican mission, the Franciscans were discussing how they might legitimately abbreviate the Rite of Baptism to accommodate the millions who sought to become Christians.

Over the past twenty-five years or so, the phrase "New Evangelization" has become a commonplace in the Catholic Church. In John Paul II's teaching, the "New Evangelization" is the Church's grand strategy for the twenty-first century and the third millennium. As he put it in the apostolic letter concluding the Great Jubilee of 2000, *Novo Millennio Ineunte* (Entering the New Millennium), the Church of the future must leave the shallow waters of institutional maintenance and, like the disciples on the Sea of Galilee, "put out into the deep" [Luke 5.4]: the roiling waters of the postmodern world, which badly needs to hear again that Jesus Christ is the answer to the question that is every human life. The Church of the future must rediscover that it does not *have* a mission (as if "mission" were one of a dozen things the Church does), but that it *is* a mission, and that everything it is and does is ordered to evangelization. Or, to put it another way, the Church of the twenty-first century must return in its imagination to Galilee and hear again the Great Commission: "Go, therefore, and make disciples of all nations, baptizing them in the name of the Father and of the Son and of the Holy Spirit, teaching them to observe all that I have commanded you" [Matthew 28.19].

In the Church of the New Evangelization, which many of us have come to call "Evangelical Catholicism," the people of the Church must understand that, on the day of our baptism, each of us received a missionary's commission. "Mission territory," in the Church of the twenty-first century, does not involve exotic locales from the pages of *National Geographic*; "mission territory" is all around us, and you enter "mission territory" every day—in your home, your neighborhood, your school; in your life as a consumer and a citizen. It's *all* "mission territory." And laypeople have a special role in all this—a role that was foreshadowed at Guadalupe. As Carl Anderson put it in an address there in 2013, "on a continent where John Paul II told us that the laity was largely responsible for the future of evangelization, Our Lady of Guadalupe shows us the way, not only as a member of the laity, but as an example of the domestic Church—as a wife and mother." The New Evangelization begins in the domestic Church that is the family.

John Paul II's call for a New Evangelization, like Pope Francis's call for Catholics to be a "Church in permanent mission," is a Marian call in another way. For as we saw in our visit to the Dormition Abbey in Jerusalem, Mary's unique role in salvation history is to be the one who always points us to her Son. What the image of Our Lady of Guadalupe reminds us is that Christ, borne by Mary, "comes to us even in the midst of our idolatries" (as Father Peter John Cameron, OP, once put it). And that is a wholly appropriate image for Christian mission in the twenty-first century, which is at least as replete with idols as early sixteenth-century Mexico.

There is the idol of money, of which Pope Francis has spoken on many occasions. It's an old idol, really, and it used to be called "avarice" or "greed." It exerts a powerful attraction in consumer societies, which often signal that we are what we have, and the more we have, the more we are.

There's the idol of pleasure, which used to be called "lust." It, too, promises a false fulfillment by turning human love into another contact sport, one of little more consequence than other games.

And then there's the idol of the Imperial Autonomous Self, the idol of "me," which is a particularly modern variant on the old capital sin of pride—the worship of "me" that so often leads to other evils that make for misery and loneliness even as they promise fulfillment and happiness.

These twenty-first-century idols are, in their way, just as bloodthirsty as the Aztec gods to whom human sacrifice was made. Twenty-first-century idols are death-dealing, too, although the form of death in question is usually spiritual death—a self-absorption in which we become the equivalent of those interstellar "black holes" that eventually collapse into themselves. The answer to idolatry remains the same, too: the true worship of that which is worthy-of-worship, the Trinitarian God who is revealed to us in friendship with Jesus Christ, the Holy One borne by Our Lady of Guadalupe.

As we've seen here, "inculturation" is that process by which the Church—adapting materials from a given culture that hint at the presence of the one, true

God—purifies those cultures so that they can become expressions of the human encounter with the Father, Son, and Holy Spirit. As Cardinal Joseph Ratzinger pointed out in a lecture in Hong Kong in 1993, this process (which he preferred to call "inter-culturality") is one that Catholicism learned from its Jewish parent:

> We may not forget that Christianity, already in the New Testament, bears the fruit of an entire cultural history, a history of acceptance and rejection, of encounter and change.
>
> Israel's history of faith, which has been taken up into Christianity, found its own form through confrontation with the Egyptian, Hittite, Sumerian, Babylonian, Persian, and Greek cultures.
>
> All of these cultures were at the same time religions, comprehensive historical forms of living. Israel painfully adopted and transformed them in the course of her struggle with God, in struggle with the great prophets, in order to make ready an ever purer vessel for the newness of the revelation of the one God. These other cultures came thereby to their own lasting fulfillment. They would all have sunk into the distant past had they not been refined and elevated by the faith of the Bible, thereby attaining permanence.

Every culture is, in principle, capable of that purification, although some, historically, have been more difficult arenas of Christian inculturation than others; think of the difficulties that Christian mission has always experienced in societies shaped by a thick, culturally transmitted Hinduism. In any event, the entire discussion about "inculturation" in the work of evangelization raises another question worth pondering: Was there, in the history of the Church, a privileged inculturation that set the baseline or standard for all the rest?

Following once again an insight from Joseph Ratzinger, let me suggest that *the Gospel's "first inculturation" in the Greco-Roman world of the first Christian centuries was decisive for all other "inculturations."* Why? Because the primitive Church's encounter with the rationality first formed in ancient Greece, and then transmitted by classical Greek and Roman culture, allowed the Church to "translate" the early *kerygma*, the basic Christian proclamation that "Jesus is Lord," into doctrine and creed. In other words, the Church's encounter with the classical world allowed later generations of Christians, who did not know the Risen Lord personally and who entered the drama of history after those who had known him in the flesh had left the stage, to meet the challenge that the First Letter of Peter had put before that first generation of converts: to be ready to "give an account of the hope that is in you" [1 Peter 3.15]. That "account" is found in the creeds of the Church, which took their permanent form in the early Church's encounter with classical reason.

Every Sunday, you recite one expression of that accounting in the Nicene Creed. You can read and study a fuller "account" in the contemporary *Catechism of the Catholic Church*. All of that was made possible by the "first inculturation," and that, I suggest, gives the first inculturation a privileged status, in the sense that no other "inculturation" can negate or substitute for the first.

Another way to think about this is through a historical counter-factual: What would have happened if the first Christian missionaries had all turned right when leaving the

Holy Land? Suppose the first "inculturation" of the Christian faith had taken place in a culture that did not have the principle of non-contradiction, which had evolved in Greek philosophy and which taught the classical world that something could not "be" and "not be" at the same time? Certain Asian philosophies can imagine something that "is" and "is not" at the same time: What would have happened to the proclamation that "Jesus is Lord" in such cultures? How could the Church have developed a coherent theology, leading to doctrine and creed, in a culture in which it made perfect sense to say both "Jesus is Lord" and "Jesus is not Lord"?

It would be going too far to say that the "first inculturation" was a matter of divine revelation. But I don't think it would be going too far to say that the "first inculturation" of the Gospel was a matter of the providential guidance of the reception of divine revelation. Moreover, as we have seen in our own cultural moment, the Christian purification of reason by revelation has helped reason maintain its grip on its own validity and preogatives—thus confirming Ratzinger's point that the encounter with the God of the Bible preserves what is best and truest in other cultures. Look at what's going on around us today. Absent two convictions—that the God of the Bible created the world through the divine reason (the *Logos*, the "Word" who was "in the beginning" [John 1.1]), and that the *Logos* imprinted a certain rationality into created things—the longstanding Western conviction that there are truths in the world and in us that we can discover by reason has gotten very wobbly. In postmodern culture, in fact, it's collapsed, such that there's only "your truth" and "my truth," but nothing recognizable as *the* truth.

The "first inculturation" has, and always will have, a privileged place in the life of the Church. And there is no contradiction between affirming that and seeing in Our Lady of Guadalupe the image of a "perfectly enculturated evangelization." For, as it has throughout the centuries, *the encounter with the God of the Bible—in the People of Israel and in the Church—is the "translator" that unlocks the deepest meaning of the world and of cultures.* That's what happened at Guadalupe, which unveiled the deepest meaning of the Náhuatl symbols found in Juan Diego's *tilma*, even as those Indian glyphs helped "translate" that Creed for the native peoples of Mexico.

Our Lady of Guadalupe, and this entire discussion of "inculturation," helps us understand what Pope Benedict XVI meant when he wrote, in the apostolic exhortation *Sacramentum Caritatis* (The Sacrament of Charity), that the Incarnation of the Son of God (who lives within the womb of the Virgin of Guadalupe) fulfilled the divine desire "to encounter us in our own concrete situation." The Triune God enters history in the person of the Son in order to redeem history and point it back to its proper trajectory. The "Word became flesh" [John 1.14] so that God might meet us where we are.

Yet the Lord meets us "where we are" not to leave us where we are, but to summon us to something higher, grander, nobler: life in the Kingdom, at the Wedding Feast of the Lamb. That summons will be increasingly countercultural in the twenty-first-century Western world, which is full of idols who call us in very different directions. But there has always been something exhilaratingly countercultural about Christianity, and that exhilaration comes from knowing that friendship with Jesus Christ purifies our desires and leads to the happiness for which we all long—and to the solidarity found in that most remarkable family, the Catholic Church.

Here, at Guadalupe, where conquerors and conquered found each other as brothers and sisters in Christ and children of the one true God, the richness of that family and its singular capacity to transcend the barriers of race, ethnicity, and class is on full and magnificent display on a poor Indian's *tilma*, miraculously transformed into a stunning icon of the divine encounter with the human in the Word made flesh, dwelling among us, "full of grace and truth" [John 1.14].

THE OLD CATHEDRAL, BALTIMORE

Freedom for Excellence

altimore is home to the most historic
Catholic building in the United States.
It goes today by the ungainly title of the
Basilica of the National Shrine of the As-
sumption of the Blessed Virgin Mary. For
Baltimoreans of my generation, though, it is, was, and always will be "the Old Cathedral." Architectural critics and
historians will confirm what seems clear as you look at the
Old Cathedral from the corner of Cathedral and Mulberry
Streets: this is one of the finest pieces of Federal period
architecture in America, a judgment reinforced by a magnificent restoration completed in 2006. The man who built
America's first Catholic cathedral intended it to be a living
metaphor—for Catholicism and America, for Catholicism
and democracy, for Catholicism and religious freedom. We
can visit his tomb in the Old Cathedral crypt, which you

can access by either of the spiral staircases behind the high altar.

John Carroll, the first and arguably the greatest of Catholic bishops in the United States, was born in Upper Marlboro, a small hamlet in southern Maryland, in 1735. His mother's family, the Darnalls, were related to the founder of the colony, Lord Baltimore, who had established "Maryland" as a place of religious freedom for his English fellow-Catholics in 1634; his father's people, the Carrolls, produced generation after generation of distinguished personalities, including John Carroll's cousin Charles Carroll of Carrollton, the last surviving signer of the Declaration of Independence. John Carroll joined the Jesuits, was educated in France, and began his priestly work in Europe. After the Jesuits were suppressed by Pope Clement XIV in 1773, Father Carroll returned to Maryland and lived with his mother in what is now suburban Washington, DC. When the American Revolution got going in earnest, Father Carroll was recruited to the patriot cause, joining his cousin Charles, Benjamin Franklin, and Samuel Chase on a fruitless mission to Canada to persuade the colonists there to join the revolt against Great Britain. On the way back home, Franklin fell gravely ill, and Father Carroll nursed him back to health; the two remained friends for the rest of their lives.

After the success of the Revolution, Father Carroll began organizing the few priests in the new country (there were scarcely more than two dozen). The Holy See named Carroll "head of the missions in the provinces . . . of the United States" in 1784, and for the next five years Carroll traveled to Catholic communities up and down the eastern seaboard, reported to Rome on the unprecedented situation of a free Church in a free society, and defended Catholics against attacks from the bigots of the day. In 1789, Pope Pius VI confirmed the choice of the American clergy and appointed John Carroll first bishop of the Diocese of Baltimore—which was to cover the entire country. Thus John Carroll became not just the first Catholic bishop in the United States, but the *only* Catholic bishop from the Atlantic to the Mississippi, and between Canada and Florida. Bishop Carroll, who became Archbishop Carroll in 1808 when his vast diocese was divided and new sees erected in Boston, New York, Philadelphia, and Bardstown (Kentucky), had cordial relations with the political leaders of his time, including George Washington and Thomas Jefferson. His episcopal headaches and heartaches came from a cantankerous clergy and from laymen who, accustomed to managing their own affairs, demanded proprietary control over their churches, too; the more ornery of the latter took their bishop to court, where he was consistently vindicated.

In the story of the Catholic Church in the United States, the adjective "first" is more often applied to John Carroll than to any other figure: first superior of the "American mission"; first bishop and first archbishop; founder of the new nation's first Catholic seminary (St. Mary's) and its first Catholic college (Georgetown); protector of St. Elizabeth Seton, and thus a founding father of the Catholic school system; first bishop to ordain a priest and to ordain other bishops in the United States; and, to come down to cases, builder of the country's first cathedral. Archbishop Carroll had a very specific idea in mind for his cathedral—it was to embody the Catholic commitment to American democracy, and specifically, to the religious freedom enshrined in the First Amendment to the Constitution. That idea dictated a distinctively American style of architecture—or, perhaps better, a distinctively American adaptation of classical forms. So Carroll employed Benjamin Henry Latrobe, who would also do important work on the U.S. Capitol, as his architect.

Latrobe's genius produced a building that is, at one and the same time, distinctively American *and* visibly linked to the Christian past. The most innovative feature in the Baltimore Cathedral was a double-dome system, whose technical specifications Latrobe seems to have discussed with Thomas Jefferson. The great outer dome of the cathedral had twenty-four large skylights; the inner dome gathered the natural light from the skylights and filtered it through a single large oculus into the interior of the cathedral. Latrobe's double-dome system was restored in 2006 (the bicentenary of John Carroll's laying of the cornerstone), so that today you can see the Baltimore Cathedral as Latrobe and Carroll imagined it—bathed in a diffused light suggestive of both freedom and transcendence.

That's John Carroll's tomb, nearest you on the lower level of the left side of the Old Cathedral crypt. Seven other archbishops of Baltimore are also buried here. Directly across from Carroll is Cardinal James Gibbons, a Baltimore native, the second U.S. cardinal, and the most prominent Catholic personality in the United States for some forty years, from the last two decades of the nineteenth century through the first two decades of the twentieth. His book *The Faith of Our Fathers* was an exceptionally successful piece of apologetics when it was first published in 1876 and is still in print today. Above Carroll rests Martin John Spalding, who came from Louisville to Baltimore (a city of southern sympathies occupied by Union troops) during the Civil War. Spalding hailed from another venerable Maryland family, and his leadership at the Second Plenary Council of Baltimore in 1867, like Gibbons's at the Third Plenary Council in 1884, helped set the patterns of Catholic life in the United States for decades. Had he not died prematurely, Spalding would almost certainly have been the first American cardinal. Next to Spalding is his predecessor, Francis Kenrick, who translated the entire Bible into English (his tempestuous brother Peter, archbishop of St. Louis, opposed the U.S. bishops' sponsorship of his brother's translation of the Bible and left Rome rather than vote for or against the decree on papal infallibility at Vatican I). Next to Gibbons is his successor, Michael Curley, a blunt, no-nonsense Irishman who raised eyebrows in Baltimore's more refined parlors but who was loved by the poor, the black, and the elderly—and who died utterly destitute in 1947, believing that no bishop should ever leave worldly goods behind him.

It's an extraordinary array of personalities, and it's fitting that they should be here, because this cathedral is where they and their fellow bishops solemnized many of their most important decisions. The seven "provincial councils" and three "plenary councils" of Baltimore, which involved all the bishops of the United States, were the largest legislative assemblies of Catholic bishops between the sixteenth-century Council of Trent and the First Vatican Council (1869–1870). The Baltimore councils, whose most solemn moments were always celebrated in Carroll's cathedral, devised the U.S. parish system, mandated Catholic schools in those parishes, regulated the sacramental life of the Church, authorized the famous Baltimore Catechism, defended Catholicism against the frequent attacks of anti-Catholic bigots, launched the Catholic University of America, and dealt with issues ranging from appropriate dress for the clergy to the laws of fast and abstinence. Until the Second Vatican Council dramatically changed the face of the Catholic Church in the United States, it's fair to say that the distinctively Catholic way of being American and the distinctively American way of being Catholic were defined here, in this building, by those councils. For here was where all the developments taking place throughout the country were distilled, and future plans laid, by the bishops of the United States.

As I mentioned in my first letter, I got acquainted with this great building very early, when, at six and a half years old, I came to the Cathedral School, then at 7 West Mulberry Street, in September 1957. I made my First Holy Communion in the Old Cathedral on May 3, 1959. I graduated from college in the Old Cathedral on May 20, 1973. My son, Stephen, was baptized here on January 31, 1988, and my daughter, Gwyneth, married Jeffrey Spaeder here on November 9, 2013. In the first years of the new millennium, I helped the project to restore the Old Cathedral to Latrobe's original design, which promises it a third century of vigorous life. But I've brought you here not for a walk down nostalgia lane—although, if you like, I can show you the precise place where Tommy Ostendorf, standing beside me in an identical white suit with short white pants and white socks, sang "Oh, small white host" off-key on May 3, 1959. Rather, I'd like to think out loud with you here about the relationship between Catholicism and democracy. There's no more fitting place to do that in the United States—which also makes this a good place to think about the meaning of freedom.

Catholics have, or should have, a different "story" about the origins of modern Western democracy than the "story" on tap in most schools today—a story that's then refracted into our politics, our courts, and the media. According to the conventional storyline, "democracy" is, by and large, a product of the Enlightenment—of Hobbes and Locke and the Glorious Revolution of 1688, which finally subordinated royal willfulness to Parliament. "Democracy," on this understanding, required the overthrow of centuries of medieval obscurantism and royal absolutism (both typically identified with the Catholic Church). Vindicated in such contemporary dramas as the American civil rights movement and the Revolution of 1989 in east central Europe, democracy is now well established wherever the institutions of democratic governance (legislatures, an independent judiciary, an accountable executive, a free press, free and open elections, etc.) flourish. That's the conventional story.

There's another, and better, way to think about the story of democracy.

A Catholic reading of this history would suggest that you'll find the deeper, sturdier roots of democracy in those often-scorned Middle Ages, rather than in Locke's seventeenth-century treatises on civil government. It's true that democracy had to supplant absolutism in Europe; it's also true that absolutism was an aberration in European history, not a natural evolution from the medieval world. The Middle Ages weren't "absolutist" in any sense of the term. On the contrary, the Middle Ages were a time of robust social pluralism. Associational life flourished in the Middle Ages through institutions like the guilds you saw memorialized in the stained glass of Chartres. Those institutions and the medieval Church (including the papacy) were powerful checks on the absolutist pretensions of kings. Royal absolutism wasn't a feature of Catholic Christendom; absolutist political tendencies got the bit in their teeth after Christendom fractured in the Reformation.

The Catholicism of the Middle Ages nourished and supported independent, voluntary associations—religious communities, guilds, fraternal societies, charitable organizations. In the medieval view of things (unlike some Enlightenment-influenced views of things), there's more to society than the individual and the state. There's what the anticommunist dissidents who made the Revolution of 1989 called "civil society," which almost everyone now recognizes is a prerequisite for a stable and effective democracy. The medieval Catholic world lived "civil society" without ever defining it as such.

Catholicism did more than support the social institutions and way of life that eventually helped make democracy possible, however. The Catholic Church *taught* the people who would become known as "European"—taught them ideas and moral truths that would later prove crucial to the success of the democratic project in the modern world.

For instance?

When Abraham Lincoln, in his Gettysburg Address, referred to a national rebirth of freedom "under God," he was unintentionally adverting to the most fundamental idea that Western civilization learned from Catholicism: that God's sovereignty transcends and stands in judgment on all worldly sovereignties. Because God is God, Caesar is not God, and neither are Caesar's successors, be they kings, presidents, prime ministers, or party general secretaries. And because Caesar and his successors aren't God, their power is limited, not absolute; in addition to Caesar's legitimate power, there are other legitimate powers in the world.

So the state *cannot* be all-there-is. Long before Enlightenment political theorists began challenging royal absolutism with ideas like Montesquieu's "separation of powers," Western civilization learned the idea of "limited government" in the school of Christian reflection. When medieval Catholic thinkers insisted on a sharp distinction between "society" and the "state," they created a vaccine against absolutism in either its royal or modern (totalitarian) form. The vaccine wasn't completely effective. But its potency may help explain why the age of absolutism was a rather short one, as these things go in history.

Medieval Catholicism also helped plant in the Western mind the idea that "consent" is crucial to just governance. Government isn't simply coercion, medieval Catholic political theory insisted; just governance requires consent. Consent would be forthcoming if governance were just. And who would judge the justice of a particular form or style of governance, or the justice of a particular act of state? The Church's claim to be able to judge princes, and the Catholic teaching that "the people" have an inherent sense of justice within them, injected another, crucial idea into the political-cultural subsoil of the West—the idea that "justice" isn't simply what those in authority say it is. There are moral standards of justice, and they are independent of governments; we can know those moral standards, and they ought to be applied in public life. All these ideas, fundamental to democracy, were nurtured in the civilization of the Middle Ages by the Catholic Church.

Medieval Catholicism taught other important lessons that are not-so-well-remembered today—like the lesson that freedom is a matter of virtue, not just of political mechanics. The idea that a free people must be a disciplined people, a people who nurture and cherish mastery of their passions, isn't exactly front-and-center in contemporary political theory. But it's part of the medieval heritage, along with all these other proto-democratic ideas. Then there's the medieval idea that what we've come to call "rights" imply responsibilities. In a culture like ours, which often thinks of "rights" as free-floating claims to do whatever one likes (so long as "no one else gets hurt"), that linkage between rights and responsibilities could stand some revisiting. Finally, we ought to reconsider what the medieval Church taught European culture about the "communitarian individual," in my friend Michael Novak's neat formulation. Yes, we're individuals who have ideas, who create things, and who enjoy inherent "rights." But none of that means much of anything without vibrant communities, whether that be family or professional group or guild or whatever. For an individual to grow into a truly human maturity requires a sense of responsibility for others, a commitment to working with others in society, and a sense of social solidarity. That's the "communitarian individual." A society that absolutizes the commons ends up crushing individual creativity and initiative. A society that absolutizes the individual will, sooner or later, come apart at the seams. It's the old Catholic *both/and* again: *both* person *and* community, each affecting the other in important ways.

I'm not suggesting that the conventional storyline on democracy is completely flawed. I am suggesting that it's incomplete. Yes, the Church, and particularly the papacy, accommodated itself to royal absolutism in Europe. Yes, several popes in the first two-thirds of the nineteenth century were deeply skeptical about democracy (in no small part because they identified "democracy," and political modernity in general, with what had happened in France after 1789, and what had subsequently happened in the Italian *Risorgimento* and the German *Kulturkampf*). And yes, the medieval Church learned a lot about the *res publica* from the Greeks (especially Aristotle). But the same medieval Church filtered that learning through its prior commitment to distinguishing the things of God from the things of Caesar. And the medieval Church embodied what it had learned in a way of life. That way of life shaped the European culture that gave birth to modern democracy. The conventional story's suggestion that the roots of modern democracy go back no farther than the seventeenth (or possibly sixteenth) century makes no historical sense. Things just don't work that way.

John Carroll, working with Benjamin Latrobe to design the first Catholic cathedral in political modernity's first democratic republic, understood that Catholics and their ideas weren't "foreign" to the American experience and experiment—no matter what the conventional storyline said, and no matter what the bigots said. Catholics *belonged* in a democracy, because the Catholic Church had formed the culture that, over time and under a welter of influences, eventually gave birth to the modern democratic project. That's why this building we're visiting deliberately evokes the spirit of the American Founding *and* the spirit of the Great Tradition formed in the West by the interaction of Jerusalem, Athens, and Rome. The two go together.

They're being torn apart today, though. And that brings us to the question of freedom, what it means and what it's for.

Catholic thinking about freedom should begin where Catholic thinking about every other facet of the moral life ought to begin—with the Beatitudes [Matthew 5.3–12]. The Beatitudes are the basic Gospel framework for thinking about the question, How should we live? Why? Because the Beatitudes point us to the eternal happiness for which the moral life, here and now, is a preparation. So here's another challenge to conventional wisdom: in the Catholic way of thinking, the moral life is not an arbitrary set of rules imposed on us by God and the Church. *The moral life involves rules for living that emerge from inside the human heart and its thirst for happiness with God.*

The basic moral question is not that familiar teenage query, "How far can I go?" The basic moral question is the adult question, "What must I do to become a good person?"—to be the kind of person who can actually enjoy living with God forever. In answering that question, we discover rules. But they emerge organically, not "from outside"; they emerge from the dynamics of *becoming a good person.*

That idea of the moral life—of a truly *human* life—leads to a very different idea of freedom.

If American popular and high culture could ever agree on a theme song that captured the idea of freedom driving much of contemporary life, it would almost certainly be Frank Sinatra's "My Way." *I did it my way* seems to sum up the widespread notion that freedom is a matter of asserting myself and my will—that freedom is really about *choice*, not about *what* we choose and *why*. Suggest that certain choices are just incompatible with human dignity and with growth in goodness, and you'll get some very strange looks these days, whether on campus or in the workplace.

Catholicism has a different idea of freedom. In the Catholic idea of freedom, freedom and goodness go together. A great contemporary moral theologian, Father Servais Pinckaers, OP, explained all this through two brilliant metaphors. Learning to play the piano, he reminded us, is a tedious, even dreary, business at first: well do I remember my own distaste for a book of technique-strengthening tortures entitled *Scales, Chords, and Arpeggios*. But after doing one's exercises for a while, what originally seemed like a burden comes into clearer focus—learning to do the right thing in the right way is actually liberating. You can play anything you like, even the most difficult pieces. You can make new music on your own. Sure, Father Pinckaers writes, anybody can pound away on a piano. But that's a "rudimentary, savage sort of freedom," not a truly human freedom. Do your exercises, master the art and discipline of playing the piano, and you discover that, by becoming a disciplined artist, you've discovered a new and richer freedom—the freedom of doing the good things you want to do with perfection.

Then there's learning a new language. You've discovered, I'm sure, that the best way to learn a new language is to listen to it and speak it. At some point, though, we've got to learn grammar and vocabulary—the "rules" that turn noise into language. There's no communication without those rules; there's only gibberish. Father Pinckaers suggests that this common experience is really a window into the truth about freedom. Yes, language means living within a set of rules, but it's the rules that give me the freedom to make new sentences, to test new ideas, to communicate. To reduce freedom to the freedom to make mistakes demeans freedom and demeans us. Freedom involves learning to avoid mistakes without having to think about it. Freedom is doing the right thing and avoiding mistakes *by habit*. And another word for "habit" is *virtue*.

I did it my way teaches us an idea of freedom that Father Pinckaers calls "the freedom of indifference." Doing things "my way," just because it's *my* way, is like banging idiotically on the piano or talking gibberish. The richer, nobler idea of freedom the Catholic Church proposes is what Father Pinckaers calls *freedom for excellence*—the freedom to do the right thing, in the right way, for the right reasons, as a matter of habit. That's the truly human way. Because that's the kind of freedom that satisfies our natural desire for happiness, which itself reflects our desire for God, who is all Good, all the way. Freedom helps us grow into the kind of people who can live with that God forever. What's all this got to do with democracy? Everything. Freedom untethered from moral truth will eventually become freedom's worst enemy. If there's only *your* truth and *my* truth and neither one of us acknowledges a transcendent referee—*the* truth—by which to settle our disagreements, then one of two things is going to happen: you're going to impose your power on me, or I'm going to impose my power on you. Persuasion, which is the life-blood of democratic politics, gives way to coercion, which is an acid eating away at democratic institutions and commitments.

We're uncomfortably close to that situation in America today. Two generations of debonair nihilism have left us with a high culture, including the university world, in which two crucial ideas—that freedom has something to do with goodness, and that goodness has something to do with fulfilling the noblest American aspirations to "equal justice for all"—are regarded as "medieval," laughable, even dangerous. That erosion of culture has, in turn, had a profound effect on our law.

When I was a small boy, the U.S. Supreme Court ringingly affirmed the inclusion of all Americans within the community of common protection and concern, in its epic 1954 *Brown v. Board of Education* decision outlawing segregation in government-supported schools. Less than forty years later, the Court was proposing a morally indifferent, content-free freedom as the official national creed of the United States, and indeed, as the very purpose of American democracy; as three justices put it in 1992, writing in *Casey v. Planned Parenthood*, "at the heart of liberty is the right to define one's own concept of existence, of meaning, of the universe, and of the mystery of human life." A decade later, the Court drew on this bizarre "mystery passage" in its 2003 decision *Lawrence v. Texas*, which suggests that the state's only interest in matters of human sexuality is protecting an unbridled license to fulfill what any configuration of consenting adults defines as personal "needs."

On this (mis)understanding of freedom, democracy is simply a set of procedures—electoral, legislative, judicial— by which "we the people" (or, more likely, they the courts) regulate the pursuit of personal satisfactions and pleasures. There's no moral core to democracy here. The Founders' "self-evident truths," which were *moral* truths, have disappeared into the ether. In this stripped-down, *I did it my way* vision of democracy, civil society is of no consequence. There's no great public moral argument about how we ought to live together, as people committed to freedom and to the truth about freedom. There are only The Rules of the Game, determined by either law or judicial fiat in order to leave unhampered my pursuit of the gratification of *me*—of my willfulness, of my self, indeed, of my selfishness.

The moral architecture of freedom in the United States is crumbling. Young Catholics have a real opportunity, and a great responsibility, to do something about that. You have to challenge the notion that, as three Supreme Court justices wrote two decades ago, linking freedom to moral truth through the law is an act of "compulsion" that denies our fellow-citizens the "attributes of personhood." And the best way to challenge that notion of content-free democracy is to ask, What's the idea of *person* here? Isn't there something terribly demeaning about reducing the "attributes of personhood" to a bundle of undisciplined desires? Aren't we better than that? Aren't we *more* than that? How are we going to have a genuine democracy if we can't talk with each other about what's good? How are we going to have a genuine democracy if, in the name of *I did it my way*, one class of citizens—consisting of those who happen to be alive—asserts a "right" to take the lives of other indisputably human creatures who happen not to have been born yet? How are we going to have a genuine democracy if the fit and healthy assert the "right" to dispose of the inconveniently elderly, terminally ill, or radically handicapped?

All of this is being asserted today in the name of a false idea of freedom. The best antidote to a bad idea is a good idea. That's your public job, as a young Catholic in the twenty-first-century United States—to challenge the freedom of indifference with freedom for excellence. A lot depends on how well you do, including the question of whether twenty-first-century American democracy remains in any sense tethered to its founding principles.

John Carroll did not simply believe that Catholicism was "compatible" with democracy. Like other imaginative U.S. Catholic thinkers of his time and ours, he had the intuition that Catholic ideas about freedom just might be crucial to the future prosperity of the American democratic experiment. Could Carroll have foreseen our circumstances today? The idea's not as far-fetched as it might at first seem. Carroll had a very clear view of what the French Revolution—the world's first experiment in totalitarianism, an experiment based on radical assertions of willfulness—had done, and meant. He knew, because he had seen, that democracy could degenerate into mobocracy, or give birth to new and even bloodier forms of dictatorship, if sufficient numbers of people bought into a corrupt idea of freedom. I can't help but imagine that he had those ideas in the back of his mind when he helped Latrobe design this magnificent building. The roots of democracy run more deeply into our civilizational soil than some suspected. This building, in which the heritage of that civilization met the bright new promise of a democratic future, reminds us that Catholics in the United States have a special responsibility for tending to democracy's deepest roots.

I hope that you, and others like you, will be skillful and dedicated cultivators of freedom, rightly understood and nobly lived.

St. Patrick's Church, Soho, London

Why Orthodoxy, Liturgy, Service, and Work for Justice Go Together

ou've probably noticed that there's been a fair amount of contention in the Catholic Church in recent decades. It can get discouraging, even off-putting. But, as always, "history is the great teacher of life," as Pope St. John XXIII said in his opening address to the Second Vatican Council. And there have been controversy and divisiveness in the Catholic Church since the days of the apostles, as the Book of Acts and St. Paul's letters readily attest.

Catholics of your grandparents' generation thought stability was one of the defining characteristics of Catholicism; like the seven sacraments, stability seemed part of the Church's God-given "constitution" (in the British sense of the term). The truth of the matter, though, is that stability is the exception, not the norm, in Christian history. There was no little contention in the primitive Church, as those who imagined Christianity as a reform movement within Judaism contended for the future of The Way with those who believed that the Resurrection had destroyed the barrier between the People of Israel and the Gentiles, such that something new had been born—a new People of God, in which the Gentiles had been grafted onto the tree of Israel. While that struggle was getting worked out, all sorts of other odd ideas kept rearing their heads, as Paul's letters to his contentious Corinthians and Galatians, and his pastoral epistles to Ephesus, Colossae, and Philippi, demonstrate.

What historians call the "early Church" was a spiky asparagus patch of theological controversy from which grew heresies with such luxuriant names as Adoptionism, Marcionism, Patripassianism, and Pneumatomachianism. There were the great debates—which not infrequently led to serious divisiveness in the Mystical Body—over the relationship between God the Father and Jesus, over a proper understanding of Mary (Could she be called "Mother of God"?), and over the relationship between divinity and humanity in the Lord Jesus. Later in the story, the Church wrestled with the question of what to do with those who had apostasized under the threat of Roman persecution: Could they be brought back into the communion of the Church, and if so, how? No sooner had those fierce and Church-dividing controversies begun to calm down than a whole new argument broke out over the relationship between God's grace and our will in the work of salvation.

And that's just in the first four and a half centuries.

The fault lines within the Catholic Church in the early twenty-first century sometimes describe real issues: What is essential, and what is peripheral, in the structure of Catholic faith? What is obligatory, and what is optional, in Catholic practice? Other fault lines fall along the cracks between different ecclesial and liturgical styles. As aggravating as they can sometimes be, and notwithstanding the sad fact that internal Catholic divisiveness and contention is an obstacle to mission—How can we be about converting the world when we're absorbed with battling each other?—most of the arguments that divide Catholics today have to be engaged. Why? Because resolving them allows what some have called the Church's "symphony of truth" to be heard as a melody, not a cacophony. That's important in itself, and it's crucial for evangelization and Christian witness. Cacophony is not, to put it gently, an aid to mission.

There is one confusing issue in twenty-first-century Catholicism that I think can be and ought to be resolved without too much difficulty, though. It's the confusion caused by those who imagine that there can be "social justice Catholicism" without orthodoxy and regular worship, on the one hand, and those who imagine that service to the poor is an optional accessory in a Catholicism essentially defined by orthodoxy and regular worship, on the other. The "Catholic *both/and*" we've discussed in these letters should have already led you to suspect that these are false dichotomies, false choices. You're right to intuit that. Now I'd like to take you to a place where young Catholics, led by a remarkable pastor, are putting all the pieces of the great Catholic mosaic together in a compelling way—and doing it in one of the last locales you might expect such a miracle to unfold.

S oho is in London's West End, which includes the British capital's theater district. It's had a rather dodgy history.

The Wikipedia entry on Soho in January 2015 noted, somewhat primly, that by the mid-nineteenth century "all respectable families had moved away, and prostitutes, music halls and small theatres had moved in." So had Father Arthur O'Leary. In that unpromising quarter of what was then the world's greatest city, he established in 1792 the first Catholic church in London since the Reformation that had not been located on some foreign embassy's territory. The parish community, named for St. Patrick, evangelist of Ireland, first worshipped in a ballroom rented from the creditors of a bankrupt Regency theatrical impresario, Teresa Cornelys, one of Casanova's many lovers.

The parish built a church in 1893, and St. Patrick's became a home for many Catholics in London's émigré community. In the 1930s, St. Patrick's was surrounded by wine bars and pubs in which inebriated intellectuals and writers argued long into the night. Their drunken revelry, like much of London's life, was interrupted by the German Blitz, which also sent a Luftwaffe bomb crashing through the ceiling of St. Patrick's; happily, the bomb buried itself in the floor without exploding.

Soho today is tough mission territory. As my colleague Stephen White once put it, twenty-first-century Soho is a "world-class spiritual wasteland . . . a playground of the middle and upper classes, a trendy night spot that sells just about anything a man could want. It's not so much a poor neighborhood as it is a wicked neighborhood. It's a place dedicated to the appetites and built on prodigality." And in the midst of that prodigality is St. Patrick's—a model

Catholic parish, a flagship of the New Evangelization, and one of the places in the Catholic world where orthodoxy, worship, beauty, social service, charity, and intense prayer all mesh together.

When I first got to know it in 2011, St. Patrick's had been led for a decade by Father Alexander Sherbrooke, a man of no small dreams whose ecclesial vision is as expansive as his striking eyebrows. In June 2011, St. Patrick's celebrated the completion of a magnificent restoration that turned a once-drab church into a golden gem of architecture and decoration: for Father Sherbrooke, like Pope Benedict XVI, believes that beauty is a privileged pathway to God in a secular age, a countersign to the ugliness that can corrode the souls of those who drink too deeply from the wells of Soho's polymorphous perversities.

The restoration of the church interior went hand-in-glove with the creation of a center for the parish's outreach to the neighborhood. While the church was being replastered, repainted, and regilded, its dank basement was dug out and a state-of-the-art community center was built there for the parish's extensive work with the homeless and the destitute. Up in the church's bell tower is a chapel for Eucharistic adoration, where volunteers pray from 7 to 11 p.m. every night, and where two telephones bring requests from all over the world to an "SOS Prayer Line"; in the first twelve years of the project, some 65,000 calls were received.

The Holy Eucharist is at the heart of St. Patrick's life, for, as Steve White put it after his eight months of work there, "the demands of discipleship in that environment leave no room for lukewarmness. Anyone who was going to leave left long ago. The Eucharist quite simply drives the life and work of the parish. This is not a theological truism but an actual fact learned from experience. And that experience is transformative." The Eucharist, in a daily rhythm of Mass and Eucharistic adoration, is the dynamic force behind the church's evangelization programs and its work with the homeless.

Eucharistic piety was also central to St. Patrick's Evangelization School, a striking experiment in young adult formation that the parish ran for a decade; its Latin acronym, SPES, is, not coincidentally, the Latin word for "hope." Each year, ten or so young people came to St. Patrick's for a kind of lay novitiate: several months of intense catechesis, spiritual formation, street evangelization, and work with Soho's down-and-outs while manning the SOS Prayer Line during adoration and participating in the parish's rich liturgical life. It was an experience straight out of the New Testament, with twenty-first-century technology providing new opportunities for young men and women to give witness to "the hope that is within" the followers of The Way [1 Peter 3.15]. And among other fruits, it produced vocations to the priesthood, the religious life, and Christian marriage as well as the parish's director of evangelization.

Father Sherbrooke had kindly invited me to give a lecture at one of the public events marking the completion of the St. Patrick's restoration and the parish's new community center, and it seemed appropriate to talk about the New Evangelization, or what I've already referred to in these letters as Evangelical Catholicism: a Catholicism that is sacramentally rich, biblically literate, robustly missionary, and committed to the service of the poor; a Catholicism that embodies what John XXIII and the Second Vatican

Council envisioned for the world Church: a new Pentecost. For that is exactly what's going on at St. Patrick's. Its
people, touched by the fire of the Holy Spirit, have been
led by Father Sherbrooke to be salt and light in the barren field that is twenty-first-century Soho—and, through
new technologies, to the wounded and bleeding casualties
of a broken culture throughout Great Britain, and indeed
throughout the world.

Perhaps a little more detail will fill in the outline of the
Catholicism-in-full that is offered at St. Patrick's, Soho.
"Open House" is an umbrella moniker for the parish's
various outreach projects to the poor and homeless in Soho
and other nearby neighborhoods. Twice a week, volunteers
prepare a two-course dinner for sixty, seventy, or sometimes
eighty guests. The volunteers come from a variety of social
strata and walks of life, but they're mainly students and young
professionals. The room is prepared for the guests, and Father
Sherbrooke leads the volunteers in prayer. After the meal, volunteers and guests spend time in intercessory prayer together;
the volunteers also help staff the SOS Prayer Line chapel,
where they bring the needs of those whom they've just fed
before the Eucharistic Lord—underscoring the close link between Catholic worship and Catholic service. "Open House"
expanded in 2014 to include an art-and-social drop-in on the
first Saturday of each month (an event where painting and
drawing lead to conversation and fellowship) and a film evening on the first Sunday of each month.

Then there's "Nightfever," which is organized by the
young adults who are drawn to St. Patrick's because of the

intensity and comprehensiveness of its Catholic life. "Night-fever" was a fruit of the 2005 World Youth Day in Cologne, after which young people began organizing evenings of candle-lit reflection and prayer in cities all over the world. As in other locales, St. Patrick's "Nightfever" involves keeping the church open throughout a long evening, during which young people (and others) are invited to enter, take a candle, accept a piece of paper with a Bible verse or story on it, and sit down to write a prayer or speak with a priest.

Complementing these other activities is the monthly "Day for the Lord," which St. Patrick's inaugurated in response to Pope Francis's invitation that one church in each diocese remain open for twenty-four hours of Eucharistic adoration, such that it was possible to spend time with the Lord at any hour in at least one local church. St. Patrick's celebrates its "Day for the Lord" on the third Friday of each month and makes confessions available throughout the night.

SPES, the St. Patrick's Evangelization School, was one of the first projects in the world to take with utmost seriousness John Paul II's proposals, in the 1990 encyclical *Redemptoris Missio* (The Mission of the Redeemer), that every Catholic should consider himself or herself a missionary; that "mission territory" is all around us; and that each of us should measure the quality of our discipleship by how well (or poorly) we're doing in offering to others the great gift we have been given—friendship with Jesus Christ. In equipping young Catholic adults for the missionary vocation implicit in their baptism, SPES was also a response to John Paul's insistent call to the young to be the apostles of the new millennium. SPES graduates testify to the program's life-transforming impact on their lives: living what we can call *all-in Catholicism* for eight, nine, or twelve months tends to energize all-in Catholicism for a lifetime.

The seamlessness of St. Patrick's all-in Catholicism is palpable. The liturgy is beautifully celebrated, with splendid music. Yet Father Sherbrooke's preaching and the parish's daily life make it clear that, while we worship God in a dignified way because God is to be worshipped, and because we have been clothed with a baptismal dignity that empowers us to offer proper worship, our worship, to be true to itself, must be completed in service and in works of charity—which may mean simply listening sympathetically on the SOS Prayer Line to a troubled soul unburden himself of the guilt or grief that is weighing him down and making him feel utterly alone. On the Solemnity of Corpus Christi, Father Sherbrooke leads a great Eucharistic procession throughout Soho, invoking the blessing of the Eucharistic Christ on the hard soil of a neighborhood in which decadence is more common than decency. But that procession is no mere showing-the-flag, so to speak. It's an invitation to come into St. Patrick's Church, to experience the beauty of the Lord, and, just perhaps, to find in that beauty the quiet invitation to a more noble way of life: to "whatever is true, whatever is honorable, whatever is pure, whatever is lovely, whatever is gracious [and] worthy of praise" [Philippians 4.8].

At St. Patrick's, Soho, there are not "social justice Catholics" *here* and "pro-life Catholics" *there*; there aren't liturgically minded Catholics *here* and activist Catholics *there*. No, it's all one Catholicism: all-in Catholicism. And in it, all the parts work together, many gifts of the same Spirit building up the Body of Christ from some very often surprising materials.

Another part of the "Catholic *both/and*" touches on Catholic social doctrine—often called the Church's best-kept secret. Like every other Christian community, the Catholic Church teaches an ethic of charity, compassion, and service, encouraging its members to be the visible agents of the divine mercy that was so close to the heart of St. John Paul II, and that Pope Francis commended to the Church and the world from the beginning of his pontificate. That's why Catholic parishes give scholarships to students from poor families so they can attend quality Catholic schools. That's why Catholic parishes sponsor blood drives, conduct used-clothing campaigns, collect canned goods for local food banks, and sign up volunteers to work in nearby centers for the homeless. That's also why Catholics and their parishes support crisis pregnancy centers and homes for unwed mothers, just as it's why Catholic parishes sponsor prayers outside abortion clinics. Other Christian communities, of course, also conduct these direct-service, charitable activities. What's different, and unique, about the Catholic Church is that it also has a "social doctrine": a distinctively Catholic way of thinking about the just society, which in turn leads to a distinctive optic on, and approach to, the poor.

Catholics have been thinking about the just society for a long time, the originating masterwork being St. Augustine's *City of God*, written after the Visigoths sacked Rome in AD 410. Medieval Catholicism had a rather well-developed vision of the just society, and as we've seen, that vision helped shape modern democracy in ways that most twenty-first-century historians and political theorists ignore, alas. Then came the late eighteenth and early nineteenth centuries, when European civilization was rocked for decades by the massive rejection of its social and political traditions that began in the radical phase of the French Revolution; since that rejection involved severe persecutions of the Church in many parts of Europe, the popes of the early and mid-nineteenth century were inclined to look at social and political modernity with a hard, even cold, eye. But in the middle years of that century, some Catholic intellectuals began to think through a Catholic approach to modern economic, social, and political life. And their work bore fruit when Pope Leo XIII launched modern Catholic social doctrine with the 1891 encyclical *Rerum Novarum*, in which he assayed the "new things" of modernity (hence the encyclical's title) through the prism of some classic Catholic principles.

It was Leo who cemented the first two key principles into the foundations of a Catholic social doctrine that has now evolved for a century and a quarter. According to Leo's *personalist principle*, or what we can call the "human rights principle," all right-thinking about society, economy, and political community begins with the inalienable dignity and infinite value of the human person: not with the tribe, the caste, the race, the party, the gender-group, the economic group, or whatever. And according to the both/and balance supplied by Leo's *principle of the common good*, or "communitarian principle," each of us, endowed with an innate dignity, should live our freedom and exercise our rights so that we contribute to the good of society, not simply to our personal aggrandizement.

Leo's third papal successor, Pope Pius XI, laid a third principle into the foundations of Catholic social doctrine. Commemorating in its title the fortieth anniversary of *Rerum Novarum*, Pius XI's own social encyclical, *Quadragesimo Anno*, taught that there was more to the just society than the individual and the state, and that a just state had to protect and honor what we call today "civil society": the free associations (beginning with the family) into which free people organize themselves in order to contribute to the common good and live out the meaning of their own dignity as citizens. And according to this *principle of subsidiarity*, Pius XI taught, concentrations of great power in the hands of central governmental authority should be carefully avoided, and decision-making in society should be left at the lowest possible social level commensurate with the common good. You can think of American federalism as one expression of this insight into multitiered public decision-making that constitutes Catholic social doctrine's "civil society principle": just as we don't ask the national government to manage the local fire department, neither do we expect the local fire department to handle national defense.

But there is more here. *Quadragesimo Anno* was written under the lengthening shadow of totalitarianism, so Pius XI was eager to defend the prerogatives and legitimate independence of the family, the religious community, business and labor groups, and other voluntary associations against the tendency of modern states to occupy all the space in society. It's a concern that is much with us in the early decades of the twenty-first century, when the totalitarian temptation has reemerged in the West, usually in more subtle forms. When the state shrinks the social space available to families, religious communities, and other free associations, turning them into de facto departments of the government, trouble inevitably follows.

John Paul II set a fourth principle into the foundations of Catholic social doctrine in his teaching on the *principle of solidarity*, which we can call the principle of "civic friendship." A truly humane and just society, John Paul taught, requires more than a legal relationship between and among its members; it needs the social glue that comes from the sense of participating in a great common enterprise. A just twenty-first-century society is not one in which individuals are left alone with their rights, related to others only by their capacity to sue each other in court. A just twenty-first-century society must be a virtuous society, John Paul II taught: and by virtuous society, he meant one in which individuals exercise their freedom to defend others' rights in pursuit of the common good, and in which the community supports individuals in their growth into personal and civic maturity.

And then there was John Paul II's important teaching on poverty and the Catholic optic on the poor.

In his 1991 encyclical *Centesimus Annus* (named for its commemoration of the centenary of *Rerum Novarum*), John Paul II taught that the wealth of nations was no longer stuff-in-the-ground or the ground itself, as in agricultural and early industrial societies. No, wealth in the third millennium, he understood, would come from the human mind: from the application of wit, insight, and entrepreneurial skill to "stuff," so that "stuff" (like silicon, once useless and worthless) becomes useful and wealth-creating (as in silicon-based microchips, the basis of the IT revolution and the greatest expansion of wealth in human history). And if that's what "wealth" is, then the work of justice is to get as many people as possible into the circles where wealth is created and exchanged. If "wealth" is a fixed pie, then justice involves equitably cutting up a fixed, limited, unchanging pie. But if wealth is expanding and expansive, then justice involves helping everyone get the skills necessary to participate in that expansion, which allows them the dignity of earning their own livings and supporting their own families.

In this twenty-first-century Catholic vision, the *empowerment of the poor* is the prime imperative of justice. Poor people are not problems-to-be-solved (and forgotten) with a welfare check; the poor are people-with-potential-to-be-unleashed, and social welfare programs must aim at unleashing that potential so that poor people become not-poor people, people who are fully participant in the life of the community, people who are living out the truth of their human dignity.

The work of empowerment—through education, counseling, medical care, and family support, for instance—does not substitute for individual works of charity. But neither do individual works of charity satisfy the Catholic call to build the free and virtuous society. It's that *both/and* again.

My friend Father Robert Barron pulled all of this together—orthodoxy, beauty, and social justice; your personal charity and your work for the just society; the Law of the Gift we've discussed before; vocational living; what places like St. Patrick's in Soho mean—in a brilliant meditation on a gospel story with which you're familiar, but from which he drew some striking insights:

> The story of the multiplication of the loaves and fishes—versions of which can be found in all four gospels—is one of the clearest exemplifications of the spiritual principle that Saint John Paul II formulated as the Law of the Gift. Here is the principle in the abstract: your being increases in the measure that you give it away. The world, of course, teaches just the opposite, that your being increases in the measure to which you hang on to what you have.
>
> Here is the spiritual "physics" behind the John Paul idea. Since God has no need of anything, whatever is given to him returns to the giver elevated and multiplied. Anything returned to God breaks, as it were, against the rock of the divine self-sufficiency and comes back, super-abundantly, to the giver. So in the gospel story, the disciples have very little—two fish and five loaves—but they return these simple gifts to the Giver of all things, and they find them multiplied unto the feeding of the five thousand. The same principle holds in regard to the Eucharist. We bring a few tiny gifts to the Lord: bread, wine, and water. But they return to us infinitely enhanced as the Body and Blood of Jesus, and they serve to feed the deepest hunger of our hearts.
>
> The Law of the Gift is on display in the lives of all the saints. St. Benedict Joseph Labre was a homeless beggar on the streets of Rome and he most likely suffered from mental illness. But what little he had he gave totally to Christ and he radiated goodness in all directions. Take even those gifts of yours that seem inadequate, and give them

to the Lord. You will find them increased, thirty, sixty, or a hundred-fold.

So: live the Catholic *both/and* in your life of faith and your public life. You need not make a choice between friendship with Jesus Christ and social justice work. Nor need you identify social justice exclusively with advocating for state-run social welfare programs. A deep, rich, liturgically nourished encounter with Christ and his Church necessarily leads to a radical life of service, which includes work for the empowerment of the poor. In this case, you really can have it all. In fact, if you don't have it all, you're likely to lose what part of it you have. *All-in Catholicism* is the Catholicism you want to embrace, and live.

LETTER NINETEEN

The Basilica of the Holy Trinity, Kraków

On Not Being Alone

 he Dominican Basilica of the Holy Trinity in Kraków is only a few hundred yards from the *Rynek Głowny*, the Old Town market square. Like a lot of Kraków, the city's Dominican priory is thick with history. St. Hyacinth (c. 1200–1257) is buried in the basilica. Hyacinth, or Jacek, as he's known here, brought his friend Dominic's new "Order of Friars Preachers" to Poland in the early thirteenth century and persuaded his kinsman, Iwo Odrowąż, Bishop of Kraków, to give the Dominicans this property as their Polish base of operations. The basilica itself dates from the latter part of the thirteenth century; the steeply gabled front, its most striking design feature, was a later addition. Tomas Torquemada, the feared Inquisitor, once stayed here. The interior was gutted by a fire in 1850; rather than going Art Nouveaux in the redecoration,

as the neighboring Franciscans had done in restoring their fire-damaged basilica, the Dominicans chose a modified Gothic style, so you can actually get a sense in here of what a medieval cathedral looked like, especially as you look up from the nave at the blue ceiling with its gold stars and delicate net vaulting. During the Second World War, the Nazis shut down the high school the Dominicans ran on the priory property and used the schoolyard as a supply depot. One of the older fathers once told me that, as a young man in the 1940s, he and other novices would sneak out into the yard at night, "appropriate" foodstuffs for the starving citizens of Kraków, and then fill the bottom third of the shipping canisters with rocks—"And that's why the Germans lost in Russia!"

When I first came to Kraków in 1991, the basilica was almost black from centuries of coal dust and decades of communist-era neglect. Ten years of cleaning and restoration brought back to glowing life the different red hues of the medieval brick as well as the decorative stone bosses on the gabled facade. Marvelous funerary monuments were restored along the four walls of the priory's former cloister; this vaulted walkway, where you can often find art students sketching, opens on one side into a fine chapter house, beneath which are buried the bones of eight centuries of Polish Dominicans. When Pope John Paul II came to the basilica in June 1999 to venerate the relics of St. Hyacinth and greet Poland's Dominican priests, brothers, and nuns, the provincial, Father Maciej Zięba, welcomed him with the words, "Holy Father, Polish Dominicans have been waiting for this moment for seven hundred seventy-seven years." I've gotten to know the place well during numerous visits. The priory

was my Kraków base when I was researching John Paul's
biography; every summer since 1994, I've taught in a seminar here on Catholic social doctrine for students from the
new democracies of east central Europe and from North
America. Many of the fathers and student brothers are good
friends of mine in that remarkable extended family that's
the Catholic Church.

The best time to come to the basilica is at 7 p.m. on a
Sunday night—not because it's quiet then but because it
isn't. The Dominicans run a vibrant chaplaincy to students
at the city's many institutions of higher learning, and the
7 p.m. Mass every Sunday is for them. I was here, for example, on June 29, 2003, the Sunday after the university
had finished its spring semester. Despite the exodus from
the universities the previous week, the basilica was completely packed, as it is every Sunday at 7 p.m., with several
thousand young people. They're everywhere—in the pews,
on folding chairs, in the old monastic choir stalls, perched
on the great marble stairway leading up to the tomb of St.
Hyacinth, sitting on the steps of the wooden Gothic con-
fessionals, spilling out into the street. There's nothing fancy
about their dress, which is in the Universal Student Mode:
jeans and t-shirts are ubiquitous. The choir—all students—
is wonderful, blending traditional Gregorian and Polish
chants and hymns with more contemporary music from the
ecumenical monastery at Taizé in France. The preaching is
demanding, intellectually and morally—but it's also punc-
tuated with wry humor. Altogether, it's a very, very impressive liturgical experience.

My hunch is that the beauty of the liturgy won't be your
most enduring memory of 7 p.m. Sunday night Mass at the

Dominican basilica in Kraków, though. What will stick in your mind's eye are the faces—for that's what everyone I bring here seems to remember most vividly. They're intense and relaxed at the same time. They're the faces of people who know that, in coming to *this* place, they've come into one of those borderlands between the human and the divine that we've been discussing. Young men and women don't look like this when they're coming to Mass primarily to obey the rules and keep their parents happy. People look like this when they're *convicted*, as an evangelical Protestant from the Deep South might say. Or, as one friend put it after his first experience of the 7 p.m. Mass, these young people participate in the liturgy, and listen to Scripture and preaching, "as if their lives depended on it."

Which, of course, they do. That's why those thousands of young adults know something that the conventional wisdom hasn't figured out yet—or, perhaps better, doesn't want to admit. And that "something" is worth thinking about.

According to the conventional storyline of modernity, which we explored in visiting King's College Chapel and Ely Cathedral, "modernization" means secularization—the withering away of traditional religious belief and practice. On this reading of things, "modernity" and "religion" are a zero-sum game: the more modern you are, the less religious you become; and the more religious you are, the less susceptible you are to modernization. At the beginning of the twentieth century, advanced thinkers widely predicted that the new century then unfolding would witness a maturing humanity, tutored by science, lose its "need" for religion.

Religious belief and practice were for children, perhaps adolescents. A mature, adult humanity had no "need" of God.

We've already talked about what happened when those predictions held true—and what happened was that great swaths of the world were turned into an abattoir, *in the name of humanism.* In the 1940s, the French theologian Henri de Lubac, who would later become an influential figure at the Second Vatican Council, tried to parse this strange and lethal phenomenon, which he called "atheistic humanism." Atheism, of course, was nothing new; the village atheist and the radically skeptical intellectual had long been stock figures in the human drama. *Atheistic humanism* was something altogether different, Father de Lubac suggested. This wasn't a matter of skeptical individuals scratching their particular itches to discomfort the neighbors or impress the faculty tenure committee. This was atheism with a developed ideology and a program for remaking the world. And its prophets—prominent among them Comte, Feuerbach, Marx, and Nietzsche—all taught that the God of the Bible was an enemy of human dignity.

Now *that,* de Lubac argued, was a great reversal. Look at the difference between the classical world—embodied in, say, the *Iliad* and the *Odyssey*—and the biblical world. In the *Iliad* and the *Odyssey,* even the greatest mortals are subjected to the whims of the (usually frivolous or mean-spirited) gods. Things are very different in the Bible. Biblical religion was a tremendous liberation from the whims of the gods or the workings-out of Fate. As Father de Lubac put it, if God had created the world and the men and women in it, and if every human being had a direct link to the Creator through worship and prayer, then men and women were no longer playthings; they were free, and they were responsible. The God of the Bible was not a willful tyrant. Nor was he a remote abstraction. Nor was he a cosmic watchmaker, content to create the world, wind it up, and then leave it to its own devices. The God of the Bible had entered history and had become our companion on the pilgrimage of life. To be in communion with this God was to be liberated from Fate, liberated for maturity, liberated for human excellence.

The phenomenon that Henri de Lubac called "atheistic humanism" turned this idea of the God of the Bible upside down and inside out. What Judaism and Christianity proposed as liberation, atheistic humanism called bondage. Which meant, in turn, that jettisoning God was the precondition to human greatness. This was neither the atheism of the intellectually fashionable nor the atheism of despair. This was atheistic *humanism,* on the march in the name of human liberation. And this new idea, de Lubac proposed, had had the gravest consequences. Brought into action in history by the great tyrants of the mid-twentieth century, this new thing had proven something—something on which you and the members of your generation should reflect very carefully. It was once said, Father de Lubac recalled, that men couldn't organize the world without God. That, in fact, is not true; atheistic humanism disproved that claim. What atheistic humanism had also proven, however, was that without God, human beings could only organize the world against each other. Ultramundane humanism, de Lubac concluded, is inevitably *inhuman* humanism, even if it imagines itself to be motivated by the highest intentions.

If this business of "atheistic humanism" seems at all familiar, it's because it's the intellectual broth in which you've been simmering for most of your life. The roughest edges, to put it gently, have been ground off the project of atheistic humanism—although it took a world war and a Cold War to finish Nazism and communism, the two most lethal expressions of this misbegotten creed. But residues remain: in the positivism Western high culture learned from Comte, the subjectivism it learned from Feuerbach, the materialism it learned from Marx, the radical willfulness it learned from Nietzsche—and in the assumption that biblical religion is for . . . children. The immature. The psychologically "needy." Our old friend John Henry Newman once wrote that genuine university life would be impossible without serious theology, because genuine intellectual life was impossible without theology. I very much doubt that you'll find that claim seriously in play at any of the prestige schools that *U.S. News and World Report* ranks every year. On the contrary—that human maturity requires "liberation" from biblical religion and its demands is as firm an orthodoxy as you'll find on many American campuses and in many American graduate schools today.

At least, that is, among the faculty. Students today are different. I meet hundreds of university undergraduate and graduate students every year; most of them have never heard of Henri de Lubac. But I think they'd be sympathetic to his analysis because of conclusions they've reached on their own: bad ideas have bad consequences; atheistic humanism is a bad idea; and the softer forms of atheistic humanism that shaped and misshaped (and in some cases wrecked) their parents' lives are ideas to be avoided. Young people today are open to biblical religion and its understanding of the human condition in ways that were difficult to imagine twenty-five, or even fifteen, years ago. It's the professoriate that's locked into the past.

I thought of these young people, their questions and their quandaries, when I was in Germany in October 2003. In front of the Catholic archdiocesan offices in Cologne is a striking bronze memorial to Edith Stein, St. Teresa Benedicta of the Cross, whom I've mentioned before—the distinguished philosopher and Carmelite nun who was martyred in Auschwitz in 1942. There are actually three life-size Edith Steins clustered in the memorial. The first is a young Jewish girl; holding the Star of David, she seems to be thinking about the God of Israel while beginning to experience skepticism about her ancestral faith. The second Edith Stein is the rising star of modern German philosophy, more determined in visage but with a split head (remarkably composed by the sculptor); faith and reason haven't been put back together, and neither has the life of Edith Stein. The third Edith Stein in the memorial is the Carmelite-and-philosopher, a woman who has found the reconciliation of faith and reason—and the integration of her own life—in Jesus Christ. This Edith Stein, Sister Teresa "Blessed by the Cross," holds that cross in front of her as she sets out on the pathway that leads to the ultimate gift of self. The third Edith Stein is the whole Edith Stein. And that wholeness is what I sense young people looking for today in a culture that tends to pull us apart (as it had once done to Edith Stein).

The story of Edith Stein suggests that the alternative to ultramundane humanism and the antidote to its lethal effects isn't to abandon the great project of Western humanism; *the alternative is Christian humanism, a humanism built on the three theological virtues of faith, hope, and love.* That's the truth and the love that seized Edith Stein and made her whole. That's what so many young people are looking for today—a humanism that is truly humanizing and humane. You can find that humanity and that wholeness in Christ. I'd guess that not many of those thousands of young people at the 7 p.m. Mass at the Dominican basilica in Kraków have ever studied Reinhold Niebuhr, who was a great preacher, if not exactly a great theologian, when he dominated one wing of American Protestantism in the mid-twentieth century. But they've sensed the truth of what Niebuhr once described as the effects of faith, hope, and love in our lives:

> Nothing that is worth doing can be achieved in our lifetime; therefore we must be saved by hope. Nothing which is true or beautiful or good makes complete sense in any immediate context of history; therefore we must be saved by faith. Nothing we do, however virtuous, can be accomplished alone; therefore we are saved by love. No virtuous act is quite as virtuous from the standpoint of our friend or foe as it is from our standpoint. Therefore we must be saved by the final form of love which is forgiveness.

As we've seen, the twenty-first-century world is not becoming more secular, except in Europe and parts of North America, which means that the secularization hypothesis has been overturned by the evidence. For better and for worse, the world of this new century and new millennium is becoming more intensely religious. As journalist

David Brooks has pointed out, recognizing that is the first step in "recovering" from the habit of secularism, or perhaps better, the habit of taking the secularization hypothesis seriously—to recognize that, as a religious person, *you're not alone*. And you're not . . . odd. The real minority, Brooks argues, are those "pockets of people in the world who do not feel the constant presence of God in their lives, who do not fill their days with rituals and prayers and garments that bring them into contact with the divine, and who do not believe that God's will should shape their public lives."

Brooks was writing for what he calls "recovering secularists," but his advice holds true for religious people who get spooked by the dominance of the secularists in our high culture. Perhaps his wisest counsel involves a question of nerve and historical perspective—If it's true that the world is becoming more, not less, religious, doesn't that mean that the world is becoming a much more dangerous place? Maybe the secularists were right on this point, at least; maybe a thoroughly secularized politics is the safest politics. But they're not right on this, as Henri de Lubac knew. The greatest slaughters of the twentieth century were not perpetrated by religions, but by atheistic humanism. Yes, there are competing visions of human destiny at work in the world, many of them religiously informed, and some of them volatile. But that's history. That's humanity. That's the way things have been, are, and always will be. "Beating the secularist prejudices out of our minds every day" is, David Brooks suggests, an essential part of trying to push history in a more humane direction. It's certainly essential in engaging those parts of the Islamic world that reject the terrorism of Al Qaeda, the Taliban, the Islamic State, and all the rest. If, as secularists seem to suggest, engaging the Islamic world means turning "moderate" Muslims into good Western secularizing liberals, then we really are condemned to a bloody clash of civilizations.

Keeping our nerve also means recognizing that, if I may borrow a splendid trope from social scientist Ben Wattenberg, the good news is that the bad news isn't all the news there is. Historian Philip Jenkins has painted a vivid portrait of the "next Christendom" in a book by that title. Yes, on the current form sheet, Western Europe, Canada, Australia, and New Zealand seem thoroughly secularized and unlikely to recover their Christian roots anytime soon. But they're the historical aberrations, not the norm.

Various expressions of Protestant Christianity are flourishing in Latin America and Africa, often in unexpected forms; on the numbers here, Jenkins suggests, Pentecostalism is the most successful social movement of the past century. At the same time, the Catholicism in which you'll spend your life is also "moving south"—south of the equator. By 2025, Jenkins estimates, almost three-quarters of world Catholicism will be found in Africa, Asia, and Latin America. Latin America is already world Catholicism's demographic center of gravity. That suggests that the dialogue about what it means to be "the Church in the modern world" between the vibrant-if-troubled Catholic Church in the United States and the Church in Latin America is going to be arguably the most important Catholic conversation of the twenty-first century. Then there is African Catholicism, which is exploding with energy and astonishing growth. In the early 1950s, there were 16 million Catholics in Africa;

there are 198 million African Catholics today, and there may be 240 million African Catholics by 2040.

These new Catholics live a Christianity that Jenkins describes as very close to the New Testament in its sensibility: here, the supernatural is as real as the natural world, Jesus embodies a divine power capable of healing the wounds of life, authority is respected, and no one is clamoring for a "democratized" Church (whatever that would mean). Might we see the day, sometime in the mid- to late twenty-first century, when African missionaries re-evangelize the old Catholic heartland of Western Europe? Will the foundations for that re-evangelization be laid in the first half of the new century by some of those Poles you've met at the 7 p.m. Dominican Mass in Kraków? It's not impossible; a considerable percentage of all European seminarians today are in Poland. Properly formed and trained, they could become a remarkably potent force for the re-evangelization of the "Old Europe" in cooperation with the lay renewal movements—often led by young people—that are some of the liveliest parts of Catholicism in France, Germany, Italy, and Spain.

So you're not alone as a young religious believer and a young Catholic. And you're not on the back side of history. You're on its cutting edge.

Thirty-five years ago, if anyone had suggested that rallies of millions of young people would become one of the signature events of the Catholic Church throughout the world, secularists would have scoffed—and so would a lot of Catholics, including senior clergymen. Pope John Paul II had a different view. Having spent much of his ministry as a young priest with young people, he believed that the next generation of Catholics was just waiting to be rallied. So he decided to rally them.

The results have been the remarkable World Youth Days of the past two decades—Rome, 1985; Buenos Aires, 1987; Santiago de Compostela, 1989; Częstochowa, 1991; Denver, 1993; Manila, 1995; Paris, 1997; Rome again, for the Great Jubilee of 2000; Toronto, 2002; Cologne, 2005; Sydney, 2008; Madrid, 2011; and Rio de Janeiro, 2013. World Youth Day 2016 will be held here, in Kraków. Each of these events has had its own special character, but each has had a similar liturgical rhythm.

World Youth Days are meant to re-create the experience of Holy Week, which is both the center of the Church's year of grace and the basic structure of the spiritual life. Thus every World Youth Day begins with a variant on Palm Sunday, during which the large "World Youth Day Cross," which has been carried around the host country for months, is solemnly processed into the site of the opening ceremony. Then there is the analogue to Holy Thursday, when the pope preaches about living lives of Gospel service. Every World Youth Day then has its "Good Friday," in which young Catholics and the pope pray together over man's redemption through the enduring mystery of the cross. The following evening there's a candle-lit vigil service, analogous to the Great Vigil of Easter on Holy Saturday evening. And every World Youth Day ends with a concluding Mass that evokes the experience of Easter Sunday and sends everyone back out into the world with the message of the Resurrection.

I think the most memorable moment of World Youth Day 1997 in Paris was the vigil. For three days, the half-million young pilgrims had been scattered in several dozen different venues throughout Paris. Now, for the vigil, they all came to the Longchamp racecourse, filling its infield and the surrounding area. The racecourse was turned into a cathedral of light as John Paul II baptized twelve young adults drawn from every continent. The French, dumbfounded at the turnout, watched this extraordinary demonstration of faith with amazement. The next night, on French national TV, Cardinal Jean-Marie Lustiger of Paris drove the message home in an interview with a still-shocked anchorman who couldn't understand what all of this was about. It was a question of generations, the cardinal suggested to his skeptical questioner. The anchorman belonged to a generation that had been raised Catholic, had lost its faith somewhere around 1968, and had been fighting Daddy, as it were, ever since. *This* generation was different, the cardinal insisted. "They grew up with nothing. They have found Jesus Christ. They want to explore all that that means." These young people, in other words, hadn't bought the conventional storyline. The anchorman was the one in a time-warp.

In Toronto in 2002, it was the Good Friday analogue that made the greatest impact on me, and I expect on many others. Toronto is a self-consciously secular city, priding itself on a "tolerance" and "diversity" that often seem to have room for everything except culturally assertive Christian conviction. Yet on the night of July 26, 2002, Toronto saw something its secularist establishment hadn't imagined possible—half a million young people making their way up University Avenue from the business district to the provincial parliament buildings and Queen's Park, devoutly praying the Way of the Cross. The Canadian Broadcasting Corporation estimated that as many as 1 billion people around the world shared that extraordinary moment, thanks to real-time television hook-ups to 160 countries. But I very much doubt if the impact anywhere was greater than in securely secular Toronto itself.

The remaining skeptics continue to suggest that World Youth Days are simply a variant on contemporary youth culture's infatuation with celebrity—in this case, the pope. No one who's attended one of these events could say that, I don't think. In his eighth and ninth decades, and as physical infirmities slowed him down, John Paul II had long since transcended the "John Paul Superstar" phase of his pontificate; Benedict XVI's papacy never had such a phase. And, in any case, at what other festival on the world youth circuit are young people challenged to lead lives of moral heroism?

During World Youth Day 2000 in Rome, the more aggressively secular Italian media contrasted the "Rome people" with the "Rimini people"—the latter being the hundreds of thousands of youngsters flocking to Italy's beaches in August—and asked what the difference was between the two groups. Surely both had a claim to defining the European future, the papers suggested. But that's hardly the point, is it? The question is what future is being defined, and whether there's any place for a call to spiritual grandeur and moral heroism in that future. Western Europe's catastrophically low birth rates demonstrate that two generations of Europeans have failed to create a future in the most elemental human sense—by creating a successor generation capable of sustaining society. It's hard to imagine that that phenomenon doesn't have at least something to do with the corrosive effects of the acids of skepticism, moral relativism, and what I once called in these letters "debonair nihilism." That so many young people were intrigued by John Paul II's call to hold the bar of spiritual and moral expectation high, and to live the Law of the Gift written on their hearts, shouldn't be considered a threat to Europe's future, or anywhere else's. In some cases, that kind of conversion may be the very precondition to any future at all.

By all means put a future World Youth Day on your schedule. World Youth Days sum up, somehow, many of the things we've been thinking through in these letters: why deciding on your "vocation," on that unique something that only you can be and do, is so important a part of becoming an adult Catholic; why stuff counts; why the real world is the world of transcendent truth and love, revealed in and through the things of this world; why "putting on" the sacramental imagination is part of becoming the fully human being you want to be. World Youth Days are great experiences of Catholic solidarity and Catholic enthusiasm. They're also great experiences of sacramentality. Here you can see, hear, touch, feel, and taste that, in the Catholic view of things, we meet God through visible, tangible, audible things—and those things include the Church itself and the sacraments the Church makes available to us. This distinctive Catholic worldliness is ever more important in a world that, by taking itself with ultimate seriousness, doesn't take itself seriously enough. Taking the world seriously doesn't mean falling into the traps of materialism and skepticism.

Taking the world seriously means taking the world for what it is—the arena of God's action, the place where we meet the love that satisfies our yearning for a love that satisfies absolutely and without reservation.

Welcome to the real world:

> . . . *you have come to Mount Zion and to the city of the living God, the heavenly Jerusalem, and to innumerable angels in festal gathering, and to the assembly of the first-born who are enrolled in heaven, and to a judge who is God of all, and to the spirits of just men made perfect, and to Jesus, the mediator of a new covenant . . .*
>
> —[Hebrews 12.22–24]

SOURCES

LETTER ONE

Citations from Flannery O'Connor are from *The Habit of Being: Letters of Flannery O'Connor*, Sally Fitzgerald, ed. (New York: Farrar, Straus, Giroux, 1979).

LETTER TWO

John E. Walsh's 1982 book *The Bones of St. Peter: The Fascinating Account of the Search for the Apostle's Body* is out of print, alas, but may be available through used bookstores or online book services. The citations from Flannery O'Connor are from *The Habit of Being*.

There's a wonderful story about the obelisk in St. Peter's Square. The obelisk had remained in place, to the left of the current St. Peter's as you face the basilica from the square, for centuries. When Pope Sixtus V ordered his architect, Domenico Fontana, to move the obelisk to the center of the Square, Fontana had a problem: no one knew how to do this. Nine hundred men, 150 horses, and 47 cranes were in the Square on September 18, 1586, to try to move and then reerect the obelisk without damaging it. Sixtus ordered that the procedure be carried out in complete silence in order not to spook the horses—and to underscore the point, he had a gallows erected in the Square, on which anyone who made a noise would be summarily hanged. As the ropes began to pull the obelisk upright, they became so taut that they began to smolder; yet no one dared to breathe a word until finally a sailor cried, *"Acqua alle funi!"* ("Water on the ropes!"), thus saving the day, and the obelisk. Pope Sixtus was so grateful that he had been disobeyed that he gave the sailor's hometown, Bordighera, the privilege of providing palms for the Palm Sunday service at St. Peter's—a tradition that continues to this day.

LETTER THREE

Citations from Jaroslav Pelikan are from *Jesus Through the Centuries: His Place in the History of Culture* (New Haven, CT: Yale University Press, 1985).

The Waugh biography cited is Martin Stannard, *Evelyn Waugh: The Later Years, 1939–1966* (New York: W. W. Norton, 1992).

Waugh's letter to George Orwell is in *The Letters of Evelyn Waugh*, Mark Amory, ed. (New York: Penguin, 1980).

Hans Urs von Balthasar's description of Catholicism as God's search for us is taken from Balthasar, *In the Fullness of Faith: On the Centrality of the Distinctively Catholic* (San Francisco: Ignatius Press, 1988).

LETTER FOUR

Pope John Paul II's vocational memoir is *Gift and Mystery: On the Fiftieth Anniversary of My Priestly Ordination* (New York: Doubleday, 1996).

Hans Urs von Balthasar's analysis of the different images or profiles shaping the Church in every age is in *The Office of Peter and the Structure of the Church* (San Francisco: Ignatius Press, 1986).

LETTER FIVE

Newman's Roman address in 1879 is cited in Ian Ker, *John Henry Newman: A Biography* (New York: Oxford University Press, 1988).

The story of Edith Stein's conversion may be found in Freda Mary Oben, *Edith Stein: Scholar, Feminist, Saint* (New York: Alba House, 1988).

David Gelernter's description of "ice-your-own-cupcake" religion is in the September 2003 issue of *Commentary*.

The citation from Newman's *Loss and Gain* is from Avery Cardinal Dulles, SJ, *Newman* (New York: Continuum, 2002).

The text of the Hartford Appeal is in *Against the World For the World: The Hartford Appeal and the Future of American Religion*, Peter L. Berger and Richard John Neuhaus, eds. (New York: Seabury, 1976).

Letter Six

Joseph Pearce's biography of Belloc is *Old Thunder: A Life of Hilaire Belloc* (San Francisco: Ignatius Press, 2002).

The citations from G. K. Chesterton's *Orthodoxy* are from the Image Books edition (Garden City, NY: Doubleday Image Books, 1959).

Chesterton's introduction to Aquinas may be found in *St. Thomas Aquinas / St. Francis of Assisi* (San Francisco: Ignatius Press, 2002).

Gerard Manley Hopkins's poem "Pied Beauty" is taken from Hopkins, *Poems and Prose* (London: Penguin, 1963).

Letter Seven

Evelyn Waugh's August 9, 1955, letter to Edith Sitwell may be found in Amory, ed., *The Letters of Evelyn Waugh.*

The citations from *Brideshead Revisited* are from the Penguin Classics edition (London: Penguin, 2000).

Douglas Lane Patey's biography of Waugh is *The Life of Evelyn Waugh: A Critical Biography* (Oxford: Blackwell, 1998).

C. S. Lewis's reference to heaven as an "acquired taste" is from the introduction to Dorothy L. Sayers's translation of Dante's *Paradiso* (London: Penguin, 1962).

The citations from Robert Bolt's *A Man for All Seasons* are from the Vintage Books edition (New York: Vintage, 1962).

Letter Eight

H. V. Morton's *A Traveler in Rome* is available in a reprint edition published by Da Capo Press; the citation is from that 2002 edition.

The "theology of the body" is outlined in my *Witness to Hope: The Biography of Pope John Paul II* (New York: Harper Collins, 1999). The entire corpus of audience addresses, and a detailed exposition of them, can be found in John Paul II, *Man and Woman He Created Them: A Theology of the Body*, translated and with an introduction by Michael Waldstein (Boston: Pauline Books and Media, 2006).

LETTER NINE

Further information on St. Mary's Parish in Greenville, South Carolina, may be obtained by visiting the parish's website, www.stmarysgvl.org.

The Second Vatican Council's description of the Church's liturgy as a participation in the heavenly liturgy may be found in *Sacrosanctum Concilium* (the Dogmatic Constitution on the Liturgy), 8.

The texts from the *Catechism of the Catholic Church* are found at #2460.

LETTER TEN

Michael Kaufman's description of the Mass for the Fatherland is taken from his book *Mad Dreams, Saving Graces: Poland—A Nation in Conspiracy* (New York: Random House, 1989).

Hans Urs von Balthasar's description of some saints as "God's prime numbers" is taken from the introduction to his book *Two Sisters in the Spirit* (San Francisco: Ignatius Press, 1992).

The Dawson citation is from Christopher Dawson, *Religion and the Rise of Western Culture* (New York: Doubleday Image Books, 1991).

John Paul II's reflections on his vocational struggles may be found in *Gift and Mystery*.

LETTER ELEVEN

Hans Urs von Balthasar's description of the cross is taken from *The Three-fold Garland: The World's Salvation in Mary's Prayer* (San Francisco: Ignatius Press, 1982).

Peter Kreeft's reflections on suffering are in *Making Sense out of Suffering* (Ann Arbor, MI: Servant Books, 1986).

Leon Kass's essay "L'Chaim and Its Limits" may be found in the May 2001 issue of *First Things*.

LETTER TWELVE

The best introduction to the New Martyrs of the twentieth century is Robert Royal's book *The Catholic Martyrs of the Twentieth Century: A Comprehensive World History* (New York: Crossroad, 2000).

John Allen brings the story into the twenty-first century, and widens the analytic lens ecumenically, in *The Global War on Christians: Dispatches from the Front Lines of Anti-Christian Persecution* (New York: Image, 2013).

Letter Thirteen

On St. Maximilian Maria Kolbe, see André Frossard, *"Forget Not Love": The Passion of Maximilian Kolbe* (San Francisco: Ignatius Press, 1991).

Jeffrey Burton Russell's *Mephistopheles: The Devil in the Modern World* (Ithaca, NY: Cornell University Press, 1986) was the fourth volume of an extensive study that also included *The Devil: Perceptions of Evil from Antiquity to Primitive Christianity; Satan: The Early Christian Tradition;* and *Lucifer: The Devil in the Middle Ages,* all published by Cornell University Press.

On the "trial of God" at Auschwitz, see Jenni Frazer, "Wiesel: Yes, We Really Did Put God on Trial," *Jewish Chronicle Online,* September 19, 2008 (www.thejc.com/news/uk-news/wiesel-yes-we-really-did-put-god-trial).

Jaroslav Pelikan's discussion of Marc Chagall's *White Crucifixion* is in *Jesus Through the Centuries,* 20.

Joseph Ratzinger's discussion of the descent into hell is taken from Edward T. Oakes, SJ, "Pope Benedict XVI on Christ's Descent into Hell," *Nova et Vetera,* English Edition 11:1 (2013), 231–252.

Letter Fourteen

Malcolm Miller's incomparable guide to Chartres is *Chartres Cathedral* (Andover, UK: Jarrold, 1996).

Hans Urs von Balthasar's analysis of the "genius" of art and what it teaches us about God may be found in *The Glory of the Lord: A Theological Aesthetics,* vol. 1, *Seeing the Form* (San Francisco: Ignatius Press, 1982).

Augustine's "Late have I loved thee" is from Book 10: xxvii (38) of the *Confessions.*

Cardinal Schönborn's analysis of icons may be found in Christoph Schönborn, *God's Human Face: The Christ-Icon* (San Francisco: Ignatius Press, 1994).

LETTER FIFTEEN

For an elegy on contemporary England's spiritual emptiness, see Philip Larkin, "Church Going," in Philip Larkin, *Collected Poems* (New York: Farrar, Straus and Giroux, 2004).

Among Peter L. Berger's many important and influential books, you should have a look at *The Sacred Canopy: Elements of a Sociological Theory of Religion* (New York: Anchor Books, 1990); *A Rumor of Angels: Modern Society and the Rediscovery of the Supernatural* (New York: Anchor Books, 1990); and *The Desecularization of the World: Resurgent Religion and World Politics* (Grand Rapids, MI: Eerdmans, 1999).

My essay on the effects of the collapse of faith in Europe, *The Cube and the Cathedral: Europe, America, and Politics Without God*, was published by Basic Books in 2005.

Brad Gregory's *The Unintended Reformation: How a Religious Revolution Secularized Society* was published in 2012 by The Belknap Press of Harvard University Press.

Mary Eberstadt's *How the West Really Lost God* was published by Templeton Press in 2013. Her equally insightful and important book *Adam and Eve After the Pill: Paradoxes of the Sexual Revolution* was published by Ignatius Press in 2012.

LETTER SIXTEEN

Our Lady of Guadalupe: Mother of the Civilization of Love, by Carl Anderson and Monsignor Eduardo Chávez (New York: Doubleday, 2009), is a good introduction to the miracle of Guadalupe and its meaning for the New Evangelization, especially in the Western Hemisphere. Paul Badde's *María of Guadalupe: Shaper of History, Shaper of Hearts* (San Francisco: Ignatius Press, 2008) is another good introduction to the icon and its meaning.

A much fuller discussion of the New Evangelization can be found in my *Evangelical Catholicism: Deep Reform in the 21st-Century Church* (New York: Basic Books, 2013).

Cardinal Joseph Ratzinger's lecture "Christ, Faith, and the Challenge of Cultures" is available at www.ewtn.com/library/curia/ratzhong.htm.

Letter Seventeen

Information on the Old Cathedral in Baltimore may be found at www
.baltimorebasilica.org.

The contributions of medieval Catholic thought and life to modern de-
mocracy are outlined in John Courtney Murray, SJ, *We Hold These Truths:
Catholic Reflections on the American Proposition* (Garden City, NY: Doubleday
Image Books, 1964).

Father Servais Pinckaers's distinction between the "freedom of indifference" and "freedom for excellence" is taken from his book *The Sources of Christian Ethics* (Washington, DC: Catholic University of America Press, 1995).

The Supreme Court's "mystery passage" is found in the 1992 case *Casey v.
Planned Parenthood*, 112 Sup.Ct.2791, at 2807.

Letter Eighteen

Information on "Nightfever" can be found at http://en.nightfever
.org/?i-341.

You can find an overview of Catholic social doctrine in the first chapter of
my book *Against the Grain: Christianity and Democracy, War and Peace* (New
York: Crossroad, 2008), which includes a number of essays on the many roles
of the Church in public life.

Father Barron's reflections on the gospel story of the multiplication of
loaves and fishes was first published in the August 2014 edition of *Magnificat*,
p. 44.

Letter Nineteen

Henri de Lubac's study *The Drama of Atheist Humanism* was published by
San Francisco's Ignatius Press in 1995.

Reinhold Niebuhr's thoughts on faith, hope, love, and forgiveness are
cited by Wilfred McClay in his essay "The New Irony of American History,"
which may be found in *First Things*, February 2002.

David Brooks's article "Kicking the Secularist Habit: A Six-Step Program" was published in the March 2003 issue of *The Atlantic*.

Philip Jenkins's book *The Next Christendom: The Coming of Global Christianity* was published by Oxford University Press in 2002.

ACKNOWLEDGMENTS

In the first years of the new millennium, Basic Books sponsored a series, *The Art of Mentoring*, in which various authorities took a page from Rainer Maria Rilke and offered vocational advice in the form of letters: thus *Letters to a Young Chef, Letters to a Young Mathematician, Letters to a Young Lawyer, Letters to a Young Actor, Letters to a Young Therapist, Letters to a Young Golfer*, and so forth. Elizabeth Maguire, the publisher of Basic Books, with whom I had worked happily on *The Courage To Be Catholic*, suggested that I join the parade and write *Letters to a Young Catholic* (which both she and I once were, back in the day). At first, I didn't think it a good idea: I had already written one book of popular apologetics and I wasn't sure I had another one in me.

The great Liz Maguire was nothing if not persistent, however, and when she asked me for the third or fourth time, I said that if I could come up with some sort of scheme for the book that made me interested in it, I'd do it. Shortly thereafter, on a long coast-to-coast flight, the idea of doing the book as a tour of the Catholic world came to me, and by the time I'd landed at LAX I had the book outlined on a legal pad. Convincing me to do the book was one of many debts I owed Liz Maguire, for I had at least as much fun writing *Letters to a Young Catholic* as I'd had in writing any other book. Liz's terribly premature death in 2006 deprived the publishing world of one of its brightest lights, and took away, until our reunion in the Kingdom, a beloved friend. So the first word to be said here is one of thanks to the late, and quite wonderful, Elizabeth Maguire. May she rest in peace.

Liz's worthy successor, Lara Heimert, was the instigator of this revised and expanded edition of *Letters to a Young Catholic*, and I thank her for her insight, counsel, and friendship. My longtime literary agent, Loretta Barrett, first facilitated my work with Basic Books; this project was the last she helped arrange for me, as she died just as this new edition was being finished. Loretta, like Liz, was both friend and colleague, and all who knew her mourn her while giving thanks for a beautiful life.

The book's first iteration was improved by suggestions from Carrie Gress and Joan Weigel and was enhanced by materials, reminiscences, contacts, references, and revisions provided by Father Peter Cameron, OP; Archbishop Charles J. Chaput, OFM Cap.; Father Derek Cross, CO; Father J. Scott Duarte; Jean Duchesne; Dr. Henry T. Edmondson III; Father Zbigniew Krysiewicz, OP; Father Roger Landry; Father Michael McGarry, CSP; Monsignor Christopher Nalty; Father Jay Scott Newman; Father Guy Nicholls, CO; Joseph Pearce; Cardinal George Pell; Mark Potter; Dr. Manfred Spieker; and Father Maciej Zięba, OP. Other friends—Cardinal Avery Dulles, SJ; Leon Kass, MD; Father Richard John Neuhaus; Father Edward Oakes, SJ; and Dr. Douglas Lane Patey—all found in the first book echoes of our conversations, for which I was very grateful indeed. Cardinal Dulles, Father Neuhaus, and Father Oakes have all gone home to God; may they, too, rest in peace.

In the course of preparing this revised and expanded edition I've incurred new debts, which it's a pleasure to acknowledge.

Archbishop Gintaras Grušas invited me to Lithuania in September 2013 to help the Lithuanian bishops conference mark the twentieth anniversary of Pope John Paul II's epic visit to a free Lithuania in 1993. That weeklong pilgrimage of remembrance gave me the opportunity to fulfill a long-standing desire to visit the Hill of Crosses in Šiauliai, and to do so with a wonderful guide, Živilė Šeporaitytė.

Father Alexander Sherbrooke is the agent of the miracle that is St. Patrick's Soho; I thank him for his hospitality and for arranging for me to meet Pauline Stuart, a fellow-traveler, so to speak, on one of the new adventures in this revised and expanded edition.

Piotr and Teresa Malecki thought I'd be interested in the striking, contemporary *Via Crucis* in Pasierbiec; they were right about that, as about so many other Polish wonders to which they've introduced me over the past decade and a half.

Father Joseph Marcello used the first edition while teaching in Connecticut and had many wise ideas about what might be done with a new edition. Joseph S. Anderson made the apt suggestion for an amplification of the book that resulted in a new tour stop at St. Patrick's Soho.

Jack Valero was the agent of my first visit to King's College, Cambridge, and for that, as for many other kindnesses, I thank him.

Mario Paredes got me to Mexico City and Guadalupe, for which I am very grateful, as I am for a friendship extending back to the mid-1980s.

Mary Eberstadt, Elizabeth Lev, and my colleagues at the Ethics and Public Policy Center each helped in their own ways to bring the new edition to fruition, as did my son, Stephen Weigel, with technical assistance.

For the past twenty-three summers I've had the privilege of teaching young Catholics, primarily from North America and the new democracies of Central and Eastern Europe, in the *Tertio Millennio Seminar on the Free Society*, which met in Liechtenstein in 1992 and 1993 and has met every summer since in Kraków. Our students have come from Australia, Belarus, Bulgaria, Canada, Colombia, the Czech Republic, Hungary, Italy, Latvia, Lithuania, Moldova, Poland, Romania, Russia, Slovakia, Slovenia, Ukraine, and the United States. Many of them will do great things for the Church and the world in the future; others are already doing so. I'm grateful for the inspiration they've been to me, and I'm happy to be able to dedicate this book to all of them, and to include, in this edition's dedication, my faculty colleagues in the seminar, wonderful teachers and mentors whose lives are living letters to young Catholics.

G. W.

November 23, 2014

Solemnity of Our Lord Jesus Christ, King of the Universe